REASON AND THE CONTOURS OF FAITH

RICHARD RICE

WIPF & STOCK · Eugene, Oregon

All Biblical quotations, unless otherwise indicated, are from the Revised Standard Version of the Bible. Copyright © 1946, 1952, 1971, 1973 by the Division of Christian Education of the National Council of the Churches of Christ in the United States of America.

Wipf and Stock Publishers
199 W 8th Ave, Suite 3
Eugene, OR 97401

Reason & the Contours of Faith
By Rice, Richard
Copyright©1991 by Rice, Richard
ISBN 13: 978-1-62564-084-0
Publication date 5/15/2013
Previously published by LSU Press, 1991

CONTENTS

Preface   vii
Introduction   1

PART ONE: *The Meanings of Faith and Reason*

1. ### The Contours of Faith   11
   Faith in General; Biblical Descriptions of Faith; The Receptive Dimensions of Faith; The Cognitive Dimension of Faith; The Concessive Quality of Faith; The Volitional Dimension of Faith

2. ### Reason and Responsible Belief   31
   Reason and Rationality; The Nature of Knowledge; The Rational Ideal; Evidence and the Sources of Knowledge; Evidence and Argument; Reason and the Rational Ideal; The Rational Ideal Reconsidered; Responsible Belief: An Alternative to the Rational Ideal

PART TWO: *Reason and the Contents of Faith*

3. ### Christian Theology   71
   Framing the Question of Faith and Reason; Definitions of Theology; Theology and the Bible; Theology and Doctrine

4. ### The Question of General Revelation   101
   The Central Topic in Natural Theology; General Revelation and Natural Theology; John Calvin on Revelation in Nature; Karl Barth's Critique of General Revelation; The Case Against Natural Theology; The Case for Natural Theology; Conclusion

5. Natural Theology: The Philosophical Question 123
   Attitudes Toward Arguments for God; The Nature and
   Purpose of Theistic Argument; The Cosmological Argument;
   The Teleological Argument; The Problem of Evil; The Moral
   Argument; The Ontological Argument; What the Proofs
   for God Accomplish; The Limits of Philosophical Theology

6. Natural Theology: The Theological Question 167
   Framing the Question of Natural Theology; Natural
   Theology as Apologetics; Natural Theology as Theological
   Foundation; Philosophy of Religion as Natural Theology;
   The Rejection of Natural Theology; Natural Theology as Part
   of the Theological System; The Need for Natural Theology;
   The Role of Natural Theology; Summary

PART THREE: *Reason and the Experience of Faith* 213

7. The Relevance of Reason to Faith 215
   Support for the Relevance of Reason to Faith; Various
   Approaches to Faith and Reason; Conclusion

8. The Contribution of Reason to Faith 247
   Variables Affecting Faith and Reason; The Role of Reason
   Within Faith; The Role of Reason Prior to Faith; The
   Limitations of Reason in Relation to Faith; Concept and
   Metaphor: Reason and the Language of Faith; Conclusion

Conclusion 285
Afterword 289
Bibliography 293
Index 301

DEDICATION

To Marlys, Jack, and the cousins

PREFACE

There are books that people feel they ought to write, and books people find they have to write. This is one of the second kind. It brings to expression a long process of intellectual ferment in an area of great importance to me, both personally and professionally. And it results from the convergence of two streams in my experience, a personal religious quest and a formal academic career—first as a student and then as a teacher.

The question of faith and reason has fascinated and perplexed me for over twenty years now. I first developed a concern with the topic as a college student. As often happens, my thinking was stimulated by encountering views which I intuitively rejected without having clearly formulated objections. I listened to several popular speakers who assured their audiences that Christian faith was eminently reasonable and that our faith was firmly grounded on rational evidence that was more than sufficient. I found this account of things inadequate to the turmoil of my own religious odyssey, and I felt that it threatened to reduce faith to a matter-of-fact conclusion of dispassionate logical investigation. I felt that faith was much more a venture and a risk than this description acknowledged.

During my ministerial internship, I found that such a view of faith was inadequate to the suffering that good people are often called to endure. It seemed impossible to me that people faced with death and tragedy would find that the evidence added up nicely in favor of time-honored religious beliefs. If they survived their experiences with their faith intact, I thought, it would be more in spite of, than because of, the accumulated evidence.

Interest in making sense of religion and in understanding the Christian faith more fully led me to graduate school, so in 1970,

I began the PhD program in Christian Theology at the University of Chicago Divinity School. While the relation between reason and the experience of faith continued to occupy my thoughts on a personal level, I was deeply involved academically with the application of reason to the contents of faith. Questions about the meaning and truth of religious claims generally and those of Christianity in particular pervaded my courses with Langdon Gilkey, Schubert M. Ogden, and David Tracy.

My concern with the issue of faith and reason intensified during the summer of 1971, when my wife and I spent several weeks touring the United States by private airplane in the company of my sister and her husband. My brother-in-law, a physician and at the time an avid amateur pilot, had just finished his internship at a hospital in Spokane, Washington. He and my sister were visiting relatives around the country before leaving for mission service in the Far East, and they invited us to fly along with them.

As the journey progressed, Jack and I found ourselves engaged in a series of long discussions about the relation between faith and reason. With his extensive scientific background and quick logical mind, he made an eloquent case for the rational approach to religion. In contrast, I vigorously emphasized the non-rational dimensions of faith. To the considerable frustration of our wives, we pursued our topic week after week, from the green hills of New England to the blue skies of the Southwest. No matter where our conversations began, we always seemed to come back to the question of faith and reason. Was faith rational or not? Jack thought Christianity was eminently reasonable. I insisted that faith could not be reduced to a logical operation.

In spite of all our time on the topic, neither of us modified his views in the slightest. Jack left for Okinawa and I returned to Chicago, each convinced his position was correct, and a little frustrated that the other had not found it persuasive. As another academic year began, our conversations repeated themselves over and over in my mind. I seemed unable to put them behind me and concentrate fully on my current classes.

Christmas vacation arrived, and as much to get the whole thing out of my system as for any other reason, I took the opportunity to write down the points that I had tried so hard to put across the previous summer. Three or four long days at the typewriter produced a manuscript of some twenty pages, in which I argued vigorously that faith is irreversibly prior to reason. Although I had written it for purely personal reasons, I wondered what others would think of the effort and sent the essay to the editors of *Spectrum* early in 1972. To my surprise, they accepted it for publication and the article appeared early in 1974 accompanied by a critique written by James Londis.[1]

My graduate program kept me pursuing other aspects of the issue. At Schubert Ogden's suggestion, I devoted my doctoral dissertation to the study of natural theology in the thought of the American philosopher Charles Hartshorne. I was impressed by Hartshorne's commitment to pursue reason to the end in matters of faith, especially when this commitment resulted in the development of powerful arguments for the reality of God. (I also felt that Christians could learn a lot from Hartshorne's view of God's nature.)[2] As I studied Hartshorne's concept of natural theology, I became increasingly interested in the questions it raises for Christian thought, and particularly for theological method. What can philosophy contribute to faith? I wondered. In particular, what is the appropriate role of philosophical reflection within Christian theology? My teachers were convinced it had a role to play. My doctoral adviser, David Tracy, often described himself as one of the few admirers of Vatican I, which affirmed the importance of reason in relation to Christian faith. I came to the conclusion that theology needed to use philosophy. Looking back, I realize that I finished my doctoral studies holding diverse, if not contradictory, views on faith and reason. On an intellectual level, I was convinced that philosophy had an important contribution to make to theology. On a personal level, I continued to feel that faith and reason were worlds apart.

My views on the topic changed considerably in subsequent years. Teaching theology and philosophy of religion at a church-operated university, I soon found that my greatest challenges arose from two quite different sorts of students—those who dismiss religion as unworthy of serious consideration, and those who feel that their religious convictions are so obviously true that they need no examination at all. For the benefit of both groups, I presented Christian faith as something that both requires and deserves careful investigation. I encouraged thinkers to believe and urged believers to think. Along the way, I also sensed the irony that one whose major academic interest lies in philosophical theology should work so hard to minimize the significance of reason for religion.

Consequently, in the summer of 1977, I worked out a modified statement of my views which I subsequently used in my philosophy of religion classes. The essay argues that there is a positive relation between faith and reason, but that rational investigation cannot produce personal religious commitment. The present proposal represents a further modification of this basic position. Sabbatical leaves during the fall quarters of 1985 and 1988 gave me an opportunity for further reading and reflection on various aspects of religious epistemology. I continue to believe that intellectual inquiry has an important relation to religious experience, but its contributions are limited and its role must be carefully defined.

This book results from the confluence of personal reflection and academic study. It covers a wide range of questions and deals with the thought of a number of diverse figures. I hope that my efforts to think through the complex nest of questions raised by faith and reason will benefit others who have found them as perplexing as I have. I also hope this discussion will stimulate the thinking of those who feel that such questions are irrelevant to the religious life.

As the foregoing comments suggest, my indebtedness in this project extends far beyond the usual academic scope and includes a much wider range of people. On the one hand, I think of the rigorous philosophical work of Charles Hartshorne. I also think of Schubert M. Ogden, one of the country's foremost philosophical theologians and a peerless teacher, who introduced me to Hartshorne's thought. I recall with gratitude the gracious guidance of David Tracy, who drew me from the brink of despair on a couple of occasions long ago, and the contributions of Brian Gerrish and Bernard McGinn to my thinking. On the other hand, I think of the early childhood influences of a religious home and school and of my years of service within a conservative and close-knit religious community. I believe that the effects of such diverse influences on my experience and my thinking have been thoroughly positive, and I hope that their sources would feel the same.

I want to thank the academic leadership of La Sierra University and the faculty of the School of Religion for freeing me from teaching responsibilities during two busy quarters to pursue this project. Even more I appreciate the way my colleagues have constantly stimulated my thinking, particularly Dalton Baldwin and Fritz Guy. Bailey Gillespie and I have discussed the experience of faith in many different settings, from southern California to the Greek Islands. He has taught me a great deal about the psychology of religion. I specially thank my friend Larry Goodwin for his careful critique of the manuscript. I learned a lot from his probing criticisms, although I doubt that he will be uniformly pleased with my attempts to respond to them.

I am indebted to the staff of La Sierra University Press, and to Edwin Zackrison in particular, for bringing this endeavor into print. My assistant, Josie Velasco, was helpful in many ways, especially in preparing the indexes. Most of all, I thank my wife Gail, who in addition to pursuing her own academic career, cheerfully manages the more important parts of our life together, while I worry over philosophical matters.

---

[1] "The Knowledge of Faith," *Spectrum: A Quarterly Journal of the Association of Adventist Forums*, Vol. 5, No. 2, pp. 19-32; James J. Londis, "Comment," Ibid., pp. 32-37. Shortly afterwards, I presented the substance of the article as a paper at the West Coast Religion Teachers' Conference. The replies to this presentation also appeared in *Spectrum*. (See Larry M. Lewis, "Perspective and Tension with Faith and Reason," Dalton D. Baldwin,

"Reason and Will in the Experience of Faith," and Eric D. Syme, "The Gift of Reason and the Aid of Revelation," *Spectrum*, Vol. 6, Nos. 1-2, pp. 77-86). In October, 1975, I presented essentially the same paper to a group of religion scholars in Chicago attending the annual meeting of the American Academy of Religion.

[2] See my book, *God's Foreknowledge and Man's Free Will* (Minneapolis: Bethany House Publishers, 1985).

INTRODUCTION

Matthew 17:2   If you have faith as a grain of mustard seed, . . . nothing will be impossible to you.
Mark 9:2   I believe, help my unbelief.
Luke 18:8   When the Son of man comes, will he find faith on earth?
Acts 16:31   Believe on the Lord Jesus, and you will be saved.
Romans 12:3   God hath dealt to every man the measure of faith (KJV).
Ephesians 2:8   By grace you have been saved through faith.

Faith is one of the most important elements in Christianity. It plays a prominent role in the Biblical writings from Genesis to Revelation, and in the New Testament, especially in the letters of Paul, it emerges as the one essential condition of human salvation. At the same time, the Bible says varied and contrasting things about faith. One of the familiar statements above suggests that everyone has a degree of faith, but according to others it represents a rare and precarious possession.

The relation between faith and reason is one of the most basic and persistent concerns in religion. No topic in the area of theology or philosophy has attracted more attention, for a longer period of time, from a greater variety of sources, or with more diverse results. The question as to how rational investigation relates to religious belief crops up century after century, and virtually all the great names in the history of Western thought have had something to say about it. There are thinkers who elevate the role of faith in our experience, and there are those who emphasize the significance of reason. Some believe that faith and reason are contradictory and incompatible; others believe that they are essentially unrelated; still others maintain that they are complementary and mutually supportive.

The question of faith and reason is not only complicated, it is urgent as well. Philosophers, theologians and intellectual historians find the issue important, of course. But the problem of faith and reason meets us on the personal level, too. It appears when we notice the contrast between the world we live in today and the ancient sources of religious beliefs. And it arises implicitly from the simple act of thinking about religion. Moreover, it is a question that everyone answers in one way or another—whether by careful reflection, by repeating something read or heard, or simply by making an unexamined assumption.

This book develops an approach to the question of faith and reason that lies between two undesirable extremes—"fideism"[1] and "rationalism." According to fideism, faith and reason are unrelated. Religious faith is a highly personal matter, and what we believe in the realm of religion is distinct from our beliefs in other areas. Many who take this position are deeply committed believers. They find the experience of faith utterly unique, and they insist that religious beliefs are too important to subject to mundane rational analysis. Consequently, they resist the intrusions of reason into the province of faith.

Others sharply divide the realms of faith and reason on the grounds that religion is strictly a matter of private preference. For them, it is not so much impossible as inappropriate to subject faith to rational analysis. A person's religion is much like one's taste in fashion or entertainment. It may be an arbitrary selection, or it may be completely determined by inheritance or upbringing. But in either case it is something to which one is perfectly entitled without having to provide rational justification. To do so, in fact, violates the very nature of the experience. We miss the whole point of religion if we subject it to the scrutiny of reason.

If fideism holds that reason has nothing to do with faith, rationalism maintains it has everything to do with it. For the rationalist, religious beliefs require rational evidence, and the responsible person believes only as much as reason supports. This approach to the relation of faith and reason yields divergent results. Some people find abundant evidence to support their religious beliefs. They are convinced that rational considerations fully justify their faith.[2] For others, the evidence for religious beliefs is insufficient, to say the least.[3] And there are some who conclude that the facts invalidate such beliefs altogether. According to the last, one cannot be a believer and a thinking person at the same time, and since responsible people must be rational, religious belief has to go.[4]

I am convinced that fideism and rationalism are both mistaken. Faith and reason are not unrelated, as fideists maintain. We cannot isolate religion from the rest of our experience. Our religious beliefs will have an inevitable effect on our other beliefs, and the converse is true as well. But even though faith and reason are related, it is inaccurate to think of faith as completely dependent on reason, as rationalists maintain. This oversimplifies the complexity of faith and misrepresents the experience of believers.

This book affirms a positive relation between faith and reason. It takes the position that certain religious beliefs can find rational support and that reason can contribute to the experience of faith in a number of different ways. It also attaches important qualifications to each of these points.

Although reason supports religious beliefs to a certain extent, the scope of the "demonstrable continuities," as we shall call them, between faith and reason is extremely limited. By no means can all of what Christians believe be established by reason. Very little can, in fact. But this little is important nonetheless, for it deals with the central religious concept in Western thought, namely, the idea of God. As we shall see, reason provides evidence for the reality of God, and it even shows that in a sense everyone believes in God.

The contributions of reason to the experience of faith are also limited but important. Rational inquiry can prepare the way for personal faith by removing some intellectual obstacles, and once faith is present reason can help conviction grow by discovering new truth and resolving doubts within the believer's life. But reason by itself cannot produce faith. Reason does not take us step by step from unbelief to the point where religious commitment is the only logical move. So, reason never fully justifies faith. As in all significant relationships, there are elements of freedom and risk in the life of faith. As we shall see, these considerations lead to the conclusion that faith as personal commitment to God is a reasonable but not a reasoned position.

We shall develop these themes in the following way. Our first task will be to formulate some careful definitions. So far we have used such words as "faith," "reason," "religion," and "evidence" rather loosely. Each expression has a wide range of meaning, which makes this possible. But this latitude is one of the factors that makes the question of faith and reason extremely complicated. Consequently, we need to define the various terms involved if we hope to make any progress in understanding the relation of faith and reason. This is the basic objective of Part 1. Chapters 1 and 2 explore the nature of faith and reason, respectively, and Chapter 3 identifies two basic ways of formulating the question of faith and reason. One deals with the relation of reason to the contents of faith; the other, with the relation of reason to the experience of faith. The major sections of the book pursue answers to these questions.

Part 2 examines the relation of reason to the contents of faith. It deals with several ways in which reason applies to religious beliefs. Theology, the topic of Chapter 3, is the application of reason to religious beliefs within the context of a religious community. Its purpose is to explore the inner dynamics of faith and the interrelation of various beliefs. As frequently described, philosophy of religion applies reason to religious beliefs from outside a religious community, or from a perspective independent of religious commitment. Unlike theology, it does not presuppose the truth of religious beliefs. Chapter 5 outlines some of the principal concerns of this activity.

Juxtaposing the concerns of theology and philosophy of religion raises two further issues. Are religious beliefs accessible to philosophical inquiry? This is the question of general revelation, the topic of Chapter 4. And, do the results of philosophical inquiry have theological significance? What role, if any, should they play in the work of theology? This is the question of natural theology in its theological form, the topic of Chapter 6.

Part 3 examines the function of reason in the experience of faith. Chapter 7 seeks to establish the relevance of reason to faith, and Chapter 8 attempts to define the faith-related functions of reason more precisely.

As these chapter descriptions indicate, this discussion deals with many of the traditional concerns of philosophy of religion. And parts of it serve as an introduction to that discipline. What is unique about our treatment in this volume is that it brings a wide range of issues together under the rubric of one comprehensive question—the relation of religious faith and rational inquiry.

The complexity of our topic and the great volume of what has been written on it require us to define the nature of this investigation with great care. Our discussion bears the following characteristics. First, its basic purpose is constructive rather than descriptive. We are less concerned with reviewing historical or contemporary treatments of the topic than in developing our own understanding. This will not prevent us from examining the work of others, of course. Not only can we learn a great deal from them, but in many cases they provide the basic terms of the discussion. But we shall attempt nothing like a survey of different views on the topic. Instead, our objective will be to formulate the question of faith and reason as carefully as we can, and then develop answers to it.

Second, the present discussion approaches the topic of faith and reason from the side of religion rather than philosophy—from inside rather than outside faith, we might say. In particular, the perspective is that of Christian faith, as distinct from other religious communities. This means that our major interest is how the question of faith and reason arises in the experience of believers and what the best answers to it might be. We will not deliberately ignore any of the basic forms the question takes, but limiting our approach in this way will help us to focus our reflections and keep the discussion within manageable bounds.

Third, our discussion is directed to the general reader rather than the expert. This is no excuse for superficiality. But since the topic is one that concerns every religious person, indeed, every thinking person, our reflections will be more helpful if they are accessible to all reflective people rather than simply to specialists.

In view of all that has been said and written on our topic, someone is bound to question the value of yet another discussion. What can we possibly have to say that has not been said before? The answer, I believe, lies in the important distinction Gabriel Marcel makes between a problem and a mystery.[5]

We approach a problem with the intention of solving it, and once we solve it we move on to other things. If your lawn mower breaks down, or your tooth aches, or you need to drill for water or send a rocket to the moon, you are confronted with a problem—a specific demand for a well-defined answer or course of action. Not all problems are easily solved, of course, and we never run out of problems to deal with. But we approach a problem by looking for a solution.

Mysteries, in contrast, are never "solved." The more we ponder a mystery, the more profound it appears, and the more complex it becomes. We never "get to the bottom" of a mystery. All our attempts to understand it only reveal greater depth. It is also characteristic of mysteries that they never lose their fascination. As a result, human problems often change from age to age, but life's great mysteries remain.

Faith and reason represent mysteries rather than problems. The task of relating these two important aspects of our experience has challenged Christians since Apostolic times, and centuries of reflection have not diminished its capacity to perplex us. This is not due to a lack of progress in understanding the issue; it is due to the fact that this relation is always central to the life of the Christian community and to the experience of the individual believer.

The purpose of this book, therefore, is not to "solve the problem of faith and reason," but to explore the mystery of their relationship. It will reach its objective if it succeeds in dispelling some of the confusion that surrounds this question and serves as a springboard for further discussion, for it is highly unlikely that unanimity on this issue will ever be achieved. The question of faith and reason is one over which reasonable minds may differ, and still be reasonable, and faithful men and women may disagree, and still be children of faith.

---

[1] From *fides*, one of the Latin words for "faith."

[2] A. Graham Maxwell takes this position. He states that God "never asks His intelligent creatures to believe anything for which He does not provide adequate evidence" (*Can God Be Trusted?* [Nashville, TN: Southern Publishing Association, 1977], pp. 44-45). He also defines faith as "having enough confidence in Him [God], based on the *more than adequate evidence* revealed, to be willing to believe whatever He says, to accept whatever He offers, and to do whatever He wishes—without reservation—for the rest of eternity" (Ibid., p. 46; italics mine).

[3] This was the view of Bertrand Russell, the great agnostic. When someone asked him what he would say if he encountered God after his death and were asked why he had not believed, Russell replied, "I'd say, 'Not enough evidence! Not enough evidence!'" (Wesley Salmon, "Religion & Science: A New Look at Hume's Dialogues," *Philosophical Studies* 33 [1978]:176; quoted in Alvin Plantinga, "Reason and Belief in God," in *Faith and Rationality: Reason and Belief in God*, ed. Alvin Plantinga and Nicholas Wolterstorff [Notre Dame: University of Notre Dame Press, 1983], pp. 17-18.

[4] This is the conclusion Wallace Matson comes to in *The Existence of God* (Ithaca, NY: Cornell University Press, 1965): "Are there any reasons for believing in the existence of a Deity . . .? As far as I can tell, there are none. . . . Is it, then, reasonable, in any sense at all, to believe that there is a Deity? Apparently it is not" (p. 239).

[5] "A problem," writes Marcel, "is something which I meet, which I find complete before me, but which I can therefore lay siege to and reduce. But a mystery is something in which I myself am involved. . . . A genuine problem is subject to an appropriate technique by the exercise of which it is defined; whereas a mystery, by definition, transcends every conceivable technique" (*The Mystery of Being*, trans. S. G. Fraser [2 vols.; Chicago: Henry Regnery Company, 1950], 1:260).

PART ONE

THE MEANINGS OF FAITH AND REASON

1

THE CONTOURS OF FAITH

The central terms involved in the question of faith and reason display a variety of meanings and apply to a wide range of human experience. Consequently, our first step in exploring the relationship of reason to the contours of faith must be to examine the different meanings of these expressions and to describe the experiences to which they refer. This chapter considers the nature of faith; the next explores the nature of reason.

Although "faith" is fundamentally a religious category, we commonly use the word in a secular sense as well. It will be helpful to review the general meaning of the term before turning specifically to its religious significance.

Faith in General

On the most basic level, "faith" is synonymous with "trust" or "confidence." It carries this meaning in statements like these: "I took the mechanic's explanation on faith"; "I have faith that my son is telling the truth about the broken window"; "I have faith in my surgeon." These utterances all express trust, but there are differences among them which illuminate some of the basic features of faith.

If a service station attendant examines the oil level in my car and says it's a quart low, I ordinarily take his word for it rather than check it myself. My trust takes the place of personal investigation. In one sense, then, faith means accepting the testimony of others rather than finding something out yourself. It involves a distinction between "having-found-out-for-oneself" and "having-taken-it-on-faith" or "having-taken-someone's-word-for-it."[1] We exercise faith in this way all the time, whenever we read a newspaper or listen to a traffic report, for example. Such faith is indispensable to education. By far most of what we know comes to us through the testimony of others, in one form or another. We would learn very little if we accepted only information that we acquired through personal investigation.

In some cases, most of them probably trivial, we accept things on faith that we could find out for ourselves if we took the trouble (like the oil level in a car's engine). But in other cases we can't investigate for ourselves, and we have to rely on someone else's testimony. If the relevant data is highly technical, we must rely on the word of others unless we have the expertise to understand or interpret it ourselves. And if the testimony involves an historical event, which cannot be repeated, we have no choice but to depend on the accounts of witnesses. This leads us to another characteristic of faith.

Faith not only involves exercising trust rather than making a personal investigation, it also involves having confidence in the absence of proof. Asked if we *know* that something unproven is so, we typically say, "No, I'm taking it on faith." Suppose my son's football breaks the kitchen window, and he tells me that his kick in that direction was an accident. There were no other children present, I didn't see him strike at the ball, and I certainly don't want him to threaten another window by reenacting the incident. So there is no way to demonstrate the truth of his claim. Nevertheless, I believe him. I have faith that he tells me the truth. As we frequently use the term, then, faith involves confidence that goes beyond the available evidence. For this reason, it is sometimes described as certainty without proof.

There is a third characteristic of faith as we often use the term. This is an element of personal commitment, or a willingness to act on one's belief. To act on a proposition, or to be willing to act on it, involves more than simply accepting its truth. It is one thing to assert that Dr. Smith is an excellent surgeon. It is quite another to ask him to perform a delicate operation on your child. For this reason, we often speak of faith as distinct from "belief," or "mere belief."

There have been many attempts to explain this distinction. One of the best known employs the expressions "belief-that" and "belief-in." *Belief-that* is mere intellectual assent, a simple acknowledgment that something is so. But *belief-in* refers to personal commitment; it involves a willingness or a decision to act on one's belief. This distinction also expresses different degrees of personal importance. When someone simply says he believes that something is the case, we do not know how important this belief may be to him. But when a person says she believes *in* something or someone, her words suggest that this is something that really matters to her. For example, a person who merely believes that Chevrolets are good cars may or may not drive one. But a person who believes *in* Chevrolets not only affirms their automotive value but probably owns one.

From what we have seen, a person begins a statement with the words, "I have faith . . ." in order to express one (or more) of several things. He may be saying that he believes something that he has not personally investigated; or that he believes something which has not and perhaps cannot be proven; or that he has enough confidence in someone or something to act on it.

The features of faith we have discerned in ordinary experience are also characteristic of distinctly religious faith. Such faith also involves belief, an absence of proof, and a decision or willingness to act. In order to give our understanding of religious faith a solid footing, let us review the central elements in the biblical descriptions of faith.[2]

Biblical Descriptions of Faith

As it appears in the Bible, faith is not just one among many ideas, it represents the central element in religious life. In the Old Testament the most important Hebrew word for faith[3] refers to "the comprehensive, exclusive and personal relation between God and man."[4] It denotes a person's trusting, obedient response to everything that God has done for human beings. This relationship with God encompasses all aspects of a person's life

(Ps 76:22), including inner attitudes and feelings as well as external conduct.[5] This relationship is also exclusive; it invalidates all other objects of religious devotion (cf. Dt 6:5; Hos 10:2). The same Hebrew word incorporates other elements, too. One of them is knowledge (Isa 43:10; Hos 4:1). Another is will, since faith involves obedience to God. And a third, paradoxically, is fear (Ex 14:31).

Isaiah emphasizes the importance of faith to the point where it becomes the only possible mode of life: "If you will not believe," he writes, "surely you shall not be established" (Isa 7:9). The same prophet recognizes that faith must overcome enormous obstacles, such as the apparent absence of God (8:17; cf. 45:15), but for him the tension between fear and hope gives faith energy and vitality. As a result, faith becomes "a superhuman, miraculous power which makes the impossible possible" (Isa 40:31).[6] In this sense, faith is closely related to a hope in God's promises that defies appearances.

The New Testament concept of faith builds on that of the Old. In general, the basic Greek word[7] means "to rely on," "to trust," "to believe."[8] To believe is to accept as credible, to regard as true (Jn 2:22). And in one important passage in particular we see that it also involves obedience, trust and hope (Rom 10:16; Heb 11). The various figures catalogued in Hebrews 11 acted on their confidence in God without visible evidence to support his promises.[9] "By faith Abraham," for example, "obeyed when he was called to go out to a place which he was to receive as an inheritance; and he went out, not knowing where he was to go" (11:8). The word also carries the meaning of "faithfulness" (2 Tim 4:7; Heb 13:7; 1 Pet 1:7).[10]

Beyond this general concept of faith, the New Testament, especially the writings of Paul, relates faith specifically to the Gospel. Faith means accepting the Christian proclamation that Jesus is Lord.[11] It involves a personal relation to Christ that leads to salvation (Rom 10:10).[12] The word "faith" can refer not only to the act of believing, but also to the contents of belief, or to *what* is believed.[13, 14] Galatians 1:23, for example, contains the expression, "preaching the faith," and 1 Timothy 1:2 describes Timothy as "my true child in the faith."

The concept of faith reaches greater significance in Paul's major writings than anywhere else. Paul accepts the general notion of faith just described. But with him, faith becomes the single decisive element in Christian experience; it represents the one indispensable condition of salvation. This is evident in the emphatic way in which he opposes faith and works: "For we hold that a man is saved by faith apart from works of law" (Rom 3:28); "For by grace you have been saved through faith.... Not because of works, lest any man should boast" (Eph 2:8-9).

As Paul describes it, faith is thus an absolute committal to God in which a person abandons all self-reliance. It is "the radical decision of the will in which man delivers himself up."[15] Some actions are incidental to a person's identity. Others may reflect his distinctive personality to a certain degree. And still others may express the very essence of his character. For Paul, faith belongs in the last of these categories.

The concept of faith also figures prominently in John's writings, where it functions somewhat differently. Here it involves a renunciation of the world and a turning to the invisible (Jn 20:29). This gives faith a miraculous character. It is an event which has its roots in the other world. It is an act or gift of God Himself: "No one can come to me unless the Father who sent me draws him" (6:44).[16] Their faith takes Jesus' followers out of the world: "because you are not of the world, but I chose you out of the world, therefore the world hates you" (15:19); "they are not of the world, even as I am not of the world" (17:14).

This radically new form of life is possible only through God's revelation, only because the light has come (1:9; 3:19). But faith does not arise because people first perceive and then respond to the truth which Jesus proclaims. Rather, faith is involved in the very perception of truth.[17] So, those who do not believe are guilty, not of rejecting the truth they have seen, but of not seeing the truth to begin with. "He who believes in him is not condemned; he who does not believe is condemned already" (3:18).

Faith and knowledge are closely related in John, but in a complicated way. They have the same objects. Both are concerned with the fact that the Father has sent Jesus (Jn 17:3, 8, 21). Both realize that he, or his teaching, is from the Father (16:27-30; 7:17). The fact that Jesus is the Christ is an object of both faith and knowledge (6:69; 20:31). At times knowledge is the consequence of faith: "we have believed, and have come to know, that you are the Holy One of God" (6:69; cf. 8:31-32). At other times faith is the result of knowledge: "now we know that you know all things . . .; by this we believe that you came from God" (16:30; cf. 17:8). So we cannot regard faith and knowledge simply as successive stages in the Christian life. In the words of Rudolf Bultmann, "Knowledge can never take us beyond faith or leave faith behind. As all knowledge begins with faith, so it abides in faith. Similarly, all faith is to become knowledge. . . . Knowledge is thus a constitutive element in genuine faith."[18]

With these biblical considerations in mind, we can identify the essential features of religious faith. As the Bible describes it, faith is fundamentally the exercise of trust or confidence in God. We can think of faith in a general sense as trust or confidence in God's ability to protect us, for example, to provide for our needs, and so forth. In the most important sense, however, faith is the exercise of trust in God as the source of salvation. To have faith is to rely completely on God's power to save, apart from any human accomplishments. "Faith" in the biblical sense is often synonymous with "saving faith." It refers to the one indispensable condition of our salvation. Such faith exhibits a threefold character. It has receptive, cognitive, and volitional dimensions.

The Receptive Dimension of Faith

Faith is receptive in several different ways. For one, it emphasizes the priority of God's activity. Faith involves a personal response to God. It presupposes that God has done something which requires human beings to react in a certain way. In a specifically Christian sense, faith is a response of trusting acceptance to God's gracious gift of salvation in Jesus Christ.

Faith is also receptive in the sense that it presupposes God's immediate personal influence. Not only is the saving activity to which faith responds a gift of God (cf. John 3:16), the response itself depends on God's power. Faith, too, is the gift of God (cf. Rom 12:3).

The recognition that faith is essentially receptive in character prevents us from viewing faith as a meritorious achievement on our part. Faith is not a personal quality or virtue which we offer to God in order to get something in return. God does not bestow salvation as a reward for faith. If he did, faith would simply be another form of works. It would represent something human beings offer to God in hopes of gaining salvation. When Paul insists that the principle of faith excludes boasting (Rom 3:27), he means that human beings have absolutely nothing which recommends them to God. So, faith does not give us a basis for making claims on God. It is not an Archimedian standpoint which enables us to exert a favorable influence on God. In the experience of salvation, God's initiative is prior to every form of human involvement, including the exercise of faith. Consequently, we cannot transform faith into a source of merit. Faith is merely the instrument by which we receive the gift of salvation. Precisely speaking, it is not faith that saves, it is God who saves through faith in Jesus Christ.

Faith is also receptive in the sense that it is focused on a specific object. Faith cannot establish its own validity; it is not "self-authenticating." Instead, authentic faith requires an object that is completely reliable. The saving quality of faith thus derives from the object of trust, not from the trust itself. Otherwise, it would make no difference what or whom we trusted, as long as we trusted in the right way, and this is hardly the viewpoint of the New Testament. For the New Testament writers, faith is not a general human experience which remains essentially the same regardless of its object. It is the specific response appropriate to a specific divine activity. It is the trusting acceptance of what God has done in Jesus Christ. For them, there is no other source of salvation (Ac 4:12).

In a familiar tale, Dumbo the baby elephant had the ability to fly by using his enormous ears, but he was completely unaware of it. Some of his friends took an ordinary feather and told him it had magical qualities. They convinced him that he could fly as long as he was holding it in his trunk. So, clasping the "magic" feather carefully, he flapped his ears and soared away. His naive confidence in the feather enabled him to use the abilities that he did not perceive. The point of the story is that Dumbo's confidence gave the feather power, not the other way around.

In Christian faith, the relationship is precisely reversed. Faith presupposes the validity of its object, but it does not establish it. The saving quality of faith derives from the object of confidence, not from the confidence itself. People sometimes speak of the "power of faith" as if it had saving significance in itself, but this is not the biblical view. Faith is valid only if its object is worthy of unconditional trust.

The Cognitive Dimension of Faith

In addition to its receptive quality, faith also includes a cognitive dimension. This refers to the fact that faith involves the intellectual aspect of human experience. As we defined it, faith in general is confidence or trust, and faith in a religious and specifically Christian sense is an act of concrete personal commitment. Our point here is that personal trust or commitment includes intellectual assent; it involves the affirmation that certain things are true. The author of Hebrews seems to touch on this point when he states, "And without faith it is impossible to please him [God]. For whoever would draw near to God must believe that he exists and that he rewards those who seek him" (Heb 11:6). A person cannot have faith in God unless he believes that God exists and that he is kindly disposed to human beings.

Using distinctions mentioned earlier, we may say that "faith" or "faith *in*" (personal trust or confidence) includes "faith *that*," or "belief-in" includes "belief-that." The two are significantly different, as we shall emphasize below, but they are also intrinsically related. People cannot believe or have faith *in* something, unless they also believe certain things about it. If a rock climber said, "I have faith that this rope will support my weight, but I don't believe it will," or a teamster said, "I have faith that these tires will last another ten thousand miles, but I know they won't," we would regard such statements as nonsensical. It would be equally ridiculous for a person to say, "I have faith in God, but I don't know that he exists." We cannot have faith in something if we do not find it believable. We cannot trust something that we do not find trustworthy.

We can also express this point by using the term "evidence." Faith, we can say, always rests on evidence. A person who has faith puts confidence in things which have rational support. Consequently, people who ignore all relevant evidence, or completely disregard contrary evidence, do not exemplify faith. To rely on something or someone in complete defiance of the evidence is not an exhibition of faith.

Furthermore, we cannot overcome a lack of credulity by force of will.[19] People cannot decide to believe something that they find inherently incredible. We could not believe that the earth is shaped like a doughnut, even if we greatly desired to. Of course, it is possible to act out of sheer desperation. People who are gravely ill sometimes resort to remedies that they know will fail, just as people cling to the railing of a sinking ship. But such behavior does not exemplify faith.

Although this point seems basic, a number of contemporary scholars deny that faith has a cognitive dimension. They regard faith as a personal attitude or perspective, or as a commitment to behave in a certain way, but they do not believe that it involves a claim to know something. Let us examine this non-cognitivist interpretation of faith and then suggest some answers to it.

In recent years the view that faith does not involve knowledge emerged in response to a particular philosophical challenge to religious belief. For much of this century the most influential figures in Anglo-American philosophy devoted themselves to the analysis of language. One of their major concerns was to achieve a criterion of cognitive meaning, or a test that one could use to find out whether a supposed statement actually makes sense or not. (A statement in this sense is an utterance that communicates information. It purports to tell us something about the way things are.)

An important attempt to achieve such a criterion was the formulation of the so-called "verification principle." According to the most famous discussion of this principle, that of British philosopher A. J. Ayer, all genuine propositions, or meaningful statements, fall into two categories. One contains the propositions of logic and mathematics. These consist of relations of ideas and provide no information about the world of experience. Mathematical and logical truth is a matter of internal consistency. Those who clearly understand the meaning of the terms involved in statements such as "Two plus two equals four" and "All bachelors are unmarried men" can see whether or not they are true. They do not need to test them in light of some sort of external evidence. Their truth (or falsity) is "analytic," or "a priori," to use technical terms. It does not depend on experience.

The other category of meaningful statements consists entirely of factual propositions, or assertions about the world we encounter through sense experience. If an utterance does not belong to the area of mathematics or logic, we can find out if it is a genuine factual statement by applying the criterion of verifiability. According to this test, "a sentence is factually significant to any given person, if, and only if, he knows how to verify the proposition which it purports to express—that is, if he knows what observations would lead him, under certain conditions, to accept the proposition as being true, or reject it as being false."[20] So, unless a statement can (at least in principle) be supported by some sort of sense experience, it is not a genuine assertion. It contains no information and really tells us nothing. In a word, it is meaningless.

When the principle of verifiability ran into difficulties, analytic philosophers made other attempts to develop a criterion of cognitive meaning. One was the criterion of falsifiability, for which Antony Flew is known.[21] According to this criterion, a statement is factually significant to a person if he or she can specify, not what factual conditions would count *for* it, but what factual conditions would count *against* it. So unless a statement falls within the area of mathematics or logic, it is meaningful only if it is incompatible with some conceivable state of affairs. Conversely, if nothing factual counts against it, it is not a statement at all. It may have the grammatical form of an indicative sentence, but it is cognitively meaningless.

When philosophers applied these criteria to religious language, the results were devastating. They concluded that statements involving the word "God" are meaningless because they do not satisfy the requirements of either category of meaningful propositions. They are not analytic statements, like those of mathematics and logic, because their truth is not directly evident from the terms involved. So they could only be meaningful in a factual sense, that is, by communicating information. But examination reveals that they do not fit in this category either. They cannot be factual statements, because they cannot be falsified. Their authors allow nothing to count against them.

Flew argues that the non-falsifiability of God-language is apparent in the way people make claims such as "God has a plan," "God created the word," and "God loves us as a father loves his children." At first glance they appear to be vast descriptions of the cosmos, but closer examination shows otherwise. God's loving the world does not prevent him from allowing children to suffer and die, and his gracious plan is evidently compatible with all sorts of human injustice and cruelty. Since believers will not specify the conditions that would falsify their claims, Flew insists that their utterances are cognitively meaningless. They contain no information at all.

A number of Christian thinkers have surrendered to this challenge to God-language. They accept the judgment that utterances about God are not assertions and tell us nothing about the way things are. But even so, several contend, God-language still serves an important function. According to one interpreter, a person's statements about God may not actually tell us anything about the world, but they express their author's perspective on the world. And since people can have radically different perspectives, such expressions are important.[22]

Another thinker argues that utterances involving God are important, even though they are not assertions, because they express moral commitment. According to Richard B. Braithwaite, religious and moral statements are fundamentally similar. Both express a person's commitment to behave a certain way, and neither communicates factual information.[23] What religion adds to morality is a collection of stories to back up the intention.[24] And it is primarily differences in their stories rather than differences in moral commitment that distinguish the world's major religions from one another. As Braithwaite describes it, the factual truth of the stories is unimportant to the purpose they serve. A person may find certain stories encouraging without believing that what they say is actually so. Accordingly, a professing Christian "both proposes to live according to Christian moral principles and associates his intention with thinking of Christian stories; but he need not believe that the empirical propositions presented by the stories correspond to empirical fact."[25]

There have been other attempts to defend religion from the verificationist challenge, including the ill-fated "death of God" proposals in the late 1960's. But none of them are adequate to the nature of religion itself. It is true that religion and morality have a good deal in common. It is also true that there are non-cognitive elements in religious experience, as our own discussion will note, and these elements are indispensable. But to conclude that we can interpret religion entirely in non-cognitive terms is profoundly mistaken, and it is particularly inadequate to Christianity.

For one thing, the faith of the early church was firmly based on the preaching of the apostles. In fact, New Testament scholars are fairly confident that we can reconstruct the basic outline of their message. One important passage provides what appears to be a formal summary of the *kerygma*, as it is often called, in four basic statements: Christ died for our sins; he was buried; he was raised on the third day; and he appeared (1 Cor 15:3-5). Central to the faith of the earliest Christians, then, is the belief that certain things happened. Their faith included the assertion that certain things were true. The content and the importance of the church's later creeds support the same conclusion. Beginning with the expression, "I believe," they contained a list of fundamental claims. Affirming the truth of certain propositions is basic to Christian experience, as the very meaning of the word "creed" suggests.[26]

Furthermore, to assimilate religion to morality as some do, ignores the New Testament insistence that the two are quite distinct. Paul's vigorous polemic against legalism represents an emphatic rejection of the notion that morality is the essence of religion. Christianity may provide powerful motivation for us to live the moral life, but its heart is the claim that our standing before God is not dependent on our success in doing so (cf. Rom 3:28; Eph 2:8-9). The intellectual contents of faith are not merely stories designed to generate enthusiasm for moral behavior. They are statements affirmed to be true.

To summarize, faith exhibits a cognitive dimension. It involves propositional affirmation. People who have faith believe certain things because they find them believable, because they find evidence to support them.

The Concessive Quality of Faith

We have just described faith as an act of personal commitment which embraces belief, meaning that faith includes the affirmation that certain things are true, or that faith rests on some degree of evidence. But the complexity of faith requires us to qualify this description. What faith affirms not only has evidence to support it, it goes beyond the available evidence. In our earlier investigation of faith in general, we saw that the word frequently expresses confidence in the absence of proof. This "concessive," or "in-spite-of," quality is intrinsic to religious faith as well. To believe something which is obvious, or for which the evidence is completely overwhelming, is not an exercise of faith. This is why the famous statement in the book of Hebrews relates faith to things "hoped for" and "unseen" (11:1).

As we shall explain in some detail in Parts 2 and 3 of this book, faith goes "beyond" the available evidence in two important ways: in the scope of what it affirms and in the degree of commitment it manifests. As we just described it, the cognitive dimension of faith means that the affirmations of faith rest to some degree on rational evidence. But it is also the case—and it is equally important to faith—that some of what faith affirms is not fully supported by the evidence. Similarly, faith exhibits a confidence which the evidence justifies to some extent, but not completely. Faith is commitment in the absence of conclusive evidence, or demonstration. In faith, then, we not only affirm that something is true, we affirm it in spite of a lack of evidence, or in spite of evidence to the contrary. And we trust without reservation, even though it doesn't make complete sense to do so.

What faith affirms, therefore, stands somewhere between obscurity, on the one hand, and complete clarity, on the other. Faith affirms things that are neither incredible nor obvious. There is always evidence to support faith, but this evidence is always less than conclusive. The concessive quality of faith means that a person can never be forced to exercise faith. Not believing will always be an option; there will always be something to support it.[27] This also means that there is constant tension between trust and doubt within the life of a religious person. Faith always has to overcome the possibility and the temptation of doubt.

This concessive quality of faith is especially vivid in some of the classic examples of religious devotion. We regard Job's experience as an outstanding demonstration of faith precisely because he maintained confidence in God in the face of enormous misfortune, when it appeared that God had abandoned him. His attitude is epitomized in the exclamation, "Though he slay me, yet will I trust him" (Job 13:15; KJV). Similarly, Abraham continued to trust God even when commanded to take the life of his only son Isaac (Gen 22). These examples indicate that men and women of faith maintain their trust even when God appears to be indifferent to their difficulties. Their confidence in God goes beyond the available evidence to support it; sometimes it goes against evidence to the contrary.

As we explore the contours of faith, we must keep in mind both its rational and concessive characteristics. Exaggerating the importance of either aspect of faith distorts the experience. Rational evidence is important to faith; otherwise, as we shall see, faith becomes intellectually irresponsible. It is also true, as we shall see in Part 3, that confidence in God will grow in a maturing Christian experience as evidence to support it accumulates. Nevertheless, we cannot conclude that all the things Christians affirm have an equal amount of evidence to support them or that the strength of a person's confidence in God is always directly proportional to the amount of evidence for it. Otherwise, we would have to regard figures like Job and Abraham as foolish for trusting God when evidence of divine love was lacking.

Although faith goes beyond the evidence in certain ways, we must not conclude that the quality of faith is inversely proportional to the amount of evidence which supports it, as if a lack of evidence automatically enhanced the quality of faith. This seems to have been the view of Tertullian, the famous Latin theologian. According to Tertullian, the statement that "the Son of God died" was "worthy of belief, because it [was] absurd"; that "He was buried and rose again" was "certain because it [was] impossible."[28] But this leads to the untenable conclusion that a lack of evidence provides a basis for faith. One may believe *in spite of* a lack of evidence, but one can hardly believe *because of* a lack of evidence. If that were so, we should have to conclude that the more ridiculous a belief, the more reason one would have to hold it, and the most reliable beliefs of all would be absurd. Faith in its highest form would then amount to an affirmation of nonsense. Such a position has little to recommend it. In fact, it is difficult to know what it could possibly mean.

Besides this important concessive quality, the cognitive dimension of faith is also distinguished by the degree of confidence or certainty characteristic of faith. When worshipers confess, "I believe in God," they express complete confidence in the object of his devotion. Their utterance is not the tentative approval of a hypothesis consistent with a certain amount of evidence which further investigation may or may not sustain. It affirms something of which they are certain. A true believer is willing to "stake his life" on the content of his faith. Those who say, "I believe," in a confessional sense, do not say, "I entertain the possibility that . . . ," or "The conclusion consistent with the present stage of inquiry is that..." They say, in effect, "I am absolutely confident."

This trusting certainty of faith is different from the theoretical certainty that scientific investigation seeks.[29] The ideal objective of scholarly inquiry is to establish a conclusion beyond the possibility of doubt, to satisfy every conceivable condition relative to its truth. In practice, of course, we never achieve this. The most we realistically hope for is a high degree of probability that our hypothesis is true. But we still pursue the ideal of absolute certainty, or "apodicticity," to use a technical term. This sort of theoretical certainty is not the certainty that characterizes faith. The certainty characteristic of faith is a matter of profound personal conviction, not the results of rational investigation. It is a certainty that goes beyond the available evidence.

The Volitional Dimension of Faith

The certainty just mentioned is closely related to another important dimension of faith. In addition to having receptive and cognitive aspects, faith is also volitional in nature. That is to say, faith involves the will. We touch on this dimension when we speak of faith as an act or a decision, and when we hold people responsible for having or not having faith.

The familiar distinction between "faith" and "belief" reflects this dimension of faith. We have seen that faith involves believing certain things. We have also seen that while there is always a degree of evidence to support these beliefs, this evidence is never coercive. Faith always affirms more than reason can support. We applied this "concessive" quality, as we called it, to the contents of faith, but it also applies to the confidence with which we hold our beliefs.

Although faith involves believing certain things, faith is not present until a person acts on his or her beliefs, or relies on them in a personal way. Merely to affirm that certain things are so is not enough. According to James, even demons are capable of that sort of belief (Jas 2:19). Faith involves personal commitment. It is more than *belief that*, it is *belief in*—concrete personal trust. To have faith is to stake your life, the meaning of your entire existence, on what you believe.

As a matter of concrete personal decision, an act of the will, faith requires freedom. There may be many factors that influence a person to have faith, but faith is never an automatic response to certain stimuli. In the final analysis it is something people have to choose to exercise or not. Moreover, faith is an act of the whole person. It is one of those major decisions in which a person's very identity is involved.

This volitional dimension of faith is closely related to the concessive quality we have described. The discrepancy between what faith affirms and what reason establishes requires us to make a personal decision. We cannot sit back and expect rational inquiry to produce faith. From another perspective, this discrepancy makes room for faith. It provides what one scholar describes as the "epistemic distance" we need to exercise personal trust in God.

According to John Hick, human beings are created with a capacity to enjoy a personal relationship with God. But such a relationship involves the exercise of trust, and trust requires the exercise of cognitive freedom. If God were so vividly present to us that his existence were undeniable, we would not be free to respond to him or not. We would have no alternative. Consequently, we need to overcome an initial separation from God if our relation to him will be one of trust, or faith.[30]

Hick's basic point is valid, although we cannot accept all the features of his account. In order for our response to God to be free, it cannot be the only position available to us as thinking people. Consequently, there must be some degree of difference between the conclusions of reason and the affirmations of faith.

Faith is a free decision, but this does not mean that it necessarily originates in an act of self-conscious deliberation. Typically, individual believers are unable to point to specific momentous occasions in their experience when they confronted the choice of trusting God or not. More likely, they recognize that whereas they now believe, there was a time when they did not. But they cannot give a step-by-step account of their progress from one position to the other.

Religious faith is not the only choice in life characterized by inscrutable origins, of course. We probably make our most important decisions in something other than a clear, self-conscious manner. For many people this is true of "falling in love." A person does not ordinarily come to love someone through a process of deliberate investigation. More likely, she becomes aware, gradually or suddenly, that she has already made the decision. She finds that strong feelings and deep commitment are already present.

In a similar way, the decision of faith need not involve a conscious wrestling with alternatives in order to be free. More often than not, people make their choice for or against God and only later become fully aware of what they have done. In describing the new birth to Nicodemus, Jesus appealed to the imperceptible movement of the wind to illustrate the nature of the Holy Spirit's work. "The wind blows where it wills, and you hear the sound of it, but you do not know whence it comes or whither it goes; so it is with every one who is born of the Spirit" (Jn 3:8).[31]

Our work in this chapter reveals that faith is a highly complex experience. It exhibits receptive, cognitive, and volitional dimensions and each dimension has various facets. To summarize our findings and prepare for the discussion to follow let us define faith as a voluntary act of complete trust in God which affirms, among other things, his existence and love in response to evidence that is helpful but not conclusive.[32]

---

[1] James F. Ross makes this distinction in *Introduction to the Philosophy of Religion* (London: The Macmillan Company, 1969), p. 74.
[2] The following comments rely on discussions of *pisteuo* and related biblical terms in volume 6 of *Theological Dictionary of the New Testament*, ed. Gerhard Kittel and Gerhard Friedrich, trans. and ed. Geoffrey W. Bromiley (10 vols.; Grand Rapids, MI: Wm. B. Eerdmans Publishing Company, 1964-1976).
[3] *aman.*
[4] Kittel, 6:196.
[5] Ibid., pp. 187-88.
[6] Ibid., pp. 189, 195.
[7] *pistis.*
[8] Kittel 6:203.
[9] Ibid., pp. 205-207.
[10] Ibid., p. 208.
[11] Ibid., pp. 208-209.
[12] Ibid., pp. 210-212.
[13] Ibid., p. 213.
[14] The famous Latin terms for this distinction are *fides qua creditur* (faith which believes) and *fides quae creditur* (faith which is believed).
[15] Kittel, 6:219.
[16] Ibid., pp. 223-24.
[17] Ibid., pp. 224-25.
[18] Ibid., p. 227.
[19] In the next chapter we discuss William James' well-known concept, "the will to believe." According to James, the will has a role to play in belief when the evidence for and against something is more or less equal. But it is not a callous disregard of overwhelmingly negative evidence.
[20] A. J. Ayer, *Language, Truth and Logic* (2d ed.; New York: Dover Publications, Inc., 1952), p. 35.
[21] See Flew's contribution to the symposium, "Theology and Falsification," in *New Essays in Philosophical Theology*, ed. Antony Flew and Alasdair MacIntyre (New York: The Macmillan Company, 1955), pp. 96-99.
[22] In his well-known reply to Flew, R. M. Hare describes a person's religious utterances as expressions of his or her *blik*, a non-cognitive or pre-rational perspective on reality. It is characteristic of bliks, Hare argues, that nothing counts against them (in *New Essays in Philosophical Theology*, pp. 99-103).
[23] "An Empiricist's View of the Nature of Religious Belief," in *Logic and God: Theology and Verification*, ed. Malcolm L. Diamond and Thomas V. Litzenburg, Jr. (Indianapolis: The Bobbs-Merrill Company, Inc., 1975), p. 138.
[24] Ibid., p. 141.
[25] Ibid., p. 143.
[26] The Latin word *credo* means, "I believe."
[27] Ellen G. White puts the point in these words, "God has never removed the possibility of doubt. . . . Those who wish to doubt will have opportunity; while those who really desire to know the truth will find plenty of evidence on which to rest their faith"

(Steps to Christ [Mountain View, CA: Pacific Press Publishing Association, 1956], p. 105).

[28] *De Carne Christi* 5 (quoted in Richard Swinburne, *Faith and Reason* [Oxford: the Clarendon Press, 1981], p. 24).

[29] Wolfhart Pannenberg puts the point this way: "Today it is time . . . to distinguish the false desire of objective certainty . . . from the trusting certainty of faith, which consists of the total committal of one's own existence in the act of trust, but which is not capable of extending the theoretical credibility of the substance of faith into an absolute theoretical certainty" (*The Apostles' Creed in the Light of Today's Questions*, trans. Margaret Kohl [Philadelphia: Westminster, 1972] p. 131).

[30] Hick's concepts of "epistemic distance" and "cognitive freedom" play a prominent role in his theodicy (*Evil and the God of Love* [rev. ed.; San Francisco: Harper & Row, Publishers, 1978], pp. 281-82).

[31] Ellen G. White observes that the work of the Holy Spirit upon the heart "can no more be explained than can the movements of the wind. . . . By an agency as unseen as the wind, Christ is constantly working upon the heart. Little by little, perhaps unconsciously to the receiver, impressions are made that tend to draw the soul to Christ." As a result, "a person may not be able to tell the exact time or place, or to trace all the circumstances in the process of conversion; but this does not prove him to be unconverted" (*The Desire of Ages* [Mountain View, CA: Pacific Press Publishing Association, 1898] p. 172).

[32] Cf. Hebrews 11:1, 6: "Now faith is the assurance of things hoped for, the conviction of things not seen. . . . And without faith it is impossible to please him. For whoever would draw near to God must believe that he exists and that he rewards those who seek him."

2

REASON AND RESPONSIBLE BELIEF

Reason and Rationality

In Chapter 1 we saw that faith includes a cognitive dimension. It involves giving intellectual assent to various claims, or affirming certain things to be true. We also noticed some important features of this dimension of faith, such as the "in-spite-of," or concessive, quality of religious beliefs and the profound confidence that characteristically attends them.

This book seeks to show that faith is intellectually responsible and that reason can contribute to faith in several important though limited ways. In order to achieve these objectives we need to develop an acceptable standard of intellectual responsibility. Accordingly, our task in this chapter is to examine the nature of human reason. Our specific concern is to find out what constitutes responsible belief, to determine the conditions which make giving assent a responsible thing to do. We should then be in a position to formulate the question of faith and reason carefully, and from there we can go on to explore the different ways in which they are related.

There is a variety of expressions that combine with "faith" or "religious belief" to identify different treatments of our topic. We read of "faith and reason," "faith and knowledge," "faith and understanding," "faith and evidence," "the justification of religious belief," and so on. The diversity points to the fact that the dimension of human experience generally referred to as "reason" is just as complex as the one designated "faith."

People often use the word "reason" in a very general sense to distinguish human beings from other forms of animal life. Although the lines between human intelligence and that of other primates are not easy to draw, man is often defined as the one "rational animal." In this sense, reason seems to refer to the distinctive activities of the human mind. It incorporates all our cognitive faculties beyond sheer sense perception and whatever subliminal modes of experience there may be. So construed, reason would include such intellectual operations as inquiring, understanding, conceiving, formulating, reflecting, marshalling and weighing evidence, judging, deliberating, evaluating, and deciding.[1] All of these are "rational" operations. They indicate that we can do more than receive and react to stimuli. We have the capacity to reflect on our experience.

We also use the word "reason" in a much narrower sense, often as a verb rather than a noun. "To reason" is to think in a careful, methodical, and coherent manner. The activity of reasoning explores relationships and interconnections. It infers from causes to effects, and vice versa. It also deduces conclusions from premises. In this capacity reason is ratiocination, or discursive reason. With our capacity for reflective thought, we can think about thinking, or reason about reasoning. The discipline of logic examines the activity of reasoning. It seeks to analyze the rules or patterns of its effective operation and express them in a formal way.

Most of the time we simply know, or assume that we know, and use our knowledge to get on with the business of living. But every once in a while someone asks us *"How* do you know?" When that happens, we ordinarily offer a few remarks on the matter in question, and that either settles the issue or sets the stage for a brief exchange of views. If I state, "The lawn needs fertilizing," and my wife asks, "How do you know?" I might say: "Because the grass is turning yellow," or "Because it's been six months since I last did it," or "Because *Better Homes and Gardens* says it's time to fertilize again." Only too happy to see me do something useful around the house, she would probably let the matter rest.

But suppose such answers fail to settle the issue. Suppose someone responds to my reasons for saying something by asking,

"How do you know that those reasons adequately support your statement?" Such a question concerns not the data I have given to support my statement, but the way in which I apply the data to the statement. It concerns the structure of my thinking, or the rules of inference I am using. A persistent questioner might ask further, not about the relevance and adequacy of any particular argument, but about the very process of giving reasons, or the nature of thought itself. With such questions we enter the area of epistemology, or the theory of knowledge.

Epistemology, then, addresses the question of what it means to know. It explores the sources, conditions and characteristics of human knowledge. Unlike psychology, however, epistemology is concerned less with the process of coming to know than with the nature of knowing itself. In other words, it concerns the reasons rather than the causes of our beliefs. As a standard work on the subject puts it, the theory of knowledge has as its subject matter "the *justification of belief*, or, more exactly, the justification of *believing*."[2] So, epistemology seeks answers to the following questions: When are we entitled to believe something? What makes a belief intellectually responsible?

In what follows we shall not attempt a full-fledged epistemology. Our objective is simply to outline the conditions of rational belief. In subsequent chapters we will examine religious belief in order to see if these conditions are fulfilled. In addition, we shall concern ourselves with propositional rather than personal knowledge; that is, with the knowledge of truths. As a form of knowledge, faith involves more than assent to propositions, as we saw in the last chapter. But "belief-in" includes "belief-that," as we also noticed, so this is an appropriate place to begin.[3]

The Nature of Knowledge

We can take an initial step toward our objective by stratifying, so to speak, some of the important elements in knowledge. Understanding occupies the most basic level. Understanding is related to meaning. I understand a statement if I know what the author means by it. I do not need to believe what someone says in order to understand it. However, the converse is not true. I can understand without believing, but I cannot believe without understanding.

Belief combines understanding with assent. If I believe something, I not only grasp its meaning, I affirm its truth as well. Philosophers generally agree that belief adds affirmation or assent to understanding, but they do not agree as to exactly what this involves. Some take the view that assent is a voluntary act, that a person decides to accept something to be true. Others maintain that belief is essentially passive. As they see it, we do not choose whether or not to believe something, we are forced to believe by what we find believable. True, we have some control over the process by which we acquire beliefs. We may never bother to look into certain topics, for example, or we may remain willfully ignorant of certain data. But we do not decide what beliefs to have. They are decided for us.[4]

There are also philosophers who take the position that assent is a matter of feeling. To believe something, they maintain, is to have a feeling of confidence or conviction about it. According to David Hume, for example, "Belief consists merely in a certain feeling or sentiment."[5] "An idea assented to feels different from a fictitious idea that the fancy alone presents to us."[6] It has more force or influence, and it seems to have greater importance as well. This view is closely related to the idea that belief is essentially passive, because we do not choose or select our feelings; they simply happen to us.

Some thinkers also define belief with reference to action. In their view, to believe something is to be prepared to act a certain way. As Richard Swinburne puts it, "To believe a proposition is to have a mental attitude towards that proposition which logically constrains the way in which the believer can seek to achieve his purposes."[7] According to this position, a person cannot believe something and fail to act in harmony with it, because for a person to believe something *means* that he or she is disposed to act in a certain way. So, if I say I believe something but fail to act in harmony with it, it turns out that I do not believe it after all.

Knowledge includes belief and goes beyond it. A person might say, "I believe that such-and-such is the case, but I do not know it is true," yet no one could say, "I know that it is the case, but I do not believe it." If we know, we also believe.

Knowledge goes beyond belief in two important ways. These appear in the venerable definition of knowledge as "justified true belief."[8] For one thing, knowledge implies the truth of what is believed. As we use the words, people may *believe* something that is false, but they cannot *know* something that is false. Consequently, since Mount Everest is 29,000 feet high, we could say, "John believes that Mount Everest is 35,000 feet high," but it would not make sense to say, "John knows that Mount Everest is 35,000 feet high." Second, knowledge involves more than just affirming something that is true; it also involves having adequate grounds for believing or accepting it. The element of justification distinguishes knowledge from "true opinion," it is sometimes said. After all, there are times when having a belief that is true is just a matter of luck or coincidence.

Suppose you suffered from abdominal pain. Your family doctor, an internist, attributed it to stomach ulcers, while your second cousin, an astrologer, said you had appendicitis. Whose diagnosis would you accept? Probably the physician's. But suppose, as things turned out, your problem was appendicitis. Would you then say that your cousin *knew* that you had appendicitis, whereas the doctor didn't? Not unless you accept the validity of horoscopes and the like. Your cousin's diagnosis, though correct, was not based on reasons that you regard as valid. He did not acquire his belief by acceptable means. Beliefs that just happen to be true do not constitute knowledge.

Knowledge, then, involves beliefs that are not only true, but are also adequately grounded. We might say that knowledge is a matter of entitlement. In order to know something you not only have to hold a belief that is true, you must also be in some way entitled to that belief. We might also say that knowledge is responsible belief. People who say, "I know," rather than merely, "I think," or "I assume," or "I believe," implicitly accept responsibility for supporting their claims. But however we express it, the point is that a claim to know something requires justification.

The Rational Ideal

In order to emphasize the importance of justification to knowledge, a number of thinkers have formulated versions of what might be called "the rational ideal." According to this principle, the extent of what we claim to know, or the degree of confidence we place in our beliefs, should be directly proportional to the strength of the supporting evidence. In the words of John Locke, the mark of those who love truth for truth's sake alone is "not entertaining any proposition with greater assurance than the proofs it is built upon will warrant."[9] David Hume declares, "A wise man . . . proportions his belief to the evidence."[10] And Bertrand Russell offers this admonition: "Give to any hypothesis that is worth your while to consider just that degree of credence which the evidence warrants."[11]

These expressions of the rational ideal focus attention on the knower. In effect, they say, people rightfully claim to know something only if they have evidence to support their claim. This emphasis on the status of the knower gives knowledge an ethical or moral dimension, as W. K. Clifford argues in his well-known essay "The Ethics of Belief." Clifford states what we are calling the rational ideal in these terms: "It is wrong always, everywhere, and for anyone, to believe anything upon insufficient evidence."[12]

Clifford supports his thesis with a memorable illustration. He describes a shipowner who persuaded himself that a passenger vessel was seaworthy without examining her sufficiently before a voyage. Reluctant to pay for the ship to be overhauled, he assured himself that her past successes and the protection of divine Providence would insure her safety. Consequently, he watched her departure with a light heart, and collected his insurance money when she went down in mid-ocean.

Even though he sincerely believed in the soundness of the ship, Clifford asserts, the owner was "verily guilty of the death of those men." He had no right to his belief on the basis of the evidence before him. He acquired it, not by careful investigation, but by stifling his doubts. Moreover, Clifford maintains, the man would have been just as guilty had the ship turned out to be seaworthy after all. In that case, "The man would not have been innocent, he would only have been not found out." As Clifford sees it, "The question of right or wrong has to do with the origin of his belief, not the matter of it; not what it was, but how he got it; not whether it turned out to be true or false, but whether he had a right to believe on such evidence as was before him."[13] Consequently, we have no right to say "I know" without sufficient evidence. Otherwise, our "pleasure is a stolen one . . . stolen in defiance of our duty to mankind."[14]

Clifford's essay has attracted a great deal of attention in the century since its publication. A number of commentators observe that it really presents two models of rational belief, not just one.[15] It emphatically asserts the rational ideal that one ought to believe nothing on insufficient evidence. But instead of discussing just what constitutes sufficient evidence, it argues for the universal obligation of inquiry. As Clifford describes it, the shortcoming of the shipowner was not that his belief was entirely without evidence—after all, the ship's previous successes should count for something—but that he failed to submit his belief to sufficient scrutiny. Moreover, on his model the passengers who boarded the ship were as guilty of their deaths as the shipowner was, because they too believed in its seaworthiness on insufficient evidence.[16]

Whatever its deficiencies Clifford's position provides us with an emphatic statement of the rational ideal: responsible people base their beliefs on sufficient evidence. In order to assess the validity of this standard, we need to examine the concept of evidence, which plays such a prominent role in its formulation.

Evidence and the Sources of Knowledge

In general terms, evidence represents the data from which reason draws conclusions. Evidence *for* a certain proposition represents data that supports it, or encourages us to believe it. Evidence *against* a proposition is data that contradicts it, or encourages us to deny it or at least to withhold assent. We sometimes speak of such data as "reasons" for or against believing something.

The strength of evidence varies considerably from one belief to another. Some beliefs enjoy the support of overwhelming evidence; others, of fully adequate evidence; still others, of a simple preponderance of evidence. In addition, there are beliefs for which the evidence is insufficient, or relative to which the evidence for and against is divided. We can describe these variations in the strength of evidence in terms of amount and type.

The testimony of two people that John was eating lunch in the University Commons at noon last Monday (and therefore could not have been shoplifting at the Mall) provides stronger evidence than the testimony of one person that he was browsing at the video store when several tapes disppeared. And the testimony of five or ten people to the same effect is that much stronger. So the accumulation of evidence contributes to its strength. But if I personally saw John in the Commons at the time in question, say, having lunch across the table from me, I would find the evidence of my own eyes completely convincing, no matter how many people said they saw him somewhere else. So the nature of evidence is also related to its strength. Some kinds of evidence seem to be much stronger than others.

Because evidence consists of knowledge, we also need to examine the nature of knowledge in order to understand the rational ideal more clearly. We know some things directly and others indirectly. We have direct knowledge of the content of our senses. When I see red, I know that I see red. The experience is self-validating, or self-authenticating. I do not conclude that I see red on the basis of something else. I know I see red because I see it, period. Likewise, when I experience pain, I know that I am in pain. It is not a conclusion arrived at through a process of investigation. My knowledge of pain is immediate and certain.

There are other examples of direct or immediate knowledge. Memory is one of them. We have immediate access to our memories of the past. This does not mean either that our memories perfectly reflect what happened or that they do not need occasional jogging. It means that when we remember, we grasp the content of memory directly.

There are less obvious things that we know directly, too. We know certain truths or propositions this way. For example, we directly grasp the truth of statements such as, "Two plus three equals five" and "All men are either married or unmarried." Philosophers describe such statements as "analytic" and "a priori." They are analytic because their truth or falsity depends entirely on the meaning of the terms involved. By nature, analytic statements do not have factual content; they do not contain any information about the physical world. These statements are *a priori* because we know them to be true or false independent of our experience of the sensory world. To see that two and three make five we do not take opinion polls or conduct laboratory experiments. We see that they must be true, given the meaning of the terms involved. Or we see that they are meaningless and therefore necessarily false.

Although the truth or falsity of analytic statements is necessary because it depends on the meaning of the terms involved, this does not mean that it is always obvious. There are times when it takes effort to grasp the meaning of the terms. I can see instantly that "$2 + 3 = 5$" is a true statement. But it takes some calculating for me to see that "$427 \times 13 = 5551$" is also true. Consequently, although some of the things we know directly are analytic truths, it would not be accurate to say that we know all analytic truths directly.

Besides certain facts, such as the content of our senses, and a number of analytic truths, we also know directly certain "self-verifying" propositions.[17] Descartes' famous words, "I think, therefore I am," provide a statement of this type. The great French thinker sought a basis for his philosophical reflections of which he could be completely certain. He discovered that it was possible to doubt every truth but one—the fact of his own doubting. "I noticed that while I was trying to think everything false, it must needs be that I, who was thinking this, was something." The indubitable reality of the thinking subject gave him the standpoint he was looking for. Since he found it "so solid and secure" that skeptics could not overthrow it, he accepted it "as the first principle of philosophy that I was seeking."[18] Other thinkers affirm the validity of Descartes' discovery. William James, for example, describes "the truth that the present phenomenon of consciousness exists" as the "one indefectibly certain truth" and the "bare starting-point of knowledge."[19]

We know other things of this type directly and intuitively, but not necessarily with clarity and vividness. As in the case of Descartes' *cogito ergo sum*, it often takes considerable reflection in order for us to ascertain the contents of our experience. This is particularly true of the most basic aspects of thought, or the utterly general features of reality. We find it difficult to think of them, not because they are generally absent from our experience, but because they are permanently present. We generally think *with* them rather than *about* them.

If you ask someone looking out her apartment window to tell you what she sees, she will probably describe the sky, the trees, other buildings, or traffic in the street below. It is unlikely that she will say she sees the window. This isn't because the window is invisible, but because the window is, so to speak, permanently visible. Ordinarily we do not notice things like windows and glasses, because we are looking through them to see other things.

It is similar with truths of the sort Descartes described. They represent our "basic beliefs"—the fundamental apprehensions and convictions without which knowledge or experience of any kind would be impossible. And it is precisely because of, rather than in spite of, the important role such beliefs play in knowledge that we ordinarily give them very little attention. Their truth is self-evident, though it may not be obvious.

Most of our knowledge probably consists of things we know indirectly rather than directly. This would include everything we accept on the testimony of others. By the very nature of the case, our knowledge of the distant past is indirect. We are dependent on the accounts of witnesses to find out what happened. This is true of most of our knowledge of the contemporary world as well. Our first-hand knowledge of anything is very limited. We rely heavily on the testimony of others for our information.

We have seen that our knowledge comprises two major categories. We know some things directly and immediately; we know others only indirectly. Many philosophers further believe that our knowledge forms a structure, in that what we know indirectly ultimately depends on what we know directly. If we are asked how we know something—let's call it 'x'—we may reply, "Because we know 'y,' and 'y' supports 'x.'" If asked how we know 'y,' we may say, "Because we know 'z' and 'z' supports 'y.'" But this cannot go on indefinitely. Sooner or later we must come to something that we know without depending on anything else. We don't know it because..., we simply know it, period. We know it on its own merits, not on the strength of something else.

This understanding of knowledge has important implications for the justification of belief. It suggests that there are two sorts of evidence for our beliefs: direct knowledge and indirect knowledge. We are therefore entitled to a belief on one of two conditions: either its content is directly known to us in one of the ways described or we can show that it ultimately derives from something we directly know. The final appeal in a line of reasoning is therefore to intuition, to what we know directly and immediately.[20]

Evidence and Argument

According to the rational ideal, a responsible belief is a *reasoned* belief. It is based on adequate evidence developed by careful investigation. An argument is the formal arrangement of evidence for a belief. It is a structured expression of the process of inferential or discursive reasoning. It is customary to distinguish two types of inferential reasoning and therefore two types of argument, namely, deduction and induction. In very broad terms, deductive reasoning moves from the general to the specific; inductive reasoning, from the specific to the general.

According to logicians, the essential function of a deductive argument is to confer truth. A valid deductive argument is one whose conclusion is true if the premises are true; that is, whose conclusion follows from the premises.[21] The classic example of deductive argument is the syllogism. It consists of a major premise, a minor premise and a conclusion. Here is a famous syllogism: (1) All men are mortal; (2) Socrates is a man; (3) therefore Socrates is a mortal. This argument is valid because the conclusion follows inexorably from the premises. The conclusion, "Socrates is mortal," is unavoidable if it is true that all men are mortal and that Socrates is a man.

The essential feature of deduction is the transmission rather than the discovery of truth. It is possible for an argument to be formally valid even though its premises are false, and it is possible for an argument to be formally invalid even though its premises are true. In the following example, the conclusion follows unavoidably from the premises, but the premises are false: All dogs are immortal; Socrates is a dog; therefore Socrates is immortal. The argument is valid, but the conclusion is false. In the next example, all three statements are true, but they do not form a valid argument because the conclusion does not follow from the premises: All dogs are mortal; Socrates is a man; therefore Socrates is mortal.

Deductive arguments reveal that our beliefs are often linked together in important ways. It is possible to hold to certain beliefs without realizing that they are related. Conceivably, a person could believe (1) that all men are mortal, (2) that Socrates is a man, and (3) that Socrates is mortal, without ever recognizing that (3) is logically required by (1) and (2). On the other hand, certain beliefs exclude others. To use our time-worn example once again, a person who maintains that Socrates was not mortal—that is, who denies (3)—cannot affirm (1) and (2) without contradicting himself or herself. These beliefs, or propositions, are connected in such way that accepting (3) is the inevitable consequence of accepting (1) and (2), and rejecting either (1) or (2), or possibly both, is the logical price of rejecting (3).[22]

Unlike deductive arguments, inductive arguments do not guarantee the truth of their conclusions, even if their premises are true. At best, they provide conclusions that are probable, or probably true. As generally understood, scientific investigation employs a type of inductive reasoning. To greatly oversimplify the process, scientists test hypotheses by examining specific natural phenomena under carefully controlled conditions. They conduct tests, accumulate data, and draw their conclusions. If, for example, large numbers of rats exposed to a certain amount of cigarette smoke for a given period of time contract lung cancer, while similar numbers of unexposed rats of the same species do not, it is reasonable to conclude that cigarette smoke caused the lung cancer of the afflicted rats, or at least contributed heavily to its development. The data further suggest that cigarette smoke will cause lung cancer in other mammals, such as human beings. As a matter of principle, the conclusions of scientific investigation are always open to revision. Even when the evidence appears to be overwhelming and the conclusion virtually assured, the most that scientific investigation can achieve is a high degree of probability—a fact the American Tobacco Institute exploits to allay fears that smoking is hazardous to our health.

To summarize, what we have called the rational ideal arises from the conviction that human beings must take responsibility for their beliefs. It claims that we are entitled only to beliefs that we can support with adequate evidence and valid arguments.

Reason and the Rational Ideal

It is not hard to see why the rational ideal attracts ardent supporters. It is clearly preferable to irrationalism. In many respects it symbolizes the triumph of human intellect over gullibility, prejudice, superstition and ignorance. Indeed, without some such ideal it is difficult to imagine any of the accomplishments we associate with civilization. To use a biblical expression, we would be "children, tossed to and fro and carried about with every wind of doctrine" (Ephesians 4:14).

The rational ideal emphasizes the role of careful investigation and considered judgment in the acquisition of knowledge. The different types of argument we just described represent highly structured forms of the sort of intellectual activity that human beings engage in all the time. If we step back from the formal procedures of deduction and induction to survey the general process of reasoning, several important features of the relation between reason and knowledge emerge.

We see that reason can clarify, confirm and extend our knowledge. By analyzing the evidence bearing on the claims we make, rational inquiry clarifies the configuration of our beliefs. Reason enables us to distinguish between things we know and things we merely believe. It winnows out certain ideas as unworthy of the appellation "knowledge" and strengthens our confidence in others. It establishes what we know more firmly. Reason also extends our knowledge by drawing conclusions from what we already know. So, reason and the rational ideal seem to be closely connected.

The crucial question for us here concerns the relation between intellectual responsibility and the rational ideal. The rational ideal has a good deal to recommend it, but it is not clear that we should accept it as our standard of intellectual responsibility.

What is clear is that insisting that we are only entitled to claims that satisfy this criterion would have a devastating effect on religious beliefs. As we shall observe in greater detail in Part 3, evidence for religious beliefs is notoriously scarce, and typically of a private rather than public character, and people do not ordinarily come to their religious convictions through a process of careful investigation. Moreover, faith by its very nature fails to satisfy the rational ideal. As we saw in Chapter 1, faith exhibits a "concessive" quality; it involves assenting to claims which go beyond the available evidence to some degree, or for which the evidence is less than conclusive. By definition, religious faith represents complete trust in God in the absence of proof or demonstration. And the rational ideal discredits any belief for which the available evidence is not conclusive. So, given the nature of faith on the one hand, and the requirements of the rational ideal on the other, we must either reject religious beliefs as intellectually irresponsible or find a different criterion of responsibility.

Over time a good many thinkers have objected to the rational ideal for one reason or another, and in recent years their voices have become louder and more numerous. In order to develop a standard of rationality appropriate for our examination of faith and reason, it will be helpful for us to review some of these criticisms.

The Rational Ideal Reconsidered

According to its detractors, those who espouse the rational ideal have one major shortcoming. They fail to appreciate the complexity of the experience or process of knowing, so their standards of responsible belief are artificially narrow and rigid. Consequently, we need to find more expansive concepts of rationality and evidence and more modest expectations of what inferential reasoning, or argument, can accomplish. A number of things support a more generous standard of responsible belief, beginning with the fact that there is more than one level of rationality.

1. Levels of rationality

The rational ideal stipulates that beliefs are reasonable only if the evidence which supports them is conclusive. But a little reflection reveals, not just one, but several sorts of belief that deserve to be regarded as rational. We apply the word "reasonable," for example, to at least three different categories of belief.[23] One, of course, contains beliefs which satisfy the rational ideal. The evidence for them is overwhelming and undeniable, and we are certain of their truth. We may even say that beliefs which lie beyond all possibility of doubt occupy the highest level of rationality.

A belief may fall short of absolute certainty, and yet lie "beyond a reasonable doubt," to use an expression familiar to us from the courtroom. In the legal system of the United States, judges instruct jurors in criminal trials to return a verdict of "guilty" if the defendant's guilt has been established "beyond a reasonable doubt." Absolute certainty is not required. A belief is reasonable, it would seem, if it lies beyond a reasonable doubt, even though the evidence for it may not be indubitable.

As we typically use the word, a belief can also be "reasonable" if it is supported by a clear preponderance of evidence, that is, if the evidence in its favor outweighs the evidence against it. To return to the legal realm, this is the standard of judgment that typically applies in civil, as distinct from criminal, cases in the United States. Jurors in such cases must determine whether the weight of evidence favors the plaintiff or the defendant. It is not necessary for either side to prove its claim "beyond a reasonable doubt," let alone beyond all possibility of doubt.

Some thinkers add a fourth category to the list of reasonable beliefs. There are those who maintain that a belief is reasonable if the evidence for and against it are evenly divided. In that case, they argue, it is no more reasonable to reject than to accept it. Others insist that we should suspend judgment when the evidence is divided and withhold both assent and denial.

British philosopher Richard Swinburne finds rationality so complex that he distinguishes no fewer than five categories of "rational belief."[24] In one sense, he argues, a belief is rational as long as it satisfies a person's own standards of reasoning. In another sense, a belief is rational only if it satisfies correct objective standards. According to the former, it was reasonable for someone living in ninth century Europe to believe that the world was flat, given the information then available and the general understanding of people at the time. But according to the latter, this belief is not rational and never has been.

Swinburne relates three additional types of rational belief to adequate investigation. A belief is rational if it is backed by investigation which people believe to be adequate by their own inductive standards. It is rational in another sense if backed by investigation which is actually adequate by these same standards. And it is rational in still another sense only if it is backed by investigation which is adequate according to true, or objectively valid, standards.

We need not examine these subtle distinctions further in order to see the necessity of accepting certain beliefs as rational even when they are not backed by investigation (beliefs falling within Swinburne's first two categories). For if we were not entitled to a belief unless we had personally investigated and verified it, the number of rational beliefs anyone held, or could ever hold, would be exceedingly small. It would be difficult, if not impossible, for us to get through the activities of a single ordinary day without accepting things we have not investigated ourselves. Furthermore, we would undoubtedly regard the behavior of people who refused to believe anything they had not investigated themselves as highly irrational. They would not fit into normal society, and it would be troublesome just to carry on a simple conversation with them.

The rational ideal, then, fails to take into account certain facts of experience. For one thing, we intuitively acknowledge different levels of rationality; we apply the word "reasonable" to various types of claims. For another, it is practically impossible for us to subject all our beliefs to personal investigation. Consequently, it seems patently *unreasonable* (pun intended) to insist that the only sort of belief that qualifies as "rational" is one which enjoys the support of conclusive evidence acquired through a process of personal investigation.

2. *Degrees of responsibility*

Something else that requires us to expand our criterion of rationality is the recognition that not everyone has the same responsibility to investigate a certain belief. Whether someone must conduct a personal investigation in order to be entitled to a belief depends on circumstances. In his article "The Ethics of Belief Reconsidered," Van A. Harvey suggests that such an obligation is "role-specific." It depends on the particular duties or responsibilities an individual has. Of the ship-owner in Clifford's illustration, Harvey observes, "He is not being asked to hold all of his beliefs on the basis of inquiry. He is responsible only for arriving at a specific range of critical judgments...."[25] As the owner of a vessel on which people's lives depend, he has an obligation to investigate its condition carefully before announcing, "This ship is seaworthy."

Similarly, if the President of the United States faces an operation, it is one thing for me as an ordinary citizen to say, "He is strong enough to survive it"; it is quite another for his personal physicians to say so. Their professional positions involve the responsibility of making sound medical judgments regarding the state of the chief executive's health. Accordingly, my belief in the President's vitality is "reasonable" if it rests on a general impression of his physical condition. Theirs, in contrast, is "reasonable" only if it is based on a careful examination of medical data. In addition, a great deal more rides on their belief than on mine. My belief may do little more than stimulate dinner table conversation. Theirs may conceivably affect the future of the world. So, whether personal investigation is required in order to establish a belief as "reasonable" depends on the sorts of obligations a person assumes.

It also depends on the relative importance of the belief within the context of the person's life. Some beliefs have more personal significance to us than others. For example, my belief that my son reached school safely this morning is more important to me than my belief that Mount McKinley is the tallest peak in North America. It would not distress me particularly to discover I was wrong about Mount McKinley. But I would be greatly concerned to find that I was mistaken about my son's safety. And if I had occasion to question either belief, I would expend a good deal more energy in the effort to ascertain the truth of the second.

Certain beliefs are also more important to us than others in the sense that they are more basic to our thought and experience. As we have seen, investigating beliefs of this nature is difficult, because they typically form the framework or structure of our thinking rather than the object of our thought. The question of whether or not we have an obligation to investigate such beliefs is an interesting one. On the one hand, it seems that intellectually responsible persons would want to subject their most basic beliefs to searching rational scrutiny. On the other hand, such activity takes a good deal of time and energy, if not a high level of academic competence in philosophy. If everyone pursued it, there would be time for little else.

Consider a biologist, for example, engaged in studying the dam building habits of beavers. She must assume a continuity between the past and the future, which is basic to scientific endeavor, but she would have no time for beavers if she devoted herself to reflecting on this belief and others like it. To get on with her scientific work, she has to leave such investigation to the philosopher of science. For purely practical reasons, then, the responsibility of examining certain beliefs may also be role-specific, to use Harvey's term. As intellectual beings, we may all have some responsibility to examine the beliefs which are central to thought and experience, but the amount of time we can afford to spend doing so depends on our other obligations.

We have just found two reasons for objecting to the rational ideal. Since the word "reasonable" applies to several different sorts of belief, and since the responsibility to investigate a specific belief depends on various things, we cannot say that a belief is reasonable only if it is conclusively established through personal investigation. There are other factors, too, that require us to seek an alternative to the rational ideal. They include the nature of evidence and the practical relation between argument and belief.

3. Public and private evidence

In a discussion of the nature of rational belief, Stephen T. Davis makes a perceptive distinction between public and private evidence.[26] Public evidence consists of data that are, at least in principle, available to any investigator. It does not depend on a privileged standpoint, or on some special experience of illumination. Scientific data provide the classic example of this type of evidence. The scientist draws conclusions from phenomena that are accessible to everyone who has the proper equipment and the necessary know-how to examine them. A well-designed scientific experiment will produce the same results anywhere in the world, no matter who conducts it, if the original conditions can be duplicated. Public evidence is available to any sufficiently observant person.

Private evidence, in contrast, is not generally available. Its perception requires a unique perspective. In fact, it is characteristic of private evidence that it cannot in principle be made public. My seeing John eat lunch in the Commons at a certain time would represent public evidence even if he and I were the only people in the room, because my experience would be available to any sighted person. But if a "vision" of John eating lunch in the Commons appears to me while I am sitting in my office, or I hear a mysterious voice say, "John is now eating lunch in the Commons," while I am driving home one day, it would represent private evidence of his whereabouts. I could not assume that other people in my situation would have the same experience.

Private evidence is typically of a highly personal nature. It includes what the French philosopher Blaise Pascal refers to as "reasons of the heart."[27] There are certain things we know in ways that are difficult to communicate to other people, or for reasons that might even sound nonsensical if we tried to express them verbally. This is characteristic of some of the most important experiences of our lives. People who are deeply in love are typically unable to describe their relationship in cool, rational terms. They can't explain their commitment by referring to evidence that any observer could see. Each believes the other worthy of great affection, and the predominant evidence which supports their belief is private.

In general, people not only allow private evidence to play a role in romantic experience, they consider it indispensable. In fact, we would question the depth of affection between people who could only cite public evidence to account for their relationship. People should love each other for reasons other than physical appearance, education, musical or athletic ability, and earning power. Love should also find other, intensely private, reasons for its existence.

In other areas, too, we appreciate the way people seem to derive knowledge from private evidence. In the realm of detective fiction, Sherlock Holmes is the master of deductive thought.[28] He drew all his conclusions from purely public evidence. What distinguished him from others, notably his companion John Watson, was an astonishing power of perception. Holmes saw things that were there for everyone to see, but he was often the only one to notice them and to appreciate their relation to the matter under investigation.

In sharp contrast to Holmes, films and television shows occasionally feature curmudgeonly old police chiefs, or rumpled detectives like Sergeant Colombo, who somehow know "whodunnit" long before the evidence is in. Intuition takes them directly to the guilty party while others tediously pursue conventional investigation. So, there are times when people act on hunches, instincts, or intuition to reach correct conclusions, and we admire such leaps of insight just as much as Sherlock Holmes' powers of deduction.

Although private evidence plays an important role in our thinking, it is not easy to determine the relative weight we should assign to it. Perhaps its significance is context-dependent, somewhat like the role-specific responsibility people have for supporting beliefs we noticed earlier. In a court of law, only public evidence is admissible. A detective's hunch may help him solve a crime, but it will not convict the criminal. The prosecutor's case must rest on publicly accessible evidence, not the intuition of a police officer. In other situations private evidence may tip the scales when public evidence is indecisive. Suppose an experienced physician has not been able to diagnose a patient's problem conclusively, but strongly suspects that a certain disease is at fault. Under the circumstances it may be wise for him to follow his intuition and prescribe an appropriate course of treatment.

Ordinarily both public and private evidence figure in our beliefs, and whether one or the other will be more prominent depends on the nature of the belief. In highly important personal matters, such as a decision to marry, private evidence will be extremely influential. At the same time, public evidence remains important, if not to the two principals involved, then certainly to their parents.

We have spoken of public and private evidence as if the distinction were clearcut and exhaustive—as if all evidence were either available to everyone or restricted to single individuals. In actuality, things are more complicated. Sometimes a number of people have highly unusual experiences of a similar kind. Because of their unpredictability, such experiences cannot be regarded as public evidence, yet because of their number and similarity they cannot be regarded as completely private either. Moreover, those who have such experiences are likely to believe the accounts of other people who claim to have had them. Such evidence is therefore neither public nor private in the strictest sense of these terms. It lies somewhere in between.

This seems to describe the evidence provided by personal religious experiences. It is not strictly public, because many people do not have religious sentiments, and those who do often find it difficult to describe their content. On the other hand, the evidence of religious experience is not entirely private, either. Large numbers of people do have experiences they regard as religious, and they find enough similarity in one another's accounts of them to form large and lasting communities. Any standard of responsible belief will have to take into account these important differences in the types of evidence that figure in our thinking.

4. The limits of argument

According to the rational ideal, argument has an important role to play in responsible belief. For a belief to be rational, it must rest on adequate evidence, and we must be able to demonstrate just how the evidence supports it. In other words, we must be able to construct valid arguments for it. This suggests that we acquire our beliefs through a process of deliberate investigation—by carefully sifting and organizing the evidence.

In the actual course of events, however, we hardly ever come to our beliefs through such a process, and seldom feel the need to defend our beliefs by means of rational demonstration. Indeed, according to many philosophers and logicians, the construction of arguments and proofs is a purely academic exercise. It has nothing to do with the ways in which we acquire or maintain our beliefs. James F. Ross, for one, describes the nature and function of philosophical arguments in the following way.

Ross maintains that a good argument is "impersonal-objective" rather than "personal-relative." As he interprets it, "A good argument proves something: it shows that its conclusion is so,"[29] and the purpose of arguments is to establish beliefs "as part of a theoretical and explanatory picture of the world." In order to accomplish this, arguments must be logically sound, and they must satisfy the general standards of scientific inquiry, namely, public accessibility and assessability.[30] But this is all that arguments can or should be expected to do. They "need not convince anyone who does not already accept the conclusion." Indeed, they "need not convert, convince, or comfort anyone."[31] According to Ross, then, it is not surprising that arguments do not generally lead people to belief, for this is not what they are supposed to do.

If Ross is correct, then the rational ideal is mistaken. Insisting that people are entitled to a belief only if they have developed a formal argument for it, ignores the facts of experience. Moreover, it puts more weight on arguments than they were meant to carry.

5. *The changing shape of evidence*

Besides the notorious ineffectiveness of arguments in changing people's minds, other phenomena also indicate that the relation between belief and evidence in our actual experience is much looser than the rational ideal allows for. According to the rational ideal, a reasonable belief rests on a solid evidential basis. Consequently, when this evidence shifts or erodes, there must be a corresponding change in the belief. But the fact is that a belief can remain relatively constant while evidence for it changes considerably.

As adults, we still hold many of the beliefs we acquired as children, but we would now support them in quite different ways. In some cases, we find that our earlier understanding was inadequate; in other cases, that it was simply wrong.

In his book on miracles, C. S. Lewis mentions a young girl who believed that poison was harmful because it contained "horrid red things" that would kill her or make her terribly sick.[32] As she grew up she no doubt retained the belief that poison was harmful, but presumably her reasons for thinking so changed. After twenty years of marriage, a man may believe that his wife is just as worthy of love as he did on their wedding day. But the evidence that supports this belief may include all sorts of things that would not have been available on the earlier occasion, such as her care for their children, her professional development, her advanced organizational skills, and conceivably her increasing physical attractiveness. Conversely, some of the evidence that supported his belief in earlier times is now utterly irrelevant, such as the verdict of his college roommate that she was "quite a catch," or the fact that she was social vice-president of the Business Club one year and played a great third base in an intramural softball league. Then again, some of what counted as evidence earlier on may have been simply erroneous. Perhaps she wasn't the cook he thought she was, or he found on the fortieth or fiftieth reading that her poems in the college yearbook were really quite dreadful.

In actual experience, then, a particular belief and a specific body of supporting evidence do not form the tight structural unit which the rational ideal mandates. Intellectual responsibility would seem to require *some* connection between evidence and beliefs, but our beliefs are not strictly dependent on or determined by the evidence. As we have seen, people's beliefs can remain constant while the evidence they find to support them shifts and changes. An even stronger challenge to the rational ideal comes from those who question the whole idea that a body of evidence provides the basis for our system of beliefs.

6. The groundlessness of belief

In recent years a growing number of thinkers have come to reject entirely the idea that our beliefs somehow rest on evidential foundations that can be discovered and formulated as arguments. Norman Malcolm, for one, calls attention to the "groundlessness" of many beliefs whose validity we would never think to question. Consider the belief we universally share that material objects do not cease to exist without some physical explanation.[33] Malcolm observes that we do not acquire this belief by examining evidence and comparing it to the contradictory proposition, and we do not seek grounds to support it now. Instead, this belief forms part of the unreflective framework of our thinking.

Framework principles or propositions like this form what Malcolm (following Wittgenstein) calls a "system." We ask questions, examine evidence, and make judgments within the system, but we do not question the system itself. Nor do we select the system after a process of rational investigation. We acquire it much as we acquire a knowledge of our native language: we grow into it and accept it trustingly. Furthermore, Malcolm insists, we must not regard the framework principles of our system as self-justifying. The notion of self-justifying reasons obscures the non-reflective character of a system. We don't accept a system of propositions because investigation reveals them to be self-evident; we simply accept it, period. In effect, then, Malcolm dismisses the notion that we are entitled to beliefs only if we have examined them carefully in light of the evidence. Such a process has little to do with the way we actually live.

We find similar objections to the rational ideal in the work of other philosophers who herald the collapse of "foundationalism." Foundationalism is "the pursuit of immediately justified propositions on which further structures of justified belief could be constructed."[34] Foundationalists maintain that all of a person's rational beliefs fall into two categories which join to form a tidy, integrated structure of knowledge. Some beliefs are mediated by other beliefs, and some beliefs are produced immediately. Mediated beliefs are rational if they are supported by immediate beliefs which are rational. And immediate beliefs are rational, according to a prevalent version of foundationalism, if they are either self-evident (e.g., $1+1=2$) or report states of consciousness about which one could not be mistaken (e.g., "I feel pain"). Beliefs of this type are "basic beliefs," because the entire structure of our knowledge ultimately rests on them. So, unless a belief is either one of our basic beliefs or, if nonbasic, is demonstrably supported by these basic beliefs, it is not a reasonable belief.[35]

According to one of its critics, Alvin Plantinga, classical foundationalism exhibits two fatal flaws. One is its inadequate concept of basic belief. By restricting basic beliefs to those that are either self-evident, incorrigible, or evident to the senses, foundationalism eliminates enormous numbers of beliefs that it never occurs to us to question—beliefs which, in Plantinga's words, "form the stock in trade of ordinary everyday life." On the foundationalist criterion, for example, I cannot accept as rational the beliefs that there are persons distinct from myself and that the universe is more than five minutes old.[36]

The other flaw is the failure of foundationalism to meet its own criterion of rationality. The belief, "all rational beliefs are either basic in one of the ways described or else supported by such beliefs," is neither basic itself nor derived from basic beliefs. So, foundationalism invalidates itself. In technical terms, its central claim is "self-referentially incoherent."[37]

The collapse of foundationalism is widely accepted among philosophers today, but there is no general consensus on what should follow it. Some thinkers maintain that there are other, non-foundationalist, ways to justify our beliefs.[38] Others insist that the very notion that our beliefs need justification is mistaken.[39] Our purpose here is not to enter into this debate, but simply to note the widespread resistance to the position we have identified as the rational ideal. However popular it may have been at one time, a viewpoint that is steadily losing adherents can hardly serve as a *standard* of responsible belief.

7. *The will to believe*

Besides the realization that our beliefs do not, for the most part, rest on evidential foundations, another, more positive, consideration also calls for an alternative to the rational ideal. This is the recognition that non-rational factors play a legitimate and important role in our beliefs. This is true not only of beliefs in general, as we shall see in this section, but also of some of the most carefully tested of all beliefs, the claims of natural science, as the next section shows.

One of the best-known accounts of this role appears in William James' famous essay "The Will to Believe," in which he responds to W. K. Clifford's essay, "The Ethics of Belief." As we have seen, Clifford insists that "it is wrong always, everywhere, and for anyone, to believe anything upon insufficient evidence."[40] So, unless there is a clear preponderance of evidence which favors a belief, people are obliged to withhold their assent.

As James observes, the basic objective of Clifford's approach is to avoid erroneous beliefs. This is highly important, James concedes, but we also have a distinct, and equally important, obligation to know the truth. As Roderick Chisholm observes, we could fulfill either obligation by itself quite easily, either by doubting everything or by believing everything.[41] The trick is to balance the two, and as James sees it, Clifford's approach fails to do so. It may protect us from error, but the price is too high. In certain situations it is preferable to run the risk of embracing error than to miss all chance at truth. James asserts, "I believe that worse things than being duped may happen to a man in this world."[42]

According to James, it is sometimes appropriate for us to let our "passional nature" influence belief when intellect alone leaves an issue undecided.[43] This is true when the option before us exhibits three important characteristics. It must be living, momentous, and forced.[44] An option is *living* for someone when both alternatives are plausible. It is theoretically possible that the universe originated fifteen minutes rather than eons ago, but this does not represent a plausible view in the minds of most people. So, in this case we do not face a living option.

An option is *momentous* when the alternatives have enormous personal significance. Is it better to write the newspaper carrier a note with pencil or ballpoint pen? The option may be living, but it is hardly momentous. In contrast, several years ago my wife and I had to decide whether our six-year-old daughter should have surgery to correct a congenital kidney problem or left alone in hopes the condition would correct itself in time. In this case the option was momentous.

Finally, an option is *forced* if failing to decide is tantamount to making a choice. My wife and I could not postpone the decision just mentioned indefinitely without selecting one of the alternatives by default. The option before us was clearly forced. When these three conditions obtain, James argues, we are rationally justified in allowing our passional nature to influence our beliefs.

The careful way in which James indicates just when it is appropriate for us to allow our passional nature to influence our beliefs discredits a popular misunderstanding of his position. It is not James' view that people are entitled to believe something just because they want to even though the preponderance of evidence is against it, still less that people can believe things simply by force of will. Instead, the will to believe as James describes it comes into play when the intellect leaves an issue undecided; that is, only when the evidence for and against a belief is evenly balanced.

8. Science and imagination

No exercise of human reason has achieved more impressive results than scientific investigation. Science has contributed more than any other factor to the emergence of our modern view of the world.[45] And some regard it as the only area of human endeavor that shows undeniable progress. For many people, scientific inquiry exemplifies the rational ideal perfectly. They regard science as a steadily growing body of information acquired through the careful, dispassionate examination of objective data. The relation between data and conclusion is clear, and the degree of confidence with which positions are advanced is directly proportional to the strength of the supporting evidence. Consequently, they take the words "rational" and "scientific" to be largely synonymous. No intellectual enterprise deserves respect unless it satisfies standards of "scientific" inquiry. There are even those who insist that evidence of a scientific, empirical, or sense-perceived nature is the only evidence that is truly rational. It is a widespread conviction, then, that scientific claims exemplify the rational ideal perfectly, and the accomplishments of science give the ideal validity.

The accomplishments of science are certainly impressive, and any examination of human cognition must take into account the features of scientific inquiry.[46] At the same time, science does not support the rational ideal the way many people seem to think it does. For reasons we have already seen, it is highly doubtful that strict scientific methods of inquiry could be applied to a broad range of human experience. Practical considerations prevent us from acquiring anything like scientific proof for everything we believe. But more significant, the actual pattern of scientific development does not fit the rationalistic conception of science widely held by supporters of the rational ideal.

In his influential book *The Structure of Scientific Revolutions*, Thomas S. Kuhn demonstrates that "normal science," as he calls it, does not lead to momentous scientific discoveries. Instead, the history of science reveals that these come about only when ordinary scientific operations reach an impasse.

According to Kuhn, the objective of normal scientific activity is not to discover some fact or truth of which humankind has been hitherto unaware. Its purpose is to fit data within the framework supplied by a paradigm. A paradigm is the prevalent conceptual framework through which scientists view the world.[47] It acquires this status by helping to solve a few important problems and promising the solution to still others. Ordinary scientific work seeks to articulate the paradigm by extending its application to broader and broader areas of data.[48]

The thesis of Kuhn's essay is that significant scientific discovery involves a breakdown in paradigms. In the course of their normal investigation, scientists often encounter anomalies—phenomena for which the accepted paradigm does not prepare them.[49] Anomalies set the stage for new discoveries by revealing inadequacies in the prevailing paradigm and leading scientists seek new paradigms to replace it. With a major shift in paradigms, a scientific revolution takes place. It represents "a displacement of the conceptual network through which scientists view the world."[50]

Kuhn's analysis of scientific revolutions reveals that the course of scientific development does not fit the popular vision of cool calculation resulting in the steady accumulation of knowledge. Instead, the advance of science is an episodic and crisis-laden affair. Scientific discovery involves leaps of insight that go well beyond what the data currently support. And the most important scientific proposals are those which stimulate the future accumulation of data, not the ones which are firmly based on data that is already developed.

The popular concept of the scientist as a detached observer objectively recording phenomena in the natural world has completely eroded in recent years. Scholars now emphasize the personal and imaginative character of scientific understanding. Michael Polanyi stresses the importance of "the personal participation of the knower in all acts of understanding." In his words, "a passionate contribution of the person knowing" represents "a vital component of his knowledge."[51]

A more recent work examines the role of metaphors in scientific knowledge. According to Mary Gerhart and Allan Melvin Russell, metaphors are intrinsic to scientific activity, and they play a constructive rather than a merely illustrative role in scientific thought. Einstein's Special Theory of Relativity, for example, represents a metaphoric fusion of the laws of motion in the field of mechanics and in the field of electromagnetism. It shows how "the creation of a metaphor distorts our world of meanings so that our understanding of nature is radically changed."[52]

These developments in the history and philosophy of science are significant for our present concern, because they show that the actual practice of science does not support a popular conception of the enterprise. There is a great deal more involved in scientific activity than the steady extraction of conclusions from the observation of data. Scientific discovery of the most radical kind displays leaps of imagination and creativity that transcend the narrow boundaries of conventional scientific investigation. Carefully considered, then, science does not support the rational ideal that all our beliefs should rest on a secure foundation of public evidence. The impressive achievements of human thought in penetrating the structure of empirical reality would never have occurred had thinkers adhered to the rational ideal as their criterion of responsible belief.

Responsible Belief: An Alternative to the Rational Ideal

All these considerations add up to a strong case against the rational ideal. As such, they both underscore the need for and point the way to an alternative standard of responsible belief. The rational ideal sets the standard of responsible belief too high. It is unrealistic to insist that we are entitled only to beliefs which we can fully establish by formally valid arguments on the basis of publicly accessible evidence. A responsible belief is not necessarily rational in this narrow sense of the word.

All the same, we must acknowledge what is valid in the rational ideal. It is the conviction that intellectual responsibility requires us to accept only beliefs which have some measure of rational support. We cannot hold our beliefs in defiance of all the evidence, or allow them to degenerate into matters of mere personal preference. Such a position is not only academically unrespectable, it is downright dangerous. And it is unethical. Rationality is a matter of morality. Responsible human beings accept responsibility for their beliefs, as for other aspects of their lives. So we do need a standard of reasonable belief.

Just as important, we need a standard of belief that is realistic. Set the standard too high, as the rational ideal does, and few beliefs qualify. Skepticism becomes the only acceptable position. To avoid this pitfall, our notions of rationality and justification must take into account the complexity of human thought and experience. Our preceding observations point the way to a more generous and realistic standard of intellectual responsibility.

It is instructive to note the way in which we ordinarily acquire our beliefs. Typically, our most important beliefs about life and reality are more or less given to us. We acquired them unreflectively under the various influences that surrounded us as we grew up, and we still hold to them because it never occurs to us to doubt them. For the most part, this is true of the way our beliefs continue to accumulate. As Van Harvey states, "we do not acquire our beliefs by being dragged and screaming, as it were, out of skepticism. Nor do we carefully weigh the evidence for every proposition recommended to us."[53] It does not strike us as irrational or irresponsible to hold beliefs which we did not obtain through deliberate investigation.

The normal process by which we come to believe suggests that it is reasonable to entertain beliefs that have not undergone deliberate rational justification. In fact, as a general rule we may consider ourselves entitled to our beliefs unless we have good reason to question them. So the burden of proof rests not on those who accept certain beliefs, but on those who reject them. At the same time, it will not do to generalize that we are entitled to any belief whatever, just so long as it has not been conclusively disproved, for this would make us vulnerable to all sorts of strange claims. The fact that not all our beliefs require rational justification does not mean that none of them do. To exchange a rationalism so rigid that it requires formal justification for everything for an irrationalism so lax it requires justification for nothing would hardly improve our intellectual situation.

Consequently, if we reject the rational ideal—the view that we are entitled to beliefs only if they have been subjected to deliberate investigation and enjoy the support of formally valid arguments resting solidly on public evidence—but we still want to be intellectually responsible, we face two important questions. Just when does a belief require rational justification? And what does adequate justification consist of?

How can we tell if a belief needs formal justification in order to acquire rational status? It depends on at least two things: the position of the believer and the nature of the belief. We have seen that the obligation to justify certain beliefs is what some thinkers call "role-specific." It arises from the distinctive responsibilities people assume. Thus, shipowners have an obligation to justify their beliefs concerning the seaworthiness of various ships, and physicians have an obligation to justify their diagnoses, which people outside these occupations may not have. It is also the case that certain beliefs raise questions for some people but not for others. Consequently, the obligation to submit a belief to rational scrutiny appears to be, at least at times, a matter of personal inclination. If certain people have doubts about a particular belief, then they should investigate it; otherwise, they have no need to worry about it.

There are also certain beliefs whose very nature seems to require, or at least invite, investigation. What about our most fundamental beliefs about reality and human experience? Do we need to examine such beliefs carefully in order to give our knowledge a solid footing? The question is a difficult one. As we have seen, it is precisely such beliefs that need no justification according to many philosophers today. If we grow up with our basic beliefs and never have cause to doubt them, why should we feel any need to establish them? Furthermore, even if we felt such a need, there is the difficulty of trying to prove beliefs of this nature. As the bases of thought and experience, such beliefs provide the ultimate grounds for other beliefs, so how can they themselves be the object of rational demonstration? We shall return to the question of proofs and basic beliefs in a later chapter. But even if some beliefs do not require rational support to be acceptable, there are others whose problematic or controversial nature demands it.

Beliefs which clearly call for rational justification are those which conflict, or appear to conflict, with other beliefs we have. This is the case, for example, when new scientific theories arise which are incompatible with previously held views. Such beliefs require justification before we are entitled to them. Other beliefs require justification, especially ones that have personal importance, when their rational status is questioned within the prevailing intellectual environment. This applies to basic beliefs, too. Although we ordinarily accept such beliefs without investigation, we may be obliged to find evidence to support them if they are challenged or attacked. It seems, then, that our obligation to justify our beliefs varies from time to time and from one belief to another.

Once we have determined that a belief requires or deserves investigation, what does it take to give it rational status? When are we entitled to accept it as a reasonable belief? The short answer is, "When the evidence supports it," but the matter is not quite so simple. As we have seen, there are levels of rationality just as there are degrees of responsibility. A belief is clearly rational under one of three conditions: (1) when it is a certainty, that is, when the evidence for it is conclusive; (2) when it lies beyond a reasonable doubt, or when the evidence for it is overwhelming; and (3) when it enjoys a clear preponderance of evidence, even though there may be considerable evidence against it. We are rationally entitled to beliefs that fall in any of these categories, although the relative confidence we have in them may vary in proportion to the strength of the evidence.

In this chapter we have considered a number of things which indicate that we may be entitled to beliefs which do not fit into these categories. They include the notion of private evidence and such non-evidential factors as the role of the passional nature in belief and the contribution of imagination to scientific theories. The presence of elements like these in our cognitive experience requires us to enlarge the notion of reasonable belief. They indicate that it is possible to support our beliefs on grounds other than publicly accessible evidence. Consequently, it may be reasonable to believe propositions which do not enjoy the decisive support of publicly accessible evidence. Just what beliefs come under this rubric must be determined on a case by case basis, but its existence provides us with an important resource as we examine the rational status of religious beliefs.

These considerations produce a more realistic criterion of responsible belief. They show that a belief may be reasonable even though it is not reasoned—acquired, that is, through a process of deliberate investigation. They also suggest that a belief requires rational justification when it is relatively important and when it conflicts with other beliefs we hold and/or is challenged by the prevailing culture in which we live. And, finally, they indicate that a belief may be justified on grounds other than a preponderance of publicly accessible evidence, including private evidence and even non-evidential factors.

In sum, these considerations give us a concept of responsible belief which is solidly rational, but considerably more generous than the rational ideal we have described. Our concept of responsible belief defines a posture which, in Hans Küng's words, is "against rationalism for rationality."[54]

The task before us now is to apply the operations of reason and the standards of rationality outlined in this chapter to the contours of faith described in Chapter 1. What happens when we apply reason to the contents of faith? Are religious beliefs intellectually responsible? And what happens when we apply reason to the experience of faith? Does rational inquiry help or hinder religious commitment? Does it even have anything to do with it? These are our central concerns in Parts 2 and 3.

---

[1] See Bernard Lonergan's "pattern of operations" in *Method in Theology* (New York: Herder and Herder, 1972), p. 6.

[2] Roderick M. Chisholm, *Theory of Knowledge* (2d ed.: Englewood Cliffs, NJ: Prentice-Hall, Inc., 1977), p. 5.

[3] For a helpful discussion of this distinction, see H. H. Price, "Belief 'In' and Belief 'That,'" in *Religious Studies*, 1 (1965):5-27; reprinted in *The Philosophy of Religion*, ed. Basil Mitchell (Oxford: Oxford University Press, 1971), pp. 141-67.

[4] Richard Swinburne maintains that belief is "involuntary," or "passive." "In general," he writes, "a man cannot choose what to believe there and then. Believing is something that happens to a man, not something that he does" (*Faith and Reason* [Oxford: Clarendon Press 1981], p. 25).

[5] *A Treatise of Human Nature*, Appendix, p. 624 (quoted in Swinburne, p. 25).

[6] *Treatise on Human Nature* (Book I, Part III, Section VII) (quoted in Vincent Brummer, *Theology and Philosophical inquiry: An Introduction* [Philadelphia: Westminster Press, 1982] p. 156).

[7] *Faith and Reason*, p. 26.

[8] Vincent Brummer, *Theology and Philosophical Inquiry*, p. 150.

[9] *An Essay Concerning Human Understanding*, Book 4, Chapter 19, §1 (in *The English Philosophers From Bacon to Mill*, ed. Edwin A. Burtt [New York: The Modern Library, 1939], p. 396).

[10] *An Enquiry Concerning Human Understanding*, Section x, Part 1 (in *The English Philosophers From Bacon to Mill*, p. 653).

[11] *A History of Western Philosophy* (New York: Simon and Schuster, 1945), p. 816

(quoted in Stephen T. Davis, *Faith, Skepticism, and Evidence: An Essay in Religious Epistemology* [London: Associated University Presses, Inc., 1978], p. 18).

[12] William Kingdon Clifford, "The Ethics of Belief," in *Lectures and Essays*, ed. Leslie Stephen and Frederick Pollock (2 vols.; London: Macmillan and Co., 1879), 2:186.

[13] Ibid., p. 178.

[14] Ibid., p. 184.

[15] Brummer, p. 194.

[16] Van A. Harvey makes this observation in "The Ethics of Belief Reconsidered," *The Journal of Religion*, 59 (1979):412.

[17] This expression is Vincent Brummer's (*Theology and Philosophical Inquiry*, pp. 184-85).

[18] *Discourse* IV, 1 (quoted in Hans Kung, *Does God Exist? An Answer for Today*, trans. Edward Quinn [New York: Vintage Books, 1981], p. 13).

[19] *The Will to Believe and Other Essays in Popular Philosophy* (New York: Dover Publications, Inc., 1956), pp. 14-15.

[20] This view of knowledge and its justification is sometimes described as "foundationalism," or "classical foundationalism" (Roderick Chisholm, *Theory of Knowledge*, 1977], p. 63).

[21] According to a standard textbook on logic, deductive arguments "are valid if their premises establish their conclusions demonstratively, but invalid otherwise" (Irving M. Copi, *Introduction to Logic* [4th ed.; New York: Macmillan Publishing Co., Inc., 1972], p. 351).

[22] Charles Hartshorne expresses this point in these words: "Rejection of an argument is always possible, on pain of rejecting one or more of the premises. Thus a proof establishes a price for rejecting its conclusion, and in this way clarifies the meaning of the latter. It helps to measure the gap between belief and disbelief" (*Creative Synthesis and Philosophic Method* [La Salle, IL: Open Court Publishing Company, 1970], p. 276).

[23] Roderick M. Chisholm makes these distinctions in *Theory of Knowledge*, pp. 7-11.

[24] Richard Swinburne, *Faith and Reason*, pp. 45-54.

[25] Van A. Harvey, "The Ethics of Belief Reconsidered," *The Journal of Religion*, 59 (October 1979): 413.

[26] *Faith, Skepticism, and Evidence*, pp. 26-30. Davis also uses the expressions "objective" and "subjective" to describe reasons that are respectively public and private.

[27] Pascal's famous *Pensées* include the following statements: "The heart has its reasons, which reason does not know" (§277), and "We know truth, not only by the reason, but also by the heart..." (§282) (*Pensées: Thoughts on Religion and Other Subjects*, trans. William F. Trotter, ed. H. S. Thayer and Elisabeth B. Thayer [New York: Washington Square Press, Inc., 1965]).

[28] Technically, Holmes worked through induction rather than deduction.

[29] *Philosophical Theology* (Indianapolis and New York: The Bobbs-Merrill Company, Inc., 1969), pp. 4, 5.

[30] Ibid., pp. 19, 20.

[31] Ibid., pp. 12, 33.

[32] *Miracles: A Preliminary Study* (New York: The Macmillan Company, 1947), p.73.

[33] Norman Malcolm, "The Groundlessness of Belief," in *Reason and Religion*, ed. Stuart C. Brown (Ithaca and London: Cornell University Press, 1977), pp. 143-157.

[34] Robin W. Lovin, "Morality Amid the Ruins: Jeffrey Stout on the Failure of Authority and Autonomy" (a review of Jeffrey Stout, *The Flight from Authority* [Notre Dame, Ind.: University of Notre Dame Press, 1981]), *Journal of Religion*, 65 (1985): 244

[35] For descriptions of "foundationalism" by two of its critics, see Nicholas Wolterstorff, Introduction, in *Faith and Rationality: Reason and Belief in God*, ed. Alvin Plantinga and Nicholas Wolterstorff (Notre Dame, Ind.: University of Notre Dame Press, 1983), pp. 2-

3; Alvin Plantinga, "Reason and Belief in God," in *Faith and Rationality*, pp. 47-59; Alvin Plantinga, "Rationality and Religious Belief," in *Contemporary Philosophy of Religion*, ed. Steven M. Cahn and David Shatz (New York and Oxford: Oxford University Press, 1982), pp. 259-264.

[36] Plantinga, "Reason and Belief in God," p. 59.

[37] Plantinga, "Rationality and Religious Belief," p. 269.

[38] Alvin Plantinga argues that belief in God is properly basic in "Rationality and Religious Belief" (*Contemporary Philosophy of Religion*), pp. 270-77; compare W. P. Alston, "Christian Experience and Christian Belief," in *Faith and Rationality*, pp. 103-34, and Nicholas Wolterstorff, "Can Belief in God Be Rational If It Has No Foundations?" in *Faith and Rationality*, pp. 135-86.

[39] This is the contention of Richard Rorty in his influential book *Philosophy and the Mirror of Nature* (Princeton, NJ: Princeton University Press, 1979).

[40] W. K. Clifford, "The Ethics of Belief," p. 186.

[41] *Theory of Knowledge*, p. 15.

[42] *The Will to Believe and Other Essays in Popular Philosophy* (New York: Dover Publications, Inc., 1956), p. 19.

[43] In James' words, "not only as a matter of fact do we find our passional nature influencing us in our opinions, but ... there are some options between opinions in which this influence must be regarded both as an inevitable and as a lawful determinant of our choice" (ibid.). This is the thesis of his essay: "Our passional nature not only lawfully may, but must, decide an option between propositions, whenever it is a genuine option that cannot by its nature be decided on intellectual grounds ..." (ibid., p. 11).

[44] Ibid., pp. 3-4.

[45] According to John Herman Randall, Jr., "It was not humanism, and it was not the Reformation, that was destined to work the greatest revolution in the beliefs of men, however triumphant they seemed for centuries; it was science" (*The Making of the Modern Mind: A Survey of the Intellectual Background of the Present Age* [New York: Columbia University Press, 1940], p. 203).

[46] Bernard Lonergan's involved studies of human knowledge pay careful attention to the features of scientific inquiry (see especially *Insight: A Study of Human Understanding* [New York: Philosophical Library, 1970]).

[47] *The Structure of Scientific Revolutions* (2d ed.; Chicago: University of Chicago Press, 1970), p. 100. Kuhn also defines a paradigm as "a set of recurrent and quasi-standard illustrations of various theories in their conceptual, observational, and instrumental applications" (ibid., p. 43).

[48] Ibid., pp. 23-24.

[49] Ibid., p. 57.

[50] Ibid., p. 102.

[51] Michael Polanyi, *Personal Knowledge: Towards a Post-Critical Philosophy* (Chicago: University of Chicago Press, 1962), pp. vii-viii.

[52] Mary Gerhart and Allan Melvin Russell, *Metaphoric Process: The Creation of Scientific and Religious Understanding* (Fort Worth: Texas Christian University Press, 1984), p. 132.

[53] "The Ethics of Belief Reconsidered," p. 410.

[54] *Does God Exist? An Answer for Today*, trans. Edward Quinn (New York: Vintage books, 1981), p. 93.

PART TWO

REASON AND THE CONTENTS OF FAITH

3
CHRISTIAN THEOLOGY

Framing the Question of Faith and Reason

Our analyses of faith and reason in the two previous chapters indicate how complicated the question of faith and reason is. In fact, they suggest that this is not really a single question at all, but a cluster of several questions. We can see how different formulations of the question of faith and reason arise by reviewing the various meanings of these words.

In a general sense, "faith" is synonymous with "trust." To take something on faith is to rely on someone else's testimony instead of finding it out for yourself. In a religious and specifically Christian sense, "faith" can refer to several things. It may refer to personal trust in God as revealed in Jesus Christ—what the apostle Paul identifies as the one essential condition of human salvation. In a broader sense, it may refer to a person's religious experience in general, and in a still broader sense, to an entire religion, with all its manifestations—beliefs, practices, teachings, and forms of devotion. We speak of Christianity, Judaism, Islam, Buddhism and Hinduism, for example, as the world's great faiths. We also use the word "faith" more narrowly to designate the beliefs, or doctrines, characteristic of a particular religion. Thus, someone might say, "According to Christian faith, Jesus is the Messiah," or, "It would violate my faith to take a human life."

The word "reason" and its related expressions apply to a large range of meanings, too. In perhaps its broadest sense, "reason" refers to our general faculty or capacity for reflective thought. This meaning lies behind our description of human beings as "rational" creatures and our appeals to people who disagree with us to be "reasonable." The word "reason" can also refer to the various operations of discursive reason, or the activity of reasoning. To reason is to think something through. On a technical level this can involve the construction of formal, logical arguments. We also speak of "reasons," of having "reasons" and giving "reasons." A reason is something which supports a conclusion. To give a reason for something is to justify it. In this sense, "reason" is closely related to "evidence," another word that displays several different meanings.

In its broadest sense, "evidence" can refer to anything that supports or conduces to belief. In a narrower sense, evidence has the connotation of public accessibility. It denotes data that are available to anyone possessing the requisite skills of observation. It is helpful to distinguish public evidence of this sort from private evidence, or evidence that is available on a much more limited basis. Evidence of a private nature can range from something accessible to only one person, such as feelings and intuitions, to data accepted within a specific group of people, such as a religious community, but not by the general public.

With these distinctions in mind, we can specify several ways of formulating the question of faith and reason. The relation between reason and faith in a general, non-religious, sense is a matter of philosophical concern. As we have seen, it falls within the purview of epistemology, the branch of philosophy concerned with knowledge. There are actually two questions that arise here. One involves the relation between rational investigation and personal intuition. The other concerns the relation between personal investigation and reliance on the testimony of others.

In this discussion we are specifically concerned with the question of faith and reason, not within the setting of epistemology, or general theory of knowledge, but in the more narrow context of religious, and specifically Christian, knowledge. Here it is a matter of importance for theology, philosophy, and personal religious experience. If we rely on the traditional distinction between the faith which believes *(fides qua creditur)* and the faith which is believed *(fides quae creditur)*, our topic divides into two major categories: the relation of reason to the contents of faith, and the relation of reason to the experience of faith. Accordingly, the following discussion contains two parts. The first examines the application of reason to Christian beliefs, or the articles of Christian faith. The second analyzes the role of rational investigation within personal religious experience.

This chapter and the three that follow are devoted to the topic of reason and the contents of faith. The distinction between public and private evidence provides a helpful way of differentiating two disciplines which involve the rational examination of religious belief. Both systematic theology and philosophy of religion apply reason to the contents of faith. As we shall see, theology explores religious beliefs from within the community of faith. In other words, its perspective is interior to faith. Theology is not concerned with religious belief, or religious beliefs, in general, but with the specific beliefs of a particular religious community. Moreover, systematic theology traditionally assumes the truth of these beliefs and sets out to analyze their inner logic and to explore their interconnections and ramifications.

To employ an earlier distinction, systematic theology appeals to private evidence to support its conclusions. It accepts the authority, or authorities, which a particular religious community accepts, and makes this authority the principal object of its reflection, the primary source of its conclusions, and the major criteria of its judgments. Thus, for example, it is essential for Christian theologians to demonstrate that the Bible supports their claims. They seek to interpret the faith of the Christian community, and this is an authority which the community accepts. In the thinking of many theologians biblical support alone is also sufficient for theological purposes. It is not necessary to appeal to any other authority.

Philosophy of religion also examines the contents of religion, but it does not assume their truth. To the contrary, it is precisely the truth of religious beliefs that philosophers question. So they do not operate on the basis of commitment to a particular religious community. Instead, the posture of philosophy is one of detachment from religious communities. We might say its perspective is exterior, rather than interior, to faith. For this reason, the claims of the philosopher must rest on public, rather than private, evidence. In fact, we can define philosophy of religion as the examination of religion from the perspective of publicly accessible evidence. The philosopher of religion must establish conclusions on the basis of common human experience, or human experience in general, not by appealing to the experience of a select group of individuals or the authority of a particular religious community. Specifically religious experiences and authorities provide material for philosophical reflection. But their "publicness" must be established before they can function as evidence for philosophical claims. The philosopher has to demonstrate that they are representative in some way of human experience in general.

From the perspective of Christian faith, this distinction between theology and philosophy of religion raises three important questions. Is Christianity open to philosophical examination? What are the results of a philosophical examination of religion, particularly of Christianity? What contribution, if any, do these results make to Christian theology? In the next three chapters, we shall deal with these questions in turn. As we shall see, there is a wide diversity of responses to each of them. Our purpose in this chapter is to review the task of systematic theology, taking special note of the role that reason plays in developing an interior view of Christian faith.

Definitions of Theology

Christian theology is one of the oldest and most important applications of reason to faith, and in some respects, it is also the most complicated. For one thing, the word is used in a variety of ways. On a general level, "theology" can refer to the activity of thinking about religious beliefs, or to these religious beliefs themselves. We use familiar expressions like "Catholic theology," "Baptist theology," and "Jewish theology" as synonyms for the beliefs of different religious communities. In a more specialized sense, "theology" refers to the discipline of reflecting carefully on religious beliefs. The history of theology as an academic exercise is long and involved. It reaches back hundreds of years and over the centuries the enterprise has taken many different forms.

Theology began early in life of the church. It may be present in the New Testament itself—some people describe the writings attributed to Paul and John as primitive examples of theology—but it was certainly underway in the work of the so-called Greek and Latin fathers, beginning in the second century and culminating in the works of Augustine in the fifth century.[1]

Building on the Augustinian heritage, medieval theology developed highly intricate forms of inquiry which reached their crowning expression during "the golden age of scholasticism" in the *Summas* of Thomas Aquinas, who sought to give theology "scientific" status in the Aristotelian sense of the term.[2] Several hundred years later the Protestant Reformation generated another outpouring of theological activity, of which John Calvin's *Institutes of the Christian Religion* is the outstanding example. Beginning with Friedrich Schleiermacher in the early nineteen century, the "father of liberal theology," theologians have wrestled with the problems which modern thought poses for Christian faith and with the further problems which attempts to solve these problems have created.

During the past few decades questions concerning the nature and purpose of theology seem to have attracted as much attention as Christian belief itself, with predictably elaborate results. Bernard Lonergan, for example, an influential Catholic scholar, portrays theology as a field encompassing field of inquiry comprising no fewer than eight "functional specialties," ranging from "research" to "communications."[3] Some people feel that theologians today are so busy talking about what theology is supposed to do that they never get around to actually doing it. The bulk of recent theological work strikes one disillusioned observer as "seemingly endless methodological foreplay."[4]

In this chapter we will not attempt to analyze the intricate methodological proposals contemporary theologians have put forward, much less to formulate one of our own. In keeping with our intention to deal with the question of faith and reason on a level accessible to the general reader, we will try instead simply to describe the basic task of theology in a way that all, or nearly all, of its practitioners would accept. Even this modest undertaking will not be easy, however, because there is no way to characterize the activity of theology which does not raise important questions.

Theology, like philosophy, is a discipline whose subject matter, purpose and method are all topics of extensive discussion. Consequently, whether or not their primary interest is theological method, the first task all theologians face is to determine the nature of their work. In order for us to develop an understanding of theology, it may be helpful for us to review some representative descriptions of the enterprise. Consider the definitions of theology formulated by six contemporary Christian theologians:

1. Paul Tillich: "Theology is the methodical interpretation of the contents of Christian faith."[5]

2. Yves Congar: Theology is "a reasoned account about God ... a body of knowledge which rationally interprets, elaborates and ordains the truths of revelation."[6]

3. John Macquarrie: "Theology may be defined as the study which, through participation in and reflection upon a religious faith, seeks to express the content of this faith in the clearest and most coherent language available."[7]

4. Thomas F. Torrance: "Theology is the positive science in which we think only in accordance with the nature of the given."[8]

5. Bernard Lonergan: Theology is "reflection on religion." It "mediates between a cultural matrix and the significance and role of a religion in that matrix."[9]

6. Schubert M. Ogden: Theology is "the fully reflective understanding of the Christian witness of faith as decisive for human existence."[10]

These characterizations of theology bring to light several important points on which theologians agree and disagree. The essence of theology is the application of reason to faith, so the mode of theological work is reflective, methodical or rational, as these quotations all indicate. Its most obvious assumption is that religion, or at least a certain aspect of it, is capable of logical expression. In addition, theological formulations should exhibit the qualities of clarity and consistency, and their contents should be arranged in a logically coherent and attractive manner. This is one implication of the familiar expression "systematic theology."

Beyond these minimal requirements of rational thought, however, theologians differ widely as to what the application of reason to faith involves. As these definitions reveal, there is significant diversity of opinion concerning the subject, purpose and object of theological reflection.

Must theologians themselves participate in the community whose faith they study? It is often the case that they do so, but does the discipline require it? According to Macquarrie's definition, the answer is Yes. The others seem to leave the question open. To be sure, one must have a sympathetic understanding of a religion in order to interpret it accurately, and this is more likely to arise from personal participation in the life of a religious community than in any other way. We might say it is characteristic of theologians to speak from "inside," rather than "outside," a religion. Consequently, scholars seeking to describe a religion other than their own typically characterize the endeavor as a form of "religious studies," rather than "theology." Someone with a Christian background might become an expert in "Islamic studies," for example, but it is unlikely that anyone other than a Muslim could ever do "Muslim theology."

On the other hand, if we make personal religious commitment a prerequisite for theological work, we propose a criterion of theological validity that is virtually impossible to apply. It is not only difficult to draw conclusions about someone's personal faith from his or her writings, the very attempt seems inappropriate. It seems tantamount to judging a person's character. Perhaps it is best to say that personal religious commitment and involvement in the life of a religious community, at least to some degree, provide the natural basis for theological work, but these do not constitute criteria of theological validity. We should not attempt to evaluate someone's religious experience on the basis of his or her theological work. According to Paul Tillich, it is possible to move within the theological circle, that is, to function as a Christian theologian, without necessarily belonging personally to the Christian community. The crucial factor is to deal with the Christian message as a matter of ultimate concern, whether or not one is personally committed to it.[11]

An important distinction for our purposes in this discussion involves the question of the truth of Christian faith. One theological approach explores the contents of Christian faith on the assumption that its claims are true, although, as we just noted, this methodological assumption is not the same as personal commitment. This perspective accepts the private evidence for Christianity. Such theological reflection operates within the boundaries defined by the contents of Scripture and the beliefs of the Christian community. This theological approach has an intra-community focus, and the terminology it employs often remains close to the traditional language of Scripture and the church. This type of theology is variously identified as "systematic," "dogmatic," "confessional" and "symbolic."

The second approach treats the truth of Christianity as something that must be established by careful investigation, rather than assumed. Instead of simply elaborating the traditional contents of faith, it subjects these beliefs to careful analysis in order to establish their intelligibility. It assigns public evidence a role in theology. Consequently, while the first approach to theology has an intra-community focus, this one has an extra-community focus. As it interprets the claims of Christianity, it bears in mind the perspective of those who are not already committed to it. This mode of theological reflection is variously designated as "constructive," "foundational," "philosophical" and "apologetic."

It is important to note that neither approach reflects on the religious experience of the theologian. It is not necessarily the case that the first approach either requires or indicates that its practitioners have the personal gift of faith, nor that those who take the second are lacking in this endowment. Whether to assume or argue that the contents of faith are true is strictly a methodological decision, not a religious one.

In Chapter 7 we will examine the issue which distinguishes these two approaches to theology. What role, if any, we shall ask, should public evidence play in Christian theology? We shall also reflect further on the relation between these two approaches. In this chapter, however, we are concerned with the attempt to understand Christian faith on its own terms. How can we develop a reflective inventory of the contents of faith? What are the doctrines of the church? Where do they come from and what do they represent?

Theology and the Bible

The widest diversity displayed in the definitions above seems to concern the object of theological reflection. It is variously identified as religion; the truths of revelation; the contents of a religious faith; the contents of Christian faith; and the Christian witness of faith. Just what, then, does theology examine? What is it the study of?

One familiar answer is "the Bible," or "the truths of revelation." According to a popular conception of the theological task, the purpose of theology is to summarize the teachings of the Bible. Consequently, the Bible represents the fundamental object of theological reflection. A conservative theological work like Millard J. Erickson's *Christian Theology* illustrates this approach.

In a section entitled, "The Process of Doing Theology," Erickson outlines "the actual task of doing theology" in nine steps, beginning with "collection of the biblical materials," "unification of the biblical materials," and "analysis of the meaning of biblical teachings." Next come "examination of historical treatments," "identification of the essence of the doctrine," and "illumination from sources beyond the Bible." The list concludes with "contemporary expression of the doctrine," "development of a central motif," and "stratification of the topics." Erickson allows for variation in the order in which these steps are taken, so he does not propose this format as an ironclad procedure for theological work. But, as these nine steps show, he insists that the development of a theological position have a firm basis in the study of biblical materials.[12]

According to this "exegetical model" of theology, the application of reason to the contents of faith consists of analyzing, summarizing and organizing the Bible's teachings, and the primary concern of theology is to represent faithfully the content of Scripture. Translating its message into the language and concepts of our time is distinctly secondary. Theological reflection begins with a study of the biblical text and characteristically remains close to the terms and concepts employed by the biblical writers themselves. As T. F. Torrance describes it, theology "is primarily concerned to unfold the objective content of revelation and is only interested in the forms of thought and language [which the church must use from age to age to proclaim the Gospel] as the expressions of that content."[13]

The exegetical approach to theology has important historical precedents. The Protestant Reformation, for example, began with Luther's recovery of the Gospel through a study of the Bible, notably the Psalms and the letters of Paul. In addition, its supporters believe, proximity to the thought and language of the biblical text minimizes the risk of losing the essential message of the Bible in the attempt to "translate" it into the thought forms of another age. At the same time, the exegetical approach to theology has its problems. One is the tendency to oversimplify the relation between the Bible and theology.

By definition, the Bible is indispensable to Christian theology. But the precise nature of the relation between the Bible and theology is complex. There are several questions relating to biblical authority that require careful consideration. First, what is there *about* the Bible in general that makes it authoritative? Second, what is it *in* the Bible that has authority? And third, just how does the Bible exert its authority? In other words, how does the Bible actually authorize various Christian beliefs?

Answers to the first of these questions generally fall into two categories—those which emphasize the role or function of the Bible in the Christian community, and those which emphasize some quality inherent in the Bible itself. In the thinking of many people, the Bible has authority for Christians because they accept it as authoritative. The familiar statement that the church created the canon suggests that the Bible derives its authority from the church. Thus construed, the authority of the Bible is not unlike that which the Constitution of the United States acquired in 1787 when the American colonies ratified it.

This functional approach to biblical authority has received considerable attention in recent years. In part, it represents a reaction to the tendency of modern biblical scholarship to emphasize the historical features of the biblical documents and to overlook their role in the community of faith. Some theologians believe that the authority of the Bible can be a matter of deliberate choice. They maintain that we can decide to regard the Bible as the Word of God, without concerning ourselves with questions about the origin of the biblical documents. Thus Charles M. Wood asserts, "We may ... read scripture *as if it were* a whole, and as if the author of the whole were God."[14]

Others find purely functional accounts of biblical authority unsatisfactory because they fail to consider the essential nature of the text. For conservative Christians the Bible is authoritative because it is divinely inspired, that is, because God was uniquely operative in its production. Since the biblical documents provide us with a record of the messages God delivered to his servants the prophets, the Bible richly merits the honored place it occupies in the Christian church. In accepting the Bible as authoritative, the early Christian church did not confer authority upon the Bible, but recognized the divine authority within it.

Besides the nature of the Bible's authority, there is the further question of just where within the Bible that authority resides. Is it to be found in specific verbal formulas, in certain literary forms, or in particular symbols or symbolic patterns? Do some biblical documents have more authority than others? Is the essential message of the Bible more apparent or accessible in some books or passages than in others? Is there a thematic center in the Bible, a material norm, or a "canon within the canon" in light of which the Bible as a whole should be read?

On a purely practical level, making distinctions within the Bible is unavoidable. The most cursory examination of its contents reveals an enormous variety of material, and nobody finds all of it equally illuminating or uplifting. For practical religious value, most modern readers will find the Psalms and the Gospels more helpful than various other portions. And for good reason certain passages are never selected for public Scripture reading or used as the bases for sermons.

Similarly, theology is concerned with certain aspects of the Bible more than others. For theological purposes, the authority of the Bible lies in its conceptual content. Christians are convinced that it contains truth claims, or information, which deserve to be believed. And the task of theology is to identify and present these claims systematically. This does not mean that only straightforward biblical propositions provide material for theology, for many of the important claims of the Bible are implicit rather than explicit. Nor does it mean that theologians agree as to what the Bible claims or which biblical claims are most important. But since theology is an intellectual enterprise, it is the intellectual content of the Bible that interests them. Theology focuses on the biblical truth which is capable of propositional formulation.

There are both liberal and conservative theologians who take this position. According to classical Protestant liberalism, the Bible expresses certain ideas (and ideals) that appeal to human reason, and this warrants our believing them. And for Schubert M. Ogden, a contemporary liberal theologian, the central object of theological interest is the meaning and truth of the Christian claims expressed in Scripture.[15] An emphasis on the cognitive content of the Bible is particularly prominent in the work of a number of contemporary evangelical theologians, such as Carl F. H. Henry, who maintains that the propositional content of the Bible is eminently reasonable because God is both author of the biblical text and creator of the human mind.[16]

Theology has two important functions to perform in its attempt to explicate the cognitive contents of the Bible. It tries to determine what the essential claims of Scripture are. Then it seeks to arrange or organize this material to form a logically coherent system of truth.

The first responsibility is complicated by the fact that the biblical documents originated under historical conditions that were so different from our own. As Gerhard Hasel observes, "The need for interpretation rests in the fact that the Bible was written in a different culture, separated from our time by the distance of many ages, and that it arose under certain specific situations."[17]

The vast historical distance that separates modern times from those of the Bible requires us to make an important distinction in the beliefs we find in the Bible. Many of the beliefs expressed in the biblical writings were part of the intellectual atmosphere of ancient times. The writers assumed their truths and made reference to them without giving them conscious consideration. They typically thought *with* these beliefs rather than *about* them. As a result, such beliefs were not the content of their teaching so much as the intellectual apparatus they acquired as part of their cultural heritage. Some of these beliefs are matters of common sense even today; some formed part of the thought-world characteristic of ancient times. In contrast, other beliefs expressed in the Bible are essential to the writers' primary concerns. Taken together, beliefs of this kind constitute the message(s) which the biblical writers sought to communicate and therefore call for acceptance in every generation.

In order to identify the essential claims of Scripture, theology must distinguish between these two sorts of belief. It must discriminate between those beliefs that are essential to the biblical message—and require assent if we are to be Christians today—and those beliefs which are incidental to these claims.

Not surprisingly, there are strong differences of opinion as to which beliefs belong in these respective categories. Most theologians would agree that a belief in something like astral influences is incidental to the point of Psalm 121, which speaks of being smitten by the moon (vs. 6) in the course of assuring us of God's abiding care. And many theologians would agree that a belief that Jesus rose bodily from the dead is essential to Christianity. But there are biblical interpreters who insist that we must accept both beliefs to be in harmony with the Bible, and there are others who regard both of them as expressions of an archaic worldview and incidental to the Bible's real message.

An appreciation of the distance between our conceptual perspective and that of the Bible lies behind the critical study of the Bible that has dominated biblical scholarship in modern times. The "historical-critical method," as it is often called, examines the contents of the Bible in light of the historical contexts in which they were written. It operates on the fundamental assumption that a text can be understood only against its background.[18]

The results of critical methods of Bible study are sometimes disturbing to conservative Christians, because they frequently reflect an antisupernaturalistic bias and conflict with traditional Christian beliefs. There are those who believe that we should reject such an approach to the Bible in order to avoid these difficulties.[19] However, many of the results of historical-critical study are compatible with a traditional view of the Bible's divine inspiration, and some of them serve to strengthen conservative beliefs. For example, an important achievement of this method for theology is the recovery of the historical sense of the Bible, which responsible biblical interpretation requires.[20]

The belief that the Bible has a human as well as a divine side also calls for a historical reading of the text. Traditional Christian doctrines of revelation emphasize the divine inspiration of the Bible. On the basis of biblical statements that "all scripture is inspired by God" (2 Timothy 3:16) and that "men moved by the Holy Spirit spoke from God" (2 Peter 1:21), they maintain that the documents of the Bible originated when God acted on the minds of his selected messengers. These same doctrines insist that although the Bible is not merely human, it is human nonetheless. Its authors wrote under the influence of God, but they also wrote as human beings and their writings reflect the personalities and the historical, religious and conceptual perspective of the authors. In order to understand the biblical documents, it is therefore essential that we study them in light of the historical contexts in which they arose.

At the same time, we must exercise caution in applying historical-critical methods of study to the biblical text, and we must closely examine the conclusions they yield in light of the biblical evidence.[21] To discredit them out of hand would be to discard a good many positive contributions to our understanding of the Bible and to adopt an obscurantist stance which, in the long run, would only weaken our theology. On the other hand, to accept the results of historical-critical study without qualification would weaken its status as the Word of God and leave us with a Bible that expresses nothing more than human ideas.

Once it has identified those beliefs in the Bible which are essential to its message, theology has the additional task of organizing or arranging them. Some of the beliefs involved in the biblical message are basic to its principal concern and others are derivative. Or, to change the metaphor, certain biblical claims are central to Christian faith while others are peripheral. And theology seeks to discover the basic pattern or framework of biblical faith. For Christians, certainly, what is central to faith is what deals with Christ, so they find the center of the Bible in its christology. In the memorable words of Martin Luther, "All the genuine sacred books agree in this, that all of them preach Christ and deal with him."[22]

People have reservations about the attempt to identify a center in the Bible. One concern is that it inevitably leads to reductionism, as it seemed to do in the case of Luther, who dismissed certain books as useless to faith.[23] Once a biblical center is identified, they fear, other biblical claims will be slighted or overlooked altogether. Another objection is that such an attempt forces the Bible into the mold of human preconceptions. Those who seek a center appear to assume a standpoint above the Bible, rather than submitting to its authority. A third objection is that the attempt to locate a center does violence to the biblical materials themselves. Their sheer diversity, many believe, thwarts all efforts to discern a pattern in the Bible.

Other people grant that the biblical materials are enormously varied and that certain beliefs are more fundamental to Christian faith than others. Yet they remain skeptical of the attempt to discern anything like a theological center, or a dominant conceptual theme, in the Bible. In their view, there is no biblical *theology*, there are only biblical *theologies*. The concerns and viewpoints of the various writers are too diverse to permit such integration. Consequently, when someone speaks of "the biblical faith," they regard it as an imposition on the biblical writings rather than a derivation from them.

In principle, of course, there will never be a final statement of "what the Bible teaches" that neither requires nor admits of further revision. No claim to knowledge can be absolute. In theology and biblical studies, as in all of human inquiry, every formulation invites criticism and further investigation. So there is good reason to deny that anyone could ever give definitive expression to the essential pattern of biblical thought. Even so, the ultimate inaccessibility of this goal should not stifle the quest for it. The fact that we can never achieve such a pattern once and for all does not mean that persistent effort will not take us closer to it.

We find support for this endeavor in the fact that the biblical writers themselves give certain beliefs more emphasis than others. The New Testament pays more attention to some portions of the Old Testament than to others, because early Christians were particularly interested in passages which helped them understand the meaning of Jesus. The apostolic church also concluded that certain aspects of the Mosaic law were not binding on Gentile converts to Christianity (Acts 15:1-19). These factors indicate that the earliest Christian community perceived a pattern of sorts in the writings of the Old Testament. Some of its legal obligations were normative for the new community of Christian faith; others were set aside. A general pattern also appears in the New Testament itself. To be sure, there are great differences within this collection of documents. But there are also ideas which all its writers accept, such as the importance of Jesus for human salvation. So, it is appropriate to distinguish levels of doctrinal significance and search for a thematic center in the Bible.

A third question about the Bible concerns its actual function in theology. How does the Bible come to bear on a theological proposal in order to authorize it? One important study of the issue is David H. Kelsey's book *The Uses of Scripture in Recent Theology*. Kelsey analyzes the work of seven different theologians and discovers a variety of ways in which the Bible functions theologically. At times, biblical material bears directly on a theological proposal. Biblical quotations provide the data from which theological conclusions are drawn. At other times, biblical material plays a less direct role. It operates in a theological discussion without actually providing the data for conclusions. To use Kelsey's terms, the biblical text variously functions in theological arguments as a "warrant" which justifies the move from certain data to a conclusion; as "backing" for a warrant; and even as "conditions for rebuttal."[24] So, the course of theological reflection does not always move from biblical text to doctrinal conclusion. The Bible is the fundamental authority for Christian theology, but it is not the only place where theological reflection originates nor the direct source from which all theological positions arise.

This is evident on a more general level as well. There are beliefs and practices related to various passages in the Bible which many Christians do not regard as biblical, in the sense of "authorized by the Bible." These include baptism for the dead, which Mormons practice, the refusal of blood transfusions advocated by Jehovah's Witnesses, and the phenomenon of glossalalia, or speaking in tongues, characteristic of Pentecostal groups. On the other hand, a solid majority of Christians strongly affirm certain beliefs and practices which do not have straightforward biblical support, such as the doctrine of the Trinity, the abolition of slavery, and the practice of monogamy. So, religious beliefs derived from biblical material are not always accepted by the church as valid, nor does every orthodox belief have an explicit biblical basis.

These observations indicate that the relation between the Bible and theology is much more complex than the exegetical model suggests. Factors other than the Bible appear to enter into theological reflection. Indeed, careful investigation would reveal that a consideration of the Bible is virtually never the only factor at work in the development of a theological position. In spite of the slogan "the Bible and the Bible only," a theological position is never a simple distillation of biblical material. In order to do justice to the concrete phenomenon of Christian faith, therefore, we need to further refine the object of theology.

Theology and Doctrine

As we have just seen, it is less than precise to identify the object of theological inquiry as simply "the Bible." This is so not only because extrabiblical factors are involved in theological development, but also because there are other scholarly disciplines which study the Bible, too, such as linguistics, history, and literary analysis, as well as sociology and anthropology. What distinguishes theology is not that it studies the Bible, but that it studies the Bible in a particular way.

Theology approaches the Bible from the perspective of Christian faith. The specific focus of theological attention is not simply the Bible, but the Bible as understood and interpreted by the community of faith. Rather than the Bible per se, then, it would be more accurate to identify the immediate object of theological reflection as "Christian belief," or, better, as "Christian doctrine."

Doctrines are beliefs, of course, but they are beliefs with special status. To quote the opening sentence of Jaroslav Pelikan's magisterial work, "The Christian Tradition," "What the church of Jesus Christ believes, teaches, and confesses on the basis of the word of God: this is Christian doctrine."[25] His definition indicates the essential characteristics of doctrine.

First, Christian doctrines are the beliefs of the church as a whole, not just of its individual members. They are beliefs held by all Christians, or at least by significant numbers of Christians. Second, doctrines are official beliefs. They are matters of public importance, not private opinion. As the word itself suggests, the doctrines of the church are the teachings of the church. They form an important part of the public expression of Christianity. Third, the doctrines of the church are those beliefs which are basic to the identity of Christianity. To be a Christian is to believe that certain things are true. The church defines itself with reference to its doctrines.

Along with these characteristics, Pelikan's definition also indicates the important relation between Christian doctrine and the Bible. Christians, as well as Jews and Moslems, are "people of the Book." In Christianity, as in these other religions, the authority for the community's beliefs lies in a collection of writings, and the various Christian doctrines represent the church's understanding of what the Bible teaches. The church's creedal formulas and confessional statements, for example, represent official summaries of biblical truth. According to one authority, "The creed is simply the Church's understanding of the meaning of Scripture." "The creeds are the record of the

Church's interpretation of the Bible in the past and the authoritative guide to hermeneutics in the present."[26]

But though the Bible is basic to Christian beliefs, the church's doctrines do not develop from a simple reading of the Bible. What Pelikan refers to as "environmental factors" always figure in the process, too. To some degree doctrines inevitably reflect the specific situation of the Christian community at the time of their formulation. The concrete experience of the church includes the relations of its members to each other and their relations to the larger world around them. Over the centuries, for example, heresy has provided a powerful stimulus to doctrinal development.[27] The New Testament canon developed in response to inadequate lists of authoritative Christian writings. And the orthodox view of Christ's nature developed in response to different christological heresies. So important, in fact, is the role which heresy has played in doctrinal development that people often describe it as the "mother of orthodoxy."

Since doctrines arise, not from the Bible alone, but from the dynamic interplay between the Bible and the living experience of the church, we can characterize the church's doctrines in two different ways. We can describe them either as formal responses on the part of the Christian community to the ongoing challenges it meets in light of the Word of God, or as the community's understanding of the Bible within the dynamic context of its concrete historical development.

This characterization of Christian doctrines with reference both to the Bible and the church requires a parallel characterization of theology. We can define theology as the attempt to formulate a coherent exposition of Christian doctrine that is faithful to the authority of the Bible and responsive to the experience of the Christian community. Theology thus involves bringing the church's experience to bear on the Bible and bringing the Bible to bear on the experience of the church. It alternately views the Bible through the community's understanding of truth, and scrutinizes the church's formulation of truth in light of the Bible.

At any given time either of these factors may figure more prominently in theological reflection than the other, but theology must keep both in mind in order to provide an adequate account of the contents of faith. Occasionally people study the Bible primarily out of a desire to learn what it teaches and seem to draw their doctrinal conclusions more or less directly from the biblical writings. Much more frequently, however, people are driven to the Bible by other concerns. In his book *Evangelicals at an Impasse: Bible Authority in Practice,* for example, Robert K. Johnston examines recent discussions within evangelical theology of homosexuality, social ethics, and the place of women in the church. He observes that the church's interaction with society and the conflict between different ecclesiastical traditions exert a major influence on theological development. In other words, the experience of the Christian community influences the way in which people read the Bible. Furthermore, he attributes the current disarray among evangelicals partly to their failure to appreciate these extra-biblical influences on their thinking. In response to this problem, Johnston calls for a "constructive evangelical theology" that will provide "a dynamic blend of Biblical, traditional, and contemporary sources."[28]

Johnston's statement also points to the important role that tradition plays in theology. Besides the Bible, the central authority for Christian belief, and the present experience of the Christian community, which inevitably affects its understanding of the Bible, as we just noted, theology must also take into account Christian tradition, or the doctrines which the church has already formulated.

The influence of established doctrines on what Christians believe is not always appreciated. But when people approach the Bible as a source of truth, they typically do so out of participation in a religious community. In fact, what a group of Christians believe is probably influenced more directly by the tradition of their community than it is by the contents of the Bible. As one contemporary theologian states, "The church, that is the geographically and sociologically describable community to which one belongs, is foremost, although not exclusively, the place where theological reflection begins."[29] This is why theologians such as Paul Tillich and John Macquarrie define theology with reference to the faith of the Christian community rather than simply to revelation, or the contents of the Bible. The doctrinal statements of different Christian denominations are more obviously expressions of the various groups' traditions than summaries of biblical exegesis.

So, even though the Bible represents the basic authority for Christian beliefs, it is not the case that Christians typically read the Bible and then form their doctrinal conclusions. Rather, they come to the Bible with a set of doctrinal beliefs already in mind, and read the Bible under their influence. The church's doctrines may not predetermine the results of biblical study, but they ordinarily pose the agenda of issues that receive attention.

Occasionally people try to sweep aside accumulated interpretations in an effort to hear what the Bible says directly. But such attempts are futile. In fact, someone who overlooks or deliberately ignores the influence of Christian tradition on the way he reads the Bible actually becomes more, rather than less, susceptible to it. As Dietrich Ritschl states, "Our questions are already shaped by two thousand years of tradition, even if we are unaware of the details of this tradition. The less one knows about it the more he is vulnerable to be influenced unduly by it."[30]

This characteristic priority of church doctrine to biblical interpretation is not necessarily negative. To the contrary, a doctrinal framework can be immensely helpful in the study of the Bible. It can prepare people for this work by suggesting which biblical themes to study. This is how John Calvin described his greatest work: "It has been my purpose in this labor to prepare and instruct candidates in sacred theology for the reading of the divine Word."[31] "Although Holy Scripture contains a perfect doctrine, ... yet a person who has not much practice in it has good reason for some guidance and direction, to know what he ought to look for in it, in order not to wander hither and thither, but to hold to a sure path, that he may always be pressing toward the end to which the Holy Spirit calls him."[32]

Noting the inevitable influence of Christian doctrine on the way we read the Bible raises the important question of Scripture and tradition. And this brings to mind the famous Reformation maxim, *sola scriptura*. People sometimes think of this as a call to eliminate everything but the Bible from theological consideration. This is not only impossible, as we have seen, but it is not faithful to the activity of the great Reformers themselves. As developed and followed by Luther and Calvin, for example, this principle represents an affirmation of the Bible's authority, rather than a procedural rule for biblical exegesis. For the Reformers themselves, the Bible was by no means the only object of theological reflection. Their writings contain references, appeals and allusions to a great variety of sources, from the writings of Augustine to the myths of pagan literature.

What *sola scriptura* stands for is the superiority of the Bible to other authorities, including ecclesiastical officers, church councils and previous doctrinal formulas. It calls for Christians to study the Bible directly in order to determine its teaching and settle doctrinal questions, rather than rely on subsequent interpretations. Accordingly, those who are faithful to this principle allow nothing to substitute for the study of the Bible, and they insist on evaluating every interpretation of the Bible by the standard of the biblical text itself. But they do not, and cannot, ignore the established teachings of the Christian community.

Given the complex relation of Christian doctrine to the Bible and to the experience of the church, it is not surprising to find different theories as to what doctrines represent. In a recent study George A. Lindbeck makes a helpful distinction between two prevalent views of doctrine. On the propositional-cognitive theory, "church doctrines function as informative propositions or truth claims about objective realities." In other words, doctrines have cognitive content; they give information about the way things are. According to this theory, doctrines may be right or wrong, and the information they provide may be true or false.

This perspective on doctrines is characteristic of traditional Christianity. Throughout its history, the vast majority of church members have assumed that the teachings of the church are reliable descriptions of ultimate realities. It is also the view of those who seek to establish the truth of Christian beliefs by appealing to rational evidence, even when their understanding of the essential claims of Christianity may be quite unorthodox. Many who reject the literal veracity of various traditional Christian beliefs nevertheless maintain that certain cognitive claims do form the basis of Christianity and that the truth of these claims can, and sometimes must, be argued for.[33]

In contrast, those who follow what Lindbeck calls the "experiential-expressive" interpretation view doctrines as "noninformative and nondiscursive symbols of inner feelings, attitudes, or existential orientations."[34] They see doctrines as arising from an underlying religious experience which could find expression in a variety of verbal formulas. Unlike cognitivists, symbolists do not attach great importance to variations in doctrinal formulations. The same doctrines can serve to express different religious meanings, and conversely, the same religious meanings can find expression in a variety of doctrinal formulas.[35] Doctrines are not so much right and wrong as they are for cognitivists. They are, rather, more adequate or less adequate expressions of religious experience.

We have suggested that doctrines and the experience of the church, as well as the Bible, are objects of theological reflection. If doctrines represent beliefs which enjoy official status in the Christian community and theology is the enterprise of reflecting on these beliefs, the relation between theology and doctrine takes several different forms. In one sense, theology is the work of the church as a whole as Christians seek to discern the teachings of the Bible in response to the concrete challenges they face in the world. In fact, the word "theology" can refer either to the church's activity in developing its beliefs or to the results of this activity, namely, the beliefs themselves. In another sense, theology is the formal enterprise of reflecting on these beliefs. As an academic exercise, theology is a second order discipline. It presupposes the beliefs of the Christian community as its primary data.

Theology in this second, more formal, sense fulfills several different functions. On one level, the task of theology is simply to describe the faith of the Christian community. It provides an inventory or catalogue of Christian doctrines. Instead of merely listing doctrines, however, theology also seeks to arrange the various doctrines of the church in a logically attractive pattern. We might say that in this capacity theology explores the "configuration of Christian belief." It seeks to determine the relative importance of different doctrines within the Christian community. For logical reasons, certain doctrines seem to be more central or basic to Christian faith than others. Most Christians would agree, for example, that the doctrines of God and Christ are more fundamental than, say, the doctrines of systematic benevolence and healthful living. They provide the foundation on which the entire structure of faith comes to rest.

Theology will also identify the type of importance which certain doctrines have. Some doctrines are more important than others in the sense that they attract more attention at a given time. Controversy always seems to heighten the importance of a doctrine. The question of believer's baptism, for example, was a matter of such great importance during the Reformation era that a number of Christians left established churches and formed new ones. Similarly, Seventh Day Baptists and Seventh-day Adventists feel that worshiping on the seventh day of the week is sufficiently important to justify separate denominational identity. The question of how important a particular belief is can be just as divisive as the question of its truth or falsity. Two people may agree, for example, that the case for adult baptism is convincing, but completely disagree as to whether the issue is important enough to justify leaving one denomination for another.

As we have seen, theology must devote attention to the actual beliefs of the Christian community, as well as to church doctrines and the Bible. Because the experience of the Christian community is constantly developing, there will always be some discrepancy between the church's formal doctrinal statements and the actual beliefs which Christians hold. Sometimes the church's formal doctrines may be "ahead" of the community's beliefs, so to speak. In the fourth and fifth centuries, for example, when the christological formulas of Nicea and Chalcedon became the official position of the church, a majority of the church's members were probably Arians. It took a while for the actual beliefs of the community to "catch up" with the official statements. In contrast, there are other times when the church's formal doctrines are "behind" the community's actual beliefs. To cite a controversial example, Christian worship manifests the deep conviction that God is genuinely affected by our praise and our petitions. Yet traditional doctrines of God have insisted on divine immutability. Here is a case where the religious intuition of Christians may be ahead of their formal doctrines, and the church's official teachings ought to be revised.[36]

However we might categorize specific doctrines, the point stands that an accurate portrayal of the church's faith will need to go beyond the church's explicit beliefs—the ones found in creeds, confessional formulas and official statements of belief—and take account of its "implicit beliefs," the beliefs expressed in the way Christians live and particularly in the way they worship. There will always be a certain amount of tension between the two, and there may be times when the church's formal doctrines do not give adequate expression to the experience of the Christian community.

As these remarks indicate, theology has a prescriptive or normative role to play, as well as a descriptive one, in relation to Christian beliefs. Theologians not only say what Christians do believe, at times they assert what they should believe.[37] For example, theologians may propose a new configuration for Christian doctrines. They may retrieve a doctrine whose significance has been overlooked and elevate it to a position of prominence. Or they may suggest that a subject of vigorous debate within certain circles is less important than it seems to many people.

Occasionally, though less frequently, theologians propose more radical doctrinal innovation. They may suggest that the church abandon a time-honored belief or embrace a new one.

Theologians justify doctrinal rearrangement and innovation in various ways. One is to argue that Christian doctrines should be consistent with each other. Some theologians see a contradiction between the affirmation that God is supremely loving and the familiar belief that divine justice demanded the death of Jesus. In order to relieve this tension, they suggest another explanation for the cross. To cite a second example, many theologians see an inconsistency between God's love and the idea that the wicked suffer the pains of hell through all eternity. In response, some argue against the idea of an everlasting hell; others, against any idea of hell at all. The former maintain that the suffering of the wicked is temporary, rather than unending. The latter reject the whole idea of divine punishment, insisting that God's love logically requires the eventual salvation of every human being.[38]

Another basis for doctrinal revision is the need to bring our doctrines into harmony with the concrete experience of Christians. As we mentioned above, aspects of practical religious experience sometimes conflict with the official teachings of the church. The intuitions and needs of practical religious experience provide a powerful warrant for theological innovation.

The most important basis for doctrinal change will always be the Bible. Most Christians accept the Bible as authoritative for faith and, as we have seen, almost as many would define the essential task of theology as that of interpreting its teachings. So, theologians who find that the church's beliefs are out of harmony with the Bible have a responsibility to identify the discrepancy and call the Christian community to make appropriate changes in its understanding of truth. At the same time, a significant change in belief is never achieved by theological pronouncement or administrative fiat. Doctrinal transformation involves change on the part of the community as a whole, and this ordinarily takes considerable time.

In this chapter we have identified and examined theology as an application of reason to the contents of faith, or the beliefs of a particular religious community. It is distinguished from other applications by the fact that it assumes the truth of these beliefs. We have seen that the essential task of Christian theology is that of biblical interpretation, in view of the authoritative status of the Bible in the church. But it also involves careful attention to interpretations that have developed in the course of the church's history and to the dynamic experience of the concrete Christian community. Within the Christian community all theological endeavor expresses the underlying convictions that Christian faith is intelligible, that its intellectual contents are important to the experience of faith, and that it is possible to express them in a logically attractive way.

We have concentrated here on different questions of theological method, because they are important to the topic of faith and reason. Moreover, as we have mentioned, they have also attracted a great deal of attention in recent times. Over the years, however, most theological discussion involves various Christian beliefs. Expounding on these, of course, would require us to do more than describe this particular application of reason to faith. We would have to go on and construct a theological system, and that is a task for another setting.

---

[1] Yves M.-J. Congar, O.P. provides an authoritative account of the development of theology in *A History of Theology*, translated and edited by Hunter Guthrie, S. J. (Garden City, N.Y.: Doubleday & Company, Inc., 1968).

[2] See Congar, chapter 4, "The Golden Age of Scholasticism," *A History of Theology*, pp. 85-143.

[3] Lonergan's eight functional specialties are: research, interpretation, history, dialectics, foundations, dogmatics, systematics, and communications *(Method in Theology* [New York: Herder and Herder, 1972]).

[4] Jeffrey Stout, *The Flight from Authority: Religion, Morality, and the Quest for Autonomy* (Notre Dame: University of Notre Dame Press, 1981), p. 147.

[5] Paul Tillich, *Systematic Theology* (3 vols.; Chicago: University of Chicago Press, 1951-63), 1:15.

[6] Congar, *A History of Theology*, p. 25.

[7] John Macquarrie, *Principles of Christian Theology* (2d ed.; New York: Charles Scribner's Sons, 1977), p. 1.

[8] T. F. Torrance, *Theology in Reconstruction* (Grand Rapids, MI: William B. Eerdmans

Publishing Company, 1965), p. 9. Torrance writes, "[I]n the teaching of Christian theology I have struggled to develop modes of inquiry and exposition that are appropriate to the nature and logic of God's self-revelation in Jesus Christ. . . . [W]e must allow the divine realities to declare themselves to us, and so allow the basic forms of theological truth to come to view and impose themselves on our understanding" (Ibid.).

[9] Bernard Lonergan, *Method in Theology*, pp. 267, xi.

[10] Schubert M. Ogden, "What Is Theology?" *The Journal of Religion* 52 (January 1972): 22.

[11] "[A] person can be a theologian as long as he acknowledges the content of the theological circle as his ultimate concern. . . . [I]t depends on his being ultimately concerned with the Christian message even if he is sometimes inclined to attack and to reject it" (Paul Tillich, *Systematic Theology* [3 vols.; Chicago: University of Chicago Press, 1951-63], 3:10).

[12] Millard J. Erickson, *Christian Theology* (3 vols.; Grand Rapids, Michigan: Baker Book House, 1983-85), 1:66-79.

[13] Torrance, *Theology in Reconstruction*, p. 147.

[14] Charles M. Wood, *The Formation of Christian Understanding: An Essay in Theological Hermeneutics* (Philadelphia: Westminster Press, 1981), p. 70; italics his.

[15] Although for Ogden, the mere Scriptural expression of certain claims is insufficient to establish their truth, the claims expressed in Scripture are the primary object of theological reflection (see "The Authority of Scripture for Theology," *Interpretation*, 30 [1976]: 242-261).

[16] *God, Revelation and Authority* (6 vols.; Waco, TX: Word Books, 1976-63), 1:213-224.

[17] Gerhard F. Hasel, "Principles of Biblical Interpretation," in *A Symposium on Biblical Hermeneutics*, ed. Gordon M. Hyde (Washington, D. C.: Review and Herald Publishing Association, 1974), p. 163.

[18] A helpful introduction to the discipline is Edgar Krentz, *The Historical-Critical Method* (Philadelphia: Fortress Press, 1975).

[19] This is Gerhard Hasel's position. He states, "The theologian or exegete must not get the impression that he can safely utilize certain parts of the historical-critical method in an eclectic manner, because there is no stopping point" (*Understanding the Living Word of God* [Mountain View, CA: Pacific Press Publishing Association, 1980], p. 26).

[20] Krentz describes this and other contributions in *The Historical-Critical Method*, pp. 63-67.

[21] In recent works two evangelical scholars give carefully qualified support to a historical-critical study of the Bible (Millard J. Erickson, *Christian Theology*, 1:82-104; Clark Pinnock, *The Scripture Principle*, pp. 130-52).

[22] "Preface to the Epistles of Saint James and Saint Jude," *Works of Martin Luther* (Philadelphia: A. J. Holman, Co., 1932), VI, 478; quoted in Schubert M. Ogden, "Sources of Religious Authority in Liberal Protestantism," *Journal of the American Academy of Religion*, 44 (1976): 406-407.

[23] Luther was especially critical of Esther and James.

[24] *The Uses of Scripture in Recent Theology* (Philadelphia: Fortress Press, 1975), pp. 139-44.

[25] Jaroslav Pelikan, *The Emergence of the Catholic Tradition (100-600)*, Volume 1 in"The Christian Tradition: A History of the Development of Doctrine" (Chicago: University of Chicago Press, 1971), p. 1.

[26] John Leith, "Creeds and Their Role in the Church," in *Creeds of the Churches: A Reader in Christian Doctrine From the Bible to the Present* (Garden City, NY: Anchor Books, 1963), pp. 8-9. Leith also observes, "The whole history of theology is the history of the interpretation of Scripture, even though the theologians do not always cite Biblical references. In general, the victories in the great theological debates have gone to those

100 Reason and the Contours of Faith

who have been the most convincing interpreters of Scripture" (Ibid.).

[27] George A. Lindbeck observes, "For the most part, only when disputes arise about what it is permissible to teach or practice does a community make up its collective mind and formally make a doctrinal decision" (*The Nature of Doctrine: Religion and Theology in a Postliberal Age* [Philadelphia: Westminster Press, 1984], p. 75).

[28] *Evangelicals at an Impasse: Bible Authority in Practice* (Atlanta: John Knox Press, 1979), pp. 76, 151-54.

[29] Dietrich Ritschl, "A Plea for the Maxim: Scripture and Tradition," *Interpretation*, 25 (January, 1971): 115.

[30] Ibid., p. 124.

[31] "John Calvin to the Reader, 1559," *Institutes of the Christian Religion*, ed. John T. McNeill, trans. Ford Lewis Battles (Philadelphia: The Westminster Press, 1960), p. 4.

[32] "Subject Matter of the Present Work," from the French Edition of 1560, *Institutes of the Christian Religion*, p. 6.

[33] I am thinking particularly of the work of Schubert M. Ogden.

[34] Lindbeck, p. 16.

[35] Ibid., p. 17.

[36] Charles Hartshorne sees a drastic difference between the religious and the predominant Western philosophical conceptions of God and argues that the "religious," as distinct from the "secular," attributes of God should receive more attention than they have ("The Two Strands in Historical Theology," *Man's Vision of God and the Logic of Theism* [Hamden CN: Archon Books, 1964], pp. 85-141).

[37] According to Bernard Lonergan, "The theologian ... has a contribution of his own to make." He is not "just a parrot with nothing to do but repeat what has already been said" (*Method in Theology*, p. 331).

[38] John Hick is a well-known proponent of this view, which he presents in two widely read books, *Evil and the God of Love* (rev. ed.; New York: Harper & Row, 1978), and *Death and Eternal Life* (New York: Harper & Row, 1976).

4

THE QUESTION OF GENERAL REVELATION

In the previous chapter we examined the particular application of reason to the contents of Christian faith which constitutes Christian theology. We noted that the complex task of systematic theology, as generally understood, applies discursive reason to the various beliefs of the Christian community from a perspective which assumes that these beliefs are true. It attempts to set forth the contents of Christian faith in a logically attractive pattern, arranging them in an appropriate sequence, and explaining their interconnections and implications. In short, it is concerned with the inner structure, or system, of Christian belief.

Although there are strong differences of opinion over the method appropriate to Christian theology, and many others concerning specific theological positions, Christians have almost always approved of this application of reason to faith. Of course, not every Christian finds the enterprise personally interesting or beneficial, and theologians are sometimes accused of trying to obscure, rather than clarify, the meaning of various doctrines. But hardly anyone seriously objects to the idea that the contents of faith are capable of logical expression and deserve to be thought through carefully.

In the remaining chapters of Part 2 our objective is to examine the contents of faith in light of public rather than private evidence. In contrast to theology, this application of reason to Christian beliefs does not take the truth of these beliefs for granted. Moreover, it raises a number of questions which are highly controversial, both inside and outside the Christian community.

The central issue here is whether the contents of Christian faith can be supported by a rational appeal to publicly accessible evidence. Are any of the contents of Christian faith available from a perspective independent of personal Christian commitment, or special spiritual insight? Do Christian beliefs have the support of evidence which is available to any intelligent person, not just members of the Christian community? To put it another way, does a strictly rational investigation of human experience lead to conclusions which are identical to some of the claims of Christian faith? Are there what we might call "demonstrable continuities" between the contents of Christian faith and the results of a rational inquiry into common human experience?

As we noted in the preceding chapter, these questions are the concern of philosophy of religion, or philosophical theology. The purpose of this discipline is to analyze the public evidence, or assess the rational case, for religious beliefs. If it turns out that public evidence supports the claims of religion, the results are sometimes described as forming a "natural theology." In contrast to dogmatic theology, or "revealed theology," natural theology formulates religious concepts from the data that reason can acquire independent of the special illumination of revelation or the privileged vantage point of faith. It presents a rational, as opposed to a confessional, account of certain religious concepts or doctrines.

The philosophical question of whether rational evidence supports the claims of religion raises two questions of a theological nature. The first concerns the nature of the beliefs themselves. Investigating religious beliefs from a rational perspective is possible only if these beliefs are open to rational inquiry. But will Christian beliefs permit such investigation? Is there anything within the contents of faith to indicate that they are perceptible apart from the standpoint of faith? Are they to any extent accessible to human beings in general, from the perspective of reason alone?

If an analysis of the contents of faith reveals that they are indeed open to rational investigation, and if the results of philosophical theology are positive, that is, if it turns out that public evidence does support religious belief, then another question arises. What is the relation between the conclusions of this investigation and the contents of faith? Can the results of such an investigation assist the Christian community in its attempt to understand what it believes? Is there a role for philosophical theology within Christian theology proper?

To complete our analysis of reason and the contents of faith, therefore, we need to address three questions in sequence. First, is Christianity open to philosophical investigation? Second, if it is, what are the results of such an investigation? And third, what contribution, if any, can these results make to Christian theology? This chapter deals with the first of these questions; the next two, with the second and third, respectively.

Our task is complicated not only because it entails a series of interrelated questions, but because each of these questions involves a different enterprise. The first question requires us to engage in systematic theology, or the formulation of Christian doctrine, since it requires us to reflect on various biblical materials. The second calls for an examination of the results of philosophical inquiry, and therefore leads into philosophy. And the third raises issues central to theological method.

The Central Topic in Natural Theology

An apparent obstacle to answering these questions is the enormous number of religious themes and concepts that present themselves for consideration. After nearly two thousand years of development, much of it rigorously intellectual, Christianity now includes an array of ideas so vast that no theologian today, no matter how capable and industrious, would presume to construct anything resembling a *summa theologica*. A single lifetime is not nearly long enough for the task.

No less remarkable than the wide range of ideas which Christianity encompasses, however, is the consensus among both theologians and philosophers over the centuries as to which of the many ideas Christian faith embodies define the essence of Christianity and form the foundation on which everything depends. Virtually all serious students of religion, whether inside or outside the Christian community, agree that the idea of God lies at the very center of Christian faith, as it does in the other great "monotheistic faiths," Judaism and Islam, as well. The concept of a supreme personal being, distinct from the world yet intimately involved in it, is basic to everything that Christians affirm. Occasionally suggestions arise that Christianity should dispense with the idea of God. But the rapidity with which they pass from serious consideration only confirms the truth of what they deny: the idea of God is essential to Christian faith. The short-lived "death of God" episode in American theology twenty years ago illustrates the point. It never attracted a serious following of any size and within a brief time its leading proponents took up other pursuits.

It is not hard to understand why. The concept of God has occupied a central place in Christianity from the beginning. God is the central figure in both Old and New Testaments, the seminal documents of Christian faith. Genesis begins with an account of his creative activity and Revelation ends with the promise of his eventual triumph over evil. Jesus defined his mission with reference to the activity of God. The first article of the Apostles' Creed, one of the oldest Christian confessions, affirms faith in "God the Father almighty, creator of heaven and earth."[1]

Some theologians believe that all of Christian faith expresses in various ways the one idea of God. For Schubert M. Ogden, for example, "the problem of God is not one problem among several others; it is the only problem there is."[2] And even though few Christians may be willing to compress all they believe into the single doctrine of God, many would agree with a friend of mine who insisted that the most important question in religion is the existence of God. "If there is a God," she reasoned, "everything else falls into place. But if God doesn't exist, then none of the rest of religion matters."

The testimony of philosophers to the importance of the idea of God is, if anything, more emphatic than that of theologians. God is widely regarded as the central religious idea. And many—supporters and detractors alike—insist that the validity of religion in its entirety stands or falls with the question of God's existence.

Another reason for concentrating on the idea of God is what Michael J. Buckley calls a "massive shifting of religious consciousness" in modern Western culture with respect to the question of God. According to Buckley, the last two hundred years have seen "the rise of a radical godlessness which is as much a part of the consciousness of millions of ordinary human beings as it is the persuasion of the intellectual." There have always been isolated figures who denied the reality of God. But atheism has grown from the radical viewpoint of an elite few to become the outlook of millions of ordinary people. And this is something without precedent in human history.[3] For several reasons, then, it makes sense for us to explore whether the contents of faith are open to rational examination with specific reference to the central religious belief in God.

If the Christian belief in God is to any extent accessible to rational investigation, two conditions must be met. There must be evidence for this belief which is universally available, and there must also exist a general human capacity to perceive such evidence. These conditions raise the well-known question of general, or natural, revelation, as it is customarily formulated within Christian theology.

General Revelation and Natural Theology

The doctrine of revelation plays an important role in Christian thought. It expresses the conviction that God has communicated himself to human beings in order to establish a personal, saving relationship with them. Christians believe that the life of Jesus is the decisive instance of divine revelation and that it represents the climax of a series of revelatory activities on God's part. In the familiar opening words of Hebrews, "In many and various ways God spoke of old to our fathers by the prophets; but in these last days he has spoken to us by a Son" (1:1-2). The prominent place which the Bible occupies in Christian life and thought indicates the importance to Christian faith of the concept of revelation. Christians traditionally view the Bible as the authoritative record of God's revelation to human beings. The New Testament contains the apostolic witness to the life of Jesus; the Old Testament, the record of God's activity in the experience of the Hebrew people which anticipated Jesus' ministry.

The question of general revelation arises out of the unique claims Christians make for the Bible and the events to which it testifies. It is the question of whether Jesus Christ and the stream of history in which he stands—that is, the Bible and the events it records—represent the only source of divine revelation. Has God revealed himself to human beings generally, independent of their contact with the Bible or the various events it records? In other words, is there general as well as special revelation? Or, as it is often put, has God revealed himself in nature as well as in history?

The question of general revelation raises the closely related but distinct question of natural knowledge of God. By itself the fact that God has manifested himself in nature does not guarantee that human beings could come to know him through this means. There is also a subjective condition that must be met. In order to acquire knowledge of God through nature, human beings must also possess the capacity to perceive and interpret this revelation correctly. There can be no natural knowledge of God without general revelation, obviously, but the existence of general revelation does not necessarily mean that such knowledge is possible. Let us examine the biblical material that bears on both questions—general revelation and a natural knowledge of God.

A number of biblical passages state that the natural world bears testimony to the reality of God. Some of the most important examples are the so-called "nature psalms," such as Psalm 19, which begins with the familiar words, "The heavens are telling the glory of God and the firmament proclaims his handiwork,"[4] and the first two chapters of Romans, where Paul states, "Ever since the creation of the world his [God's] invisible nature, namely, his eternal power and deity, has been clearly perceived in the things that have been made."[5] According to the account in Acts of his first missionary journey, Paul told the inhabitants of Lystra, a town in Asia Minor, that God "did not leave himself without witness" in past generations, but provided them with "rains and fruitful seasons, satisfying your hearts with food and gladness."[6]

Further biblical support for the concept of general revelation can be found in certain descriptions of human behavior. In his famous sermon at the Areopagus, as recorded in Acts 17:22-31, Paul described the religiosity of his hearers as an expression of their awareness of the true God, the Creator, whom they worshiped as unknown (vs. 23). And according to his analysis of paganism (Rom 1-2), Paul found in the moral sensitivity of those who have never had the benefit of special revelation an indication that they were nevertheless aware of the imperatives of God's law (2:14-15). As the New Testament describes it, then, human behavior provides evidence that men and women are instinctively aware of God's universal sovereignty and moral demands.

In addition to its numerous references to the created world and to human experience, the Bible also speaks of the character of God in a way which supports the concept of general revelation. In the words of 1 Timothy 2:4, God "desires all men to be saved and to come to the knowledge of the truth." And according to 2 Peter 3:9, he does not wish "that any should perish, but that all should come to repentance." If God's unchanging desire for the salvation of all human beings—the "universal salvific will of God," as Karl Rahner expresses it[7]—is more than an empty notion, it must be that God is somehow active in the life of every human being for the purpose of bringing salvation.

In another important biblical statement, the fourth Gospel refers to Jesus as "the true light that enlightens every man."[8] This famous description implies that every human being somehow benefits from the manifestation of God in Jesus Christ, even in the absence of an explicit knowledge of the Gospel.[9] So, biblical support for the view that publicly accessible evidence to some extent corroborates the contents of Christian faith includes indications of divinity in the natural world, human moral and religious experience, and God's gracious disposition toward human beings.

In addition to specific biblical statements, the very idea of God which the Bible expresses makes the concept of general, or natural, revelation plausible. The most fundamental designation of God is "creator." The first verse of the Bible speaks of God as creating the heavens and the earth.[10] Echoing this emphasis, early Christian creeds describe God as "creator of all things, visible and invisible."[11] According to the biblical concept of creation, God's power not only accounts for the origin of the universe, it also sustains everything that exists, as the following verse indicates: "Thou hast made heaven, the heaven of heavens, with all their host, the earth and all that is on it, the seas and all that is in them; and thou preservest all of them."[12] To use philosophical language, the Bible depicts God as the supreme reality, the final explanatory factor. He is the ultimate metaphysical principle.[13]

As the power that sustains the universe moment by moment, God is the source of all life. The Bible closely associates God's creative activity with his life-giving power. According to Romans 4:17, for example, God "gives life to the dead and calls into existence the things that do not exist." Several of the Psalms associate this life-giving power with the breath, or "spirit," of God: "By the word of the Lord the heavens were made, and all their host by the breath of his mouth"; "when thou takest away their breath, they die and return to their dust. When thou sendest forth thy Spirit [or "breath"], they are created."[14] Paul's quotation from Greek poetry in his sermon at the Areopagus may be the Bible's clearest affirmation of God as the power which sustains human life: "In him we live and move and have our being."[15]

As the ultimate power of being and the momentary source of all life, God must be a factor in the experience of every human being. To be aware that there is a supreme power from which we constantly derive our existence—a power in whom we live and move and have our being—is to be aware of the reality of God. This awareness may be vague and imprecise—as Paul recognized, people may acknowledge it only as something "unknown"—but it is nevertheless one form which the knowledge of God can take.

These considerations indicate that the Bible supports an affirmative answer to the question of general revelation. Besides the "special revelation" recorded and embodied in the Bible, God has manifested himself in the structure of reality, in the processes of nature and in human experience. So, we conclude that certain aspects of Christian faith, in particular certain elements in the Christian view of God, are accessible to all human beings and have the support of publicly accessible evidence.

John Calvin on Revelation in Nature

As we observed above, the presence of divine revelation in nature does not necessarily mean that human beings enjoy a natural knowledge of God. Even if God has revealed himself to humankind in some "general" way, there can be no "natural knowledge of God" unless human beings are capable of discerning this revelation and somehow responding to it. Two "classic" treatments of this issue have been especially influential in Christian thought, and it will be helpful for us to consider them briefly here. John Calvin, the great Reformer, accepts the concept of natural revelation, but rejects that of natural theology. Karl Barth, the famous neo-orthodox theologian, not only rejects natural theology, but objects to the notion of general revelation, as well.

In his monumental *Institutes of the Christian Religion,* Calvin divides our knowledge of God into two parts, knowledge of God the Creator and knowledge of God the Redeemer. We obtain the second only from Scripture, he argues, but the first has two sources, Scripture and the natural world.[16] Nature contains two types of evidence for God's existence. One is the innate awareness of divinity, or *sensus divinitatis,* which is intrinsic to human nature. This sense of divinity is the "seed of religion," the root of the universal presence of religion in human cultures.[17] It consists of the ineradicable conviction that there is a God and that he is our maker.[18]

A second source of evidence for God's existence is "the whole workmanship of the universe," which abounds with "sparks of his glory,"[19] and represents "a mirror of his deity." Calvin finds "innumerable miracles" in "this magnificent theater of heaven and earth."[20] Within the ordinary course of nature we find the heavenly host and the structure of the human body. Outside it, we find the administration of human society, with displays of both justice and mercy.[21] Indeed, so forceful is such evidence that "it ought not to escape the gaze of even the most stupid tribe" of human beings.[22]

Besides the objective component in our knowledge of God which this evidence provides, Calvin also identifies an indispensable subjective component. To obtain knowledge of God, he insists, one must exhibit a genuine religious attitude toward him. This attitude consists in piety—"that reverence joined with love of God which the knowledge of his benefits induces."[23]

According to Calvin, there is a widespread lack of piety among human beings, and the result is a general absence of the true knowledge of God. Without the proper attitude toward God, human beings inevitably misconstrue the natural evidence of his existence. Our innate sense of divinity never leads to more than a confused knowledge of God, because it is invariably distorted, either by superstition or rebellion.[24] Likewise, the external manifestations of God's reality fail to produce a true knowledge of God because of human stupidity and dullness. In sum, "we lack the natural ability to mount up unto the pure and clear knowledge of God."[25] As a result, the net effect of the abundant evidence of God's creative power is to render us inexcusable in our ignorance.

Because of our inability to interpret accurately the natural evidence of God's reality, we need "another and better help" to direct us to the Creator. To meet this need God put forth his Word, which represents "a more direct and more certain mark whereby he is to be recognized." In fact, since the evidence for God in the natural universe inevitably fails because of human weakness, Scripture is indispensable in attaining a true knowledge of God. Consequently, it is here, with the Sacred Scriptures, that our quest for true knowledge of God the Creator must begin. "No one," insists Calvin, "can get even the slightest taste of right and sound doctrine unless he be a pupil of Scripture."[26]

Although natural evidences by themselves are ineffective in leading to a true knowledge of God, they are by no means useless. For once we have the Bible, we can clearly see the evidences of God in nature. In a memorable analogy, Calvin compares the Scriptures to spectacles, which enable those weak in vision to see distinctly what they would otherwise find inscrutable. Similarly, Scripture, "gathering up the otherwise confused knowledge of God in our minds, having dispersed our dullness, clearly shows us the true God."[27] The knowledge of God obtained from the Bible thus complements the evidence provided by nature and enables us to see it clearly as a manifestation of God's creative power.

For Calvin, then, there is general revelation because nature contains abundant testimony to its divine source. But there is no true natural knowledge of God, because human beings lack piety and inevitably misinterpret this testimony. With the assistance of the Bible, however, the evidence in nature becomes clear to us and contributes to our knowledge of God as Creator.

Karl Barth's Critique of General Revelation

The most emphatic rejection of general revelation in the history of Christian thought comes from the twentieth century theologian Karl Barth, who declares himself "an avowed opponent of all natural theology."[28]

The concept of revelation plays a central role in Barth's massive theological proposal, and his opposition to natural theology, and to the related concept of general revelation, arises from his understanding of the distinctive nature and content of Christian revelation. As Barth describes it, several elements in the Christian concept of revelation make it utterly incompatible with anything like a natural knowledge of God. First of all, the nature of revelation is intensely personal. It is anything but an impersonal, objective transmission of information from one party to another. In his revelation, God discloses himself as a person, and in doing so he establishes a concrete relation with human beings. As a person, God is "one Who knows and wills, Who acts and speaks, Who as an 'I' calls me 'Thou' and Whom I can call 'Thou' in return."[29]

Given the personal nature of its source, divine revelation can be received only within the perspective created by the impact of the revelation itself. The knowledge of God is available only to one who is grasped by it and through this experience becomes a new person.[30] In other words, "knowledge through revelation" is nothing less and nothing other than "knowledge of faith."[31]

Barth not only asserts that we can know God only if we have a personal relationship with him, he also insists that we can know God only in Jesus Christ, who is "the eternal Son of God in the flesh, the one and only God in whom we have been called to believe."[32] "In the revelation of God in Jesus Christ," he states, "God and man meet, and therefore are really together."[33] So, the perspective of faith which is essential to a knowledge of God is nothing other than Christian faith, and it is only through Christ that anyone enjoys a personal relation with God. "Apart from and without Jesus Christ we can say nothing at all about God and man and their relationship one with another."[34]

Barth rejects the idea of natural theology because he finds it completely opposed to the concept of revelation just described. Natural theology presupposes the existence of an "original revelation" of God to man different from his revelation in Jesus Christ—a revelation which we possess simply by virtue of our humanity. It also presupposes an "original relation" or union between God and man, likewise independent of Jesus Christ.[35] Because the concept of such a theology radically conflicts with the theology based on God's revelation in Christ, the two are completely incompatible. The principle that God can be known only within the perspective of Christian faith invalidates the basic premise of natural theology, that human beings possess an independent standpoint from which thoughts may be formed about God. Christian theology and natural theology are therefore completely opposed to each other, and we are forced to choose between them.[36] Barth is adamant: the denial of God's revelation in Jesus Christ necessarily follows, "even if we only lend our little finger to natural theology."[37]

Barth's critique of general revelation goes far beyond the position of the Reformers, as he acknowledges.[38] Calvin would agree with Barth that God can be known only because he reveals himself. He would also agree that God can be known only because he reveals himself in Jesus Christ. But he would not agree with Barth that God reveals himself only in Jesus Christ. For Calvin, the natural world does contain divine revelation. Nevertheless, both theologians espouse a view of revelation which leads them to reject the possibility of a natural knowledge of God. For Calvin it is not a practical possibility; for Barth it is not even a theoretical possibility.

If Calvin and Barth are correct in rejecting the idea of a natural knowledge of God, then we are left with a negative answer to the question of reason and the contents of faith. For their position is that reason apart from faith can know nothing of God. Without an explicit familiarity with the contents of special revelation, human beings cannot attain a knowledge of God.

The Case Against Natural Theology

We can summarize the case against natural theology by reviewing the central points in Calvin and Barth's critiques and noting some additional criticisms closely related to them.

The most pervasive objection to the idea that human beings enjoy a natural knowledge of God is the one which Calvin raises. The effects of sin on our cognitive faculties make it impossible for us to perceive God's revelation in creation. As we have seen, Calvin accepts—indeed, he waxes eloquent in describing—the testimony to God in the natural world. But he rejects the notion that this evidence can provide a basis for reliable human knowledge of God. The fault is not with the stars, we might say, but with ourselves. On its own merits, the evidence is adequate to convey a clear concept of God's creative power, but we lack the ability to discern it. Sin has damaged our cognitive faculties to such a degree that we cannot see the evidence clearly, and we inevitably misinterpret it.

Human behavior seems to support this objection. Instead of responding to the evidence of God's creative power, human beings characteristically pervert its meaning and rebel against God. So, it seems, there is good reason to question whether any of the contents of faith are available to human beings independent of special revelation, or apart from the specific perspective of faith.

A related objection to the concept of a natural knowledge of God is the interesting idea that the revelation in creation was never intended to provide it. The idea of general revelation, the argument goes, misconstrues the purpose of the natural evidences of divinity. True, God has manifested himself in the natural world. As Paul states, "his invisible nature, namely, his eternal power and deity, has been clearly perceived in the things that have been made."[39] But the purpose of these manifestations is not to lead humans to a true knowledge of God. As Paul's next statement and the following passages indicate, it is to render them inexcusable in their sin: "So they are without excuse." Therefore, it is wrong to regard the evidence of divinity in nature as providing a natural knowledge of God. It was never intended to do so.

As we found in the case of Karl Barth, another objection to the concept of a natural knowledge of God is that it contradicts the central Christian belief that Jesus Christ is the only means of human salvation. If God can be known outside His revelation in Jesus Christ, then Christ cannot be the sole means of salvation; there must be some other basis for a saving relationship with God.

Another objection is that the existence of a natural knowledge of God would render Christian mission superfluous. As Barth argues, the universal availability of knowledge of God implies the universal availability of salvation. And this undercuts the particularism essential to Christianity, with its distinctive claims for Jesus. It also renders meaningless the task of Christian mission. If men and women can be saved without a knowledge of Christ, then why should Christians bother to preach the Gospel? Why not let everyone find God in his or her own way?

The Case For Natural Theology

Much of what Calvin and Barth have to say about the nature of revelation is very helpful. And their critique of natural theology is an important caveat against claiming too much for reason. But their rejection of a natural knowledge of God, particularly as Barth formulates it, goes too far. It is not only difficult to reconcile with the biblical statements we considered earlier, but it is not required by their central concerns. In what follows we will try to show that the most helpful elements in their view of revelation do not necessarily invalidate the concept of a natural knowledge of God. Let us address the objections just mentioned one by one.

The crux of the first objection lies in its assessment of "natural man," specifically, his cognitive faculties. It infers from the fact that sin has damaged our capacity to perceive God's revelation in nature that we will always rebel against God unless we have an explicit knowledge of his revelation in Jesus Christ. This inference is questionable, however. It seems to assume that special revelation is a necessary condition for the possibility of faith, and that rebellion is the inevitable response to general revelation.

Calvin's analysis of religious knowledge into subjective and objective factors is helpful here. It allows for a possibility he does not seem to have considered, namely, that the Holy Spirit can evoke a response of faith to general revelation. Calvin maintains, remember, that divine revelation cannot produce a knowledge of God unless human beings respond to it with piety. And he attributes the human failure to gain a knowledge of God from the revelation in creation to a lack of piety—a lack which makes it necessary for God to provide "another and better help." But although he accounts for the failure of general revelation to produce a knowledge of God by referring to the subjective aspect of religious knowledge, Calvin attributes the success of special revelation to its objective aspect—its superior content.

What Calvin does not say is important here. He does not say that there is something inherently defective or inadequate in the contents of general revelation. The fact that it does not lead to a knowledge of God is wholly due to the improper response of human beings. Nor, on the other hand, does he assert that the effectiveness of special revelation is due to the piety of its recipients. Instead, he attributes it to the superior content of special revelation. Calvin seems to assume, then, that there is a strict correlation between special revelation and faith, and that general revelation and rebellion always go together, too. But his twofold analysis of religious knowledge allows for two other possibilities.

One is a lack of piety in the response of men and women to special revelation. The other is the presence of piety in their response to general revelation. The former is certainly conceivable. In fact, it is sadly true that many people reject the revelation of God in Jesus Christ, just as many reject his revelation in creation.

Is it possible for human beings to respond positively to the revelation of God in creation, even though many of them do not? Calvin's twofold division of both subjective and objective aspects of religious knowledge allows for the possibility, but is it actually, or merely theoretically possible? Is it conceivable that human beings influenced by the Holy Spirit could respond to the revelation in creation with piety?

According to the Bible, it is. There is biblical evidence that human beings can respond positively to God's revelation in creation. Jesus commended a Syrophoenician woman for her faith.[40] And Cornelius and his household are described as fearing God before they gained a knowledge of the Gospel.[41] So, it seems possible that the Holy Spirit may influence the mind of someone who has no access to the contents of Christian faith, enabling him or her to respond appropriately to whatever divine revelation is available.

Can we speak of a natural knowledge of God, then? It depends on what we mean by "natural." If we mean, Can human beings acquire a knowledge of God from the evidence in nature?, the answer is Yes. There are sound reasons for claiming that this is indeed possible, and there is evidence that it happens from time to time. If, on the other hand, we mean, Can human beings achieve a knowledge of God apart from divine assistance?, the answer must be No. Without the influence of the Holy Spirit knowledge of God is never possible, not even in response to special revelation.

To answer the question of a natural knowledge of God, therefore, we must consider more than the typical human response to God's revelation in creation. If we understand "natural man" as man in sin, completely separated from God, then we do not describe men and women as they actually exist. For one thing, God provided human beings with a Savior as soon as sin entered the world. For another, as we have seen, the Bible describes God as desiring the salvation of all humankind and Christ as enlightening every human being. In addition, there is the evidence just cited that certain individuals have indeed responded positively to God without enjoying an explicit knowledge of the contents of Christian faith. So the possibility does exist of attaining a knowledge of God on the basis of general revelation.

In light of this evidence, it appears that the "natural man," in the sense of one whose cognitive resources consist only of his sin-damaged faculties, is an abstraction. It refers not to human beings as they do exist, but to human beings as they would exist, were not God universally at work in human lives. Consequently, we can acknowledge the effects of sin on human reason and still claim that at least some of what Christians believe is available to those who have not made an explicit response to the contents of the Gospel.

The argument that there is no natural knowledge of God because the result of natural revelation is to render human beings inexcusable in their sin draws heavily on the first two chapters of Romans, where Paul describes the large-scale response of the pagan world to the revelation in nature. According to Paul, idolaters have misapprehended the divine revelation in the natural world, rebelled against it, and polluted themselves with immoral practices to which God in his wrath "gave them up."

This objection mistakes the practical consequences of the natural evidences of divinity for the original purpose of these data. Granted, the effect of these evidences has been to render human beings inexcusable in their sin. This is certainly Paul's argument. But it does not necessarily follow that this was the fundamental purpose of the revelation in nature.

Paul is directly concerned, it is important to notice, with the actual role natural revelation has played in the course of God's dealings with humanity; he does not speak to the question of its original purpose. Consequently, the conclusion that these manifestations were designed only to condemn humans, to render them inexcusable in sin, is unwarranted. To the contrary, if indeed God wills the salvation of all people, and is everywhere at work to bring them to this experience, he manifests himself only in order to save. Whenever he reaches out, he seeks to restore human beings to harmony with himself. Consequently, all revelation is salvific in purpose. The notion of a revelation whose purpose is to condemn is incompatible with the idea of divine love.

Barth's rejection of the notion of a natural knowledge of God arises from a deep commitment to the uniqueness of Jesus as the source of revelation and salvation. But the concept of general revelation and a sense of Jesus' uniqueness are not incompatible as Barth insists. The objection that a natural knowledge of God would represent another source of salvation confuses two different questions: whether anyone can be saved without Christ, and whether anyone can be saved without explicit knowledge of Christ. It overlooks the possibility that the salvation available only through Christ could be experienced by someone who lacks an explicit knowledge of the Gospel.[42] The conclusion is therefore unwarranted that an affirmation of natural knowledge of God is a denial of Christ as the exclusive means of salvation.

The objection that a natural knowledge of God would render Christian mission unnecessary also involves a confusion. It rests on the mistaken assumption that an explicit knowledge of the Gospel is either indispensable or inconsequential for salvation. If anyone can be saved without hearing the Gospel, this line of reasoning goes, then no one really needs to hear it. The neglected consideration here is that while some may be able to respond positively to God without actually hearing of Christ, others may never be able to do so. In other words, from the possibility that some may come to faith in God in the absence of an explicit knowledge of Christ it by no means follows that everyone is capable of doing so. Many people may very well be lost without hearing the Gospel who might otherwise have been saved. So, the imperative of Christian mission loses none of its force with the idea of a natural knowledge of God.

Besides, there are other important reasons for Christian mission. For one thing, Christ commands his disciples to evangelize,[43] and for dedicated followers that is reason enough. For another, those who preach the Gospel benefit from the endeavor, not just those who hear. And in the third place, even if some may be able to respond to God positively without an explicit knowledge of Christ, their lives will be immeasurably enriched by actually hearing the Gospel and entering into the community of Christ's followers. There is no compelling reason, then, why the mission of the church loses significance on the view that some of the contents of faith are available from the perspective of common experience.

Conclusion

Our theological inquiry leads us to conclude that the contents of faith are open to investigation from a perspective which does not presuppose their validity. We find support within the contents of faith themselves both for general revelation and for the possibility of a natural knowledge of God, and none of the objections to these ideas are convincing.

In order to clarify the stage of the discussion we have reached, it will be helpful to indicate just what the concept of a natural knowledge of God does and does not involve. In basic terms it is the idea that human beings can know something of God on the basis of our common experience in the world. Put negatively, it means that not all knowledge of God presupposes a personal faith commitment in response to an explicit awareness of the contents of special revelation.

This is obviously a minimal claim. All it asserts is the possibility of such knowledge, on the basis that the contents of faith do not in principle exclude it. In other words, the existence of natural knowledge of God is not incompatible with the beliefs that God has revealed himself with unique and decisive clarity in Jesus Christ and that the purpose of this revelation is achieved only when human beings respond to the offer of salvation which this revelation extends.

We have seen that the contents of Christian faith themselves indicate that to some extent they have the support of publicly accessible evidence. Some of the beliefs involved in Christian commitment are available from the standpoint of common human experience, quite apart from special revelation or the specific perspective of personal faith. Specifically, the belief in God, which is central to Christian faith, is corroborated by the evidence of nature and human experience—evidence available to every thinking person. At least some of what Christians believe is therefore continuous with the conclusions any intelligent, attentive human being might achieve.

In addition to the question of its possibility, which has occupied us here, another important question concerning general revelation is its relation to the special revelation which it presupposes. On most accounts, special revelation surpasses general revelation in both clarity and comprehensiveness. According to Calvin, for example, Scripture represents "another, better help" than the revelation of God in creation. It tells us more about God than we could ever learn from the natural world alone and what it says about God is more clearly and forcefully expressed. Calvin's position is also instructive, because he does not take the view that special revelation renders general revelation superfluous. So the two are complementary, rather than redundant. Enriched with the insights of special revelation, believers can turn with great appreciation to the manifestations of God in the natural world.

This is getting ahead of our story, however. Before we can answer the question of how the contents of reason are related to the contents of faith, we must determine what the contents of reason are. This is our task in the next chapter.

---

[1] I have quoted from the version appearing in *Creeds of the Churches: A Reader in Christian Doctrine From the Bible to the Present*, ed. John H. Leith (Garden City, New York: Anchor Books, 1963), p. 24.

[2] *The Reality of God and Other Essays* (New York: Harper & Row, Publishers, 1966), p. 1.

[3] Michael J. Buckley, S.J., *At the Origins of Modern Atheism* (New Haven: Yale University Press, 1987), p. 28.

[4] Others are Psalms 8, 104, and 148.

[5] Romans 1:20.

[6] Acts 14:17.

[7] Karl Rahner, *Do You Believe in God?* trans. Richard Strachan (New York: Paulist Press, 1969), p. 11.

[8] John 1:9.

[9] This was apparently Ellen G. White's view, for in commenting on John 1:9, she makes the following statement: "As through Christ every human being has life, so also through Him every soul receives some ray of divine light" (*Education* [Mountain View, CA: Pacific Press Publishing Company, 1903], p. 29).

[10] Genesis 1:1.

[11] See the Creed of Nicea and the Constantinopolitan Creed.

[12] Nehemiah 9:6.

[13] Ellen G. White puts the point this way: "All created beings live by the will and power of God. They are dependent recipients of the life of God. From the highest seraph to the humblest animate being, all are replenished from the source of life" (*The Desire of*

The Question of General Revelation   121

Ages [Mountain View, CA: Pacific Press Publishing Association, 1989],p. 785).

[14] Psalm 33:6; 104:29-30.

[15] Acts 17:28.

[16] *Institutes of the Christian Religion,* trans. Ford Lewis Battles (2 vols.; Philadelphia: Westminster Press, 1970), Bk. I, ch. ii. par. 1.

[17] Ibid., Bk. I, ch. iii, par. 1; Bk. I, ch. iv, par. 1.

[18] Ibid., Bk. I, ch. iii, par. 3.

[19] Ibid., Bk. I, ch. v, par. 1.

[20] Ibid., Bk. I, ch. vi, par. 1. In a similar vein, Ellen G. White begins her best known book with the statement, "Nature and revelation alike testify of God's love" *(Steps to Christ* [Mountain View, CA: Pacific Press Publishing Association, 1956], p. 9).

[21] *Institutes,* Bk. I, ch. v, pars. 2, 7.

[22] Ibid., Bk. I, ch. v, par. 1.

[23] Ibid., Bk. I, ch. ii, par. l.

[24] Ibid., Bk. I, ch. iv, pars. 1-2.

[25] Ibid., Bk. I, ch. v, pars. 11, 15.

[26] Ibid., Bk. I, ch. vi, par. 2.

[27] Ibid., Bk. I, ch. vi, par. 1.

[28] Karl Barth, *The Knowledge of God and the Service of God According to the Teaching of the Reformation: Recalling the Scottish Confession of 1560,* trans. J. L. M. Haire and Ian Henderson (London: Hodder and Stoughton Publishers, 1938), p. 6.

[29] Ibid., p. 33.

[30] Ibid., p. 104.

[31] Ibid., pp. 25-26.

[32] Ibid., p. 21.

[33] Ibid., p. 36.

[34] *Church Dogmatics: A Selection,* trans. and ed. G. W. Bromiley (Edinburgh: T. &. T. Clark, 1961; New York: Harper Torchbooks, 1962), p. 50.

[35] *Knowledge of God,* p. 9.

[36] Ibid., pp. 103-104.

[37] *Church Dogmatics: A Selection,* p. 56.

[38] Barth argues that developments in the last four hundred years have demonstrated more fully than the Reformers themselves realized how completely their central insights require the repudiation of natural theology *(Knowledge of God,* p. 8).

[39] Romans 1:20.

[40] Mark 9:28.

[41] Acts 10:1-2. In this connection, it is significant that Ellen G. White speaks of individuals among the heathen "who worship God ignorantly," and whose "works are evidence that the Holy Spirit has touched their hearts" *(The Desire of Ages,* p. 638; cf. *Christ's Object Lessons* [Mountain View, CA: Pacific Press Publishing Association, 1900], p. 385).

[42] See, for example, Edward Heppenstall, "Has the Natural Man Access to God Apart From Jesus Christ or Special Revelation?" The Second Edward Heppenstall Endowment Lecture (Privately published, 1974).

[43] Matthew 28:19-20; Acts 1:8.

5
NATURAL THEOLOGY: THE PHILOSOPHICAL QUESTION

In Chapter 4 we asked if faith is open to reason. Our question was whether the contents of faith contain anything to indicate that they might be perceptible from the standpoint of our common human experience, or enjoy the support of public evidence. Moreover, we asked this question with specific reference to God, a central element in Christianity, if not its most important and comprehensive aspect. Is the object of Christian faith accessible to public inquiry? Our conclusion was affirmative. The biblical writers found evidence for God in the created world generally and in human experience in particular. So, this evidence establishes the possibility of a natural theology.

Having determined that faith permits reason to look at its contents, we now undertake that inspection. Moving from inside to outside a perspective of religious commitment, we shall examine the contents of faith from the vantage point of reason alone. Our general purpose in this chapter is to see what reason has to say about the contents of faith. Once again we shall focus on the concept of God. In the words of Thomas Aquinas, "We are aiming, then, to inquire, in a rational way, into the things human reason can disclose concerning God."[1] In particular, we hope to see if belief in God is intellectually responsible according to the notion of responsible belief developed in Chapter 2.

Attitudes Toward Arguments for God

What does reason have to say about the contents of faith? What public evidence, if any, supports the belief in God which is central to religious faith? Attempts to answer this question over the years have been numerous and widely diverse. But for centuries people have pursued the subject by constructing, analyzing and criticizing various "proofs for the existence of God." These several arguments—families of arguments, really—are the most famous and highly disputed exercises that philosophical reasoning has ever produced. Every textbook in philosophy discusses them, and every philosopher seems to have strongly-held opinions about them. Historically, God's existence has been the central concern of western philosophers who thought about religion. So, if there is public evidence for the contents of faith, we should find it here.

The arguments for the existence of God, or "theistic proofs,"[2] as they are often called, present a formidable landscape for exploration. Let us begin our discussion by reviewing some of the things that complicate this task. For one thing, each of the arguments has been formulated in a variety of different ways, especially the most popular of them, namely, the ontological, cosmological, and teleological arguments. One study of the ontological argument, for example, is appropriately entitled, "the many-faced argument."[3] Another lists no fewer than ten different versions of the proof.[4] The history of the arguments is also highly complex. Each argument rose and developed in its own way. By most accounts the ontological argument originated with Anselm, a churchman of the eleventh century.[5] In contrast, the cosmological argument goes back at least to the days of classical Greek philosophy.[6]

Serious thinkers not only disagree as to how the proofs are best formulated, they also differ as to what type of reasoning the various proofs employ. It is customary to distinguish between *a priori* and *a posteriori* arguments, which can be roughly explained as meaning "before" and "after" experience, respectively. *A priori* arguments proceed by appealing solely to the requirements of concepts, while *a posteriori* arguments depend to some extent on our experience of the world.[7] Everyone describes the ontological argument as *a priori* in character, but agreement ends there. David Hume, the great critic of the arguments, described the cosmological argument as *a priori* and the teleological as *a posteriori*.[8] William L. Rowe, a contemporary philosopher of religion, states that the cosmological and teleological arguments are *a posteriori*.[9]

And Charles Hartshorne, another contemporary thinker, insists that all theistic proofs, not just the ontological argument, must be *a priori*. [10]

Scholars also disagree over the relationship between the different arguments. William Paley, who gave the teleological argument one of its most popular expressions, insisted that any one of the many examples of design in nature suffices to prove the existence of God.[11] In his famous critique of the classical proofs, Immanuel Kant maintains that the arguments are interrelated. According to his analysis, the cosmological argument presupposes the ontological argument.[12] Charles Hartshorne agrees. As we shall see, he insists that all theistic arguments are really phases of one comprehensive, or "global," argument for the existence of God.[13]

The popularity of the theistic arguments ebbs and flows. This is true of the arguments both individually and as a whole. Naturally, different thinkers assess the relative strength of each argument differently. Although Kant, for example, rejected all three classical arguments—the ontological, cosmological, and teleological proofs—he expressed admiration for the last of them, the "physico-theological proof," as he called it.[14] And he formulated yet another argument for God's existence on the basis of human morality. The ontological argument is particularly controversial. It is both warmly admired and thoroughly disdained. For some, it constitutes a kind of intellectual sleight of hand, moving from premises that are unassailable to a conclusion that is unacceptable.[15] But for others, it represents one of the most significant achievements in Western thought, "an incomparably brilliant and cogent course of reasoning,"[16] to quote an avid supporter.

Interest in the general question of the existence of God also rises and falls. Sometimes the question generates animated philosophical discussion and occupies the best philosophical minds around. At other times, nobody seems to care. A few years ago a popular magazine reported a new flurry of activity in philosophical circles involving the arguments for God.[17] It was a notable departure from the preoccupation with language and its uses characteristic of philosophers in England and America for most of this century.

Finally, there are profound differences of opinion as to what the proofs accomplish. For many, the proofs are dismal philosophical failures. They are shot through with logical flaws, and none of them succeeds in demonstrating that God exists. For others, the proofs are on the right track, but they need careful adjustment, and in some cases major renovation, in order to achieve their objective. For surprisingly few, the proofs do just what they ostensibly set out to do, namely, provide a convincing case for the reality of God.

Then there are varying reactions to the whole idea of arguing for God's existence. For some people, the possibility of believing in God rests heavily on the success of attempts to formulate effective proofs. But for others such arguments are utterly irrelevant to belief in God. Whether or not you believe in God, they insist, has nothing to do with the outcome of philosophical debates.

Whatever we think of the proofs, individually or together, we must admire their resiliency. These several arguments, formulated at different points in time, repeatedly subjected to searching scrutiny and not infrequently to withering criticism, have a remarkable capacity for survival. No matter how rigorous the criticism, they always seem to rise, phoenix-like, from the ashes. Just when most people have written them off as mistaken in principle, or failing in practice, "another look" at the proofs in general, or a new formulation of one of them, comes along to ignite discussion all over again.

Since our purpose in this chapter is to determine whether publicly accessible evidence in fact supports belief in God, the proofs for God require our close examination, but we must carefully limit our objectives in discussing them. Our purpose in the following pages is to assess the overall case for theism, not to prove that God exists. We can hardly attempt to reformulate the proofs ourselves, nor does space allow us to survey in any depth the current stage of philosophical discussion. After all, there are entire books devoted to a single theistic argument.[18] But even though we cannot hope to demonstrate that God exists within the space of a few pages, we can get a pretty good idea what the evidence for theism consists of. And this should be enough for us to determine whether or not belief in God is intellectually responsible.

The Nature and Purpose of Theistic Arguments

Before we turn to the individual arguments for God, it will be helpful for us to clarify what such arguments can and cannot do. A familiar objection to theistic proofs in general is that they are either unnecessary or ineffective. Those who already believe in God don't need them, and those who don't believe in God never find them convincing. And since they are unable to generate belief within those who do not believe, the arguments are useless.

This objection is by no means limited to the "man on the street." Philosophers often make the same observation. John Hick, for example, insists that "to prove something means to prove it *to* someone," and concludes that many theistic proofs fail by this criterion, because "they necessarily beg the question, in that a person who accepts their premises already acknowledges the reality of God."[19] "They can only be probative to those who need no proof." The assumption here is that the function of an argument is psychological, that its purpose is to produce belief, to convince people of something they would otherwise find unacceptable.

But there are good reasons to reject this notion of what an argument is supposed to do. We must remember that validity and persuasiveness are different. An argument is a logical exercise, not a persuasive device, so we should evaluate arguments by logical rather than psychological criteria. In a helpful discussion of this issue, James F. Ross rejects the "person-relative" concept of a good argument, as he calls it, in favor of the "impersonal-objective" one.[20]

Ross insists that "the function of a good argument is to establish its conclusion," and that philosophy "is concerned solely with producing a good argument for a given conclusion without concern for whether or not anyone employs this reason in selecting his beliefs." Accordingly, an argument need not "convert, convince, or comfort" anyone in order to be good. Indeed, it need not even be worthwhile or significant.[21] Instead, a good argument must meet the following standards. First of all, it must be sound; it must be formally valid and have true premises. As we saw in Chapter 2, a valid argument is one which confers truth from premises to conclusion.[22] In addition to soundness, a good argument must also have premises which are characterized by both accessibility, or impersonalness, and methodical assessability.[23] As Ross describes it, philosophical accessibility is similar to the accessibility characteristic of scientific evidence. It means that the argument's premises are practically and not merely logically perceptible, if not to everyone, at least to someone other than the author of the argument.

Assessability, too, reflects the character of scientific arguments, which seek to incorporate conclusions into an accepted body of knowledge. It prevents us from employing as premises in our arguments just anything we know to be true or anything that is merely logically possible. It requires us to use premises "which are generally known in [our] time or which are decidable through investigation conducted according to the methods of philosophers."[24] For Ross, then, a good argument is one whose form is valid and whose premises are not only true but also, to use our terms, public rather than private. It will be helpful to keep Ross' description of a good argument in mind as we review the proofs for God's existence.

The purpose for making a clear distinction between the soundness and persuasiveness of an argument is not to exclude arguments from playing any role in the larger context of religious life. To the contrary, in Part 3 of this book I will argue that rational activity, including the formulation of arguments, has an important contribution to make to faith. The reason for this distinction is to prevent someone from imposing unrealistic demands on arguments for the existence of God. Given the variations in human mentality, plus the welter of factors that influence personal belief, it isn't possible to construct an argument for anything significant that would be convincing to everyone. And since we require nothing of the kind of arguments in other areas, it is inappropriate to apply such a criterion to arguments for the existence of God. Just because you can think of someone who would not find a particular theistic argument convincing does not mean that the argument is bad.

Although arguments for God should not be evaluated for their persuasive effectiveness, the familiar remark that they are unneeded by those who do believe in God and unhelpful to those who don't is an exaggeration. It assumes that all human beings fall into two distinct groups, confirmed believers and confirmed unbelievers. Even if some people are so entrenched in their positions that rational suasion is likely to have little effect on their views, this is hardly true of everyone. Other people are undecided as to whether or not God exists. And most who are strongly inclined toward either belief or unbelief are not completely impervious to rational considerations. So, if it is misguided to think of arguments for God's existence as attempts to persuade people to become believers, it is simplistic to reject them on the grounds that they could never contribute to the process.

By the way, I have been using the terms "proof" and "argument" interchangeably, but the two expressions have different connotations for some people. As we often use the words, it is one thing to *argue* for something, but quite another to *prove* it. An argument attempts to establish a conclusion, but a proof actually does so. It not only offers evidence, it achieves conviction. The word "proof" suggests conclusiveness, overwhelming force, unanswerability. A proof is a "knock-down argument" which only a blockhead could reject. So, it sounds as if the stakes are higher if we try to "prove" God's existence, rather than merely "argue" for it. But this distinction rests on the assumption that the purpose of arguments or proofs for God's existence is one of persuasion, and we have just rejected this view as mistaken. So we shall continue to use the terms interchangeably with reference to logical attempts to establish the reality of God.

Since arguments for the existence of God are exactly that—arguments—we need to remember just what an argument is as we consider the different theistic proofs. In Chapter 2 we saw that an argument establishes a relationship between different beliefs, or propositions. It demonstrates that beliefs have consequences. If we embrace certain beliefs, we must accept other beliefs, too, and conversely, rejecting some beliefs requires us to reject others as well. To cite the most basic forms of argument, if A implies B, then we must accept B if we accept A, and we must reject A if we reject B.

With this in mind we can state the basic strategy of arguments for God's existence rather simply. With one important exception, all theistic proofs are attempts to show that belief in God is logically connected to certain other beliefs. Each argument seeks to link belief in God to other beliefs in such a way that they must be accepted or rejected together. To use a financial metaphor, the proofs put a logical price tag on theism. If a certain belief logically entails belief in God, then believing in God is the logical price of accepting that belief, and rejecting that belief is logically the price of rejecting belief in God.

The crucial elements in each proof are obviously the premises—the beliefs which the proof seeks to connect with God. With poorly chosen premises, it is possible to construct a perfectly valid argument for the existence of God that is utterly worthless. Consider this argument: (a) if Texas is larger than Rhode Island, then God exists; (b) Texas is larger than Rhode Island; (c) therefore, God exists. Or consider this argument: (d) God spoke to me in a dream last night; (e) if God speaks, he obviously exists; (f) therefore, God exists.

The form of each argument is valid; its conclusion follows inexorably from the premises. But neither proof has philosophical merit. In the first example, the initial premise is contrived. There is no evident relationship between God's existence and the size of various states. Consequently, the premise is just as controversial as the conclusion, if not more so. In the case of the second argument, the first premise lacks what Ross calls "accessibility." Hearing God speak is proof positive that he exists, but unless the experience is widely available, it does not provide an acceptable basis for an argument.

A good argument is one whose premises are less controversial than its conclusion. Otherwise, the argument doesn't get us anywhere. It may show that beliefs are connected, but it does not provide any real support for its conclusion. This is clearly the flaw in an argument like the following: (h) if the Holy Spirit exists, God the Father exists; (i) the Holy Spirit exists; (j) therefore, God the Father exists. According to Christian doctrine, the reality of God involves the Holy Spirit. But apart from the perspective of Christian faith, the existence of the Holy Spirit is just as problematic as that of God the Father, so it does not provide a helpful place to begin a theistic argument.

Antony Kenny makes an interesting comment on this point. If we are trying to provide reasons for a belief, he maintains, it is not enough just to show that this belief is logically linked to other beliefs we have. The beliefs we offer as reasons—that is, the beliefs we argue *with*—must be more basic to our thinking than the belief we are arguing *for*. This point has two consequences. It means, as we just noted, that one belief does not provide good evidence for another if the two are equally controversial. This is the basic problem with the "Holy Spirit argument." Because the existence of the Holy Spirit is just as dubious as the existence of God the Father, for those who doubt the latter, it cannot provide a reason for it.

For Kenny, this difference in status between premise and conclusion also means that one belief cannot be a reason for another if both beliefs are equally basic within our cognitive structure. He argues, for example, that his belief "There is an Australia" is not based on reasons because none of the beliefs he could use to support the claim are better known to him or more basic than it is.[25] Kenny offers these comments in reply to the antifoundationalist position we briefly described in Chapter 2.

As we have seen, foundationalism is the view that we are rationally entitled to beliefs only if they are either self-evident, evident to the senses, or based directly or indirectly on beliefs of this sort. Classical foundationalism rejects belief in God because it does not fit any of these categories. Anti-foundationalists counter that this account is inadequate to the nature of knowledge. As a matter of fact, they observe, we hold many beliefs that don't fit any of these categories, and we are perfectly entitled to them. So, belief in God can function as a basic belief within the structure of our thinking in the same way that other beliefs do. Consequently, we don't need to prove our belief in God in order to be entitled to it.

Kenny agrees that foundationalism does not provide an adequate account of human knowledge. But he insists that this does not rule out the importance of theistic arguments. After all, not everyone's noetic or cognitive structure is the same.[26] All of us have basic beliefs—beliefs so intrinsic to our cognitive structure that there is nothing beyond them which could be offered as reasons—and God may function as a basic belief for many people. But this is hardly true of everyone. So, it may be necessary for us to give reasons for beliefs that are basic for us, because they are not basic for others.

As we look at the arguments for God we need to keep in mind the characteristics of good philosophical arguments we have just discussed. First, a good argument is formally valid; truth in its premises guarantees truth in its conclusion. Second, the premises of a good philosophical argument are publicly accessible. They are not dependent on unique or private insight. Furthermore, as Kenny observes, there is an asymmetry between premises and conclusion. A good argument moves from the better known to the lesser known. Its premises are less controversial than its conclusion.

The premises of the best-known arguments for God, and ultimately of all effective theistic proofs, contain the type of beliefs we referred to above as "basic beliefs." Such beliefs function within our noetic structure without depending on anything further for justification. Anti-foundationalists have shown that basic beliefs vary from person to person. For given individuals, they may include factors as diverse as belief in God and, as in Kenny's case, belief in Australia. As we just saw, what is basic in one person's noetic structure is not necessarily basic in another's. Now, the beliefs which good theistic proofs involve are basic not just for certain individuals but for everyone. These basic beliefs comprise our most fundamental convictions about experience and reality. They form the building blocks of our cognitive structure. As Kenny notes, there must be some beliefs which we all share or our thinking would have nothing in common, and this is clearly not the case. The strategy of theistic proofs is to show that basic beliefs of this sort logically support belief in God.

The task of identifying such beliefs is not an easy one, because it is characteristic of such beliefs that we are largely unaware of them. This is not because they seldom enter our thinking, but because they are always part of it. We typically find it difficult to think *about* our basic beliefs because we are always thinking *with* them. Similarly, we find it difficult to argue for them, because they are part of what gives meaning to the very ideas of "argument" and "evidence." If they don't make sense, nothing makes sense. So we can't appeal beyond these beliefs to something more basic, because they are the ultimate reasons we have for everything we believe, if we carried our arguments to the highest level of abstraction.

The importance of developing theistic arguments from basic beliefs arises from the very concept of God. The great monotheistic faiths—Judaism, Christianity and Islam—describe God as creator. They hold that God brought the world into existence and that divine power sustains it moment by moment. If God is thus involved in the whole of reality, then he cannot be something within reality, a mere part of the universe. Either everything testifies in some way to God, or nothing does. This is why the most effective arguments—some would say the only appropriate arguments—for God appeal to the basic beliefs which comprise our cognitive framework.[27] They are the only features of our experience whose generality corresponds to God's status in the universe.

With this account of philosophical arguments in mind, let us turn to some of the individual arguments for God. We will review four of the best-known theistic proofs. In each case, we will identify the basic belief(s) to which the proof appeals; analyze the essential steps in the argument; note the principal criticisms raised against it; and suggest a reply. After a brief look at the proofs, we will ask what they realistically accomplish—individually and together. While far from conclusive, this overview will give us a good idea of what reason finds when it looks at the contents of faith. And we should be able to see if belief in God fits the general description of responsible belief we outlined in Chapter 2.

The Cosmological Argument

With one significant exception, the most important arguments for the reality of God involve our basic beliefs about the nature of reality and human behavior. The cosmological and teleological arguments are examples of the first type. Both draw upon features of our experience of the world. The cosmological argument cites the dependent nature of things and concludes that God is the ultimate explanation for their existence. The teleological argument appeals to the order we find in the world and concludes that God is the supreme intelligence behind it.

The cosmological argument begins with the observation that everything in the world around us, including ourselves, owes its existence to something else. This is true of chairs, tables, houses, trees, animals, stars, electrons, and so on. Everything we experience exhibits a dependent, or contingent, character. Nothing is self-explanatory; nothing is its own reason for being. Moreover, we find that the same is true about the causes of each particular thing. They, too, owe their existence to something else. In fact, if we seek an explanation for any particular phenomenon we find ourselves following a cause-effect sequence, with each cause requiring yet another cause beyond itself.

How far can this cause-effect sequence extend before we have an explanation for whatever it is we are asking about? It depends on the kind of cause we have in mind. Some causes are co-existent with their effects, others are not. In one sense, I owe my existence to my parents, who owe their existence to my grandparents, who owe their existence to my great-grandparents, and so on. In another sense, I owe my existence to a physical environment that contains oxygen and certain other chemicals, is neither too hot nor too cold, and has atmospheric pressures that are neither too high nor too low. This environment, in turn, owes its existence to certain astronomical conditions—the distance of the earth from the sun, the speed of the earth's rotation, the absence of meteoric showers in this part of the galaxy, et cetera.

My ancestors and my environment are both causes of my existence in the sense that I would not be here without them, but my relationships to them are different. My ancestors account for my origin, but not my survival. I need them to explain how I got here, but they do not have to continue existing in order for me to exist. My parents are still living, but their parents and all my other ancestors have died. The situation with my physical environment is quite different. It explains my existence right now—not just how I came to be, but why I continue to exist. Any drastic change in the temperature, pressure, or chemical composition of my surroundings, and my life would suddenly end. So there are causes that come and go, as far as their effects are concerned, and there are causes that must continue as long as their effects exist.

Let's shift the focus of attention to the universe in its entirety, the totality of dependent things. Since everything it contains depends on other things for its existence, the universe as a whole must owe its existence to something else. Moreover, the "cause" of its existence must be something whose own existence does not depend on anything outside itself, otherwise it would simply be another item in the universe of dependent reality. "In order to explain existence," to quote F. C. Copleston, "we must come to a being which contains within itself the reason for its own existence, that is to say, which cannot not exist."[28] If the universe is intelligible, therefore, if we are to make sense of it, then there must be an ultimate explanatory factor, a "world cause," which is self-existent. There must exist a being on which everything else depends, and which contains within itself its own power of existence. Such a being, the cosmological argument concludes, is appropriately identified as "God."

There is a difference in the sort of causes one might invoke to explain the world's existence. We can ask what brought it into existence to begin with, or we can ask what holds it together and keeps it going right now. In other words, we can ask about its originating cause or its sustaining cause. According to most interpreters of the cosmological argument, it is not the origin but the continuation of the universe that requires an explanation, and the thrust of the argument is that a self-existent being must exist right now in order to explain the continuing existence of the universe. As they see it, the cosmological argument does not take us back in time to the ultimate beginning of things. Instead, it takes us up, as it were, through different levels of reality until we finally reach the one thing on which everything depends.

Mortimer Adler, for example, takes this tack in a popular presentation of the cosmological argument. Adler describes the cosmos, or universe, as radically contingent. Since every individual thing within the universe could cease to exist, the universe as a whole could cease to exist. What prevents this from happening? Only a being whose existence is not contingent, but necessary. In Adler's words, "the cosmos, radically contingent in existence, would not exist at all were its existence not caused." And this cause must be a supernatural, "exnihilating factor," which keeps the whole cosmic show from simply vanishing. It is "necessary to posit the existence of God, the supreme being, in order to explain . . . the actual existence here and now of a merely possible cosmos."[29]

We can express the cosmological argument in its simplest form with this scheme: (1) the world is an effect; (2) effects presuppose causes; (3) so there must be a world cause, which is God. Only the existence of God, then, explains why there is something, rather than nothing. Putting it this way, we can see that the cosmological argument involves several crucial—and, in the eyes of its critics, highly questionable—moves. One is applying to the world as a whole the dependent quality, or "effect" character, of things within the world. Another is the insistence that this characteristic of reality requires an explanation. And a third is the identification of this transcendent world cause with the God of religion.

Critics of the argument object to the concept of the world as an effect. They argue that it is illogical to take a characteristic of individual things within the world, like dependence, and apply it to the world as a whole. In logical terms, this involves the fallacy of composition—attributing to a group of things a characteristic of its individual members. Bertrand Russell once raised this point in an exchange with Frederick Copleston. "The whole concept of cause," he asserted, "is one we derive from our observation of particular things; I see no reason whatsoever to suppose that the total has any cause whatsoever."[30] Those who reject the proof sometimes argue in relation to the second move mentioned above, namely, that the world needs no explanation. Its existence is simply brute fact. They insist, to quote Russell again, that "the universe is just there, and that's all."[31]

Another objection to the cosmological argument is that it begs the question. The very notion that the world is an effect presupposes the concept of a world-cause, and accepting the idea of a world-cause is virtually identical to believing in God. This is how John Hick criticizes the argument. Its force, he maintains, depends on ruling out the idea that the world is ultimately inexplicable in order to drive us to the conclusion that God exists as the only acceptable alternative. But this exclusion rests upon a faith in the ultimate rationality of existence; and it is just this larger faith which the atheist refuses. "Faced with this absence of metaphysical faith," Hick concludes, "the theistic arguer is disarmed." "Since the cosmological argument thus requires a premise which is not granted by those to whom the argument is primarily directed, it follows that from their point of view it begs the question."[32]

While some people maintain that the notion of a world-cause is too close to the idea of God for the cosmological argument to be effective, others object to the argument on grounds that the two concepts are too far apart. They see too much distance between a "necessarily existing cause of the cosmos" and the supreme object of religious devotion to justify identifying the two. So the argument fails as a proof for the existence of *God*.

These objections do not, I believe, invalidate the cosmological argument. First of all, to contend that the universe is just there, period, as brute fact, and that the very notion of a world-cause is meaningless, imposes an arbitrary limit on the scope of human inquiry. What's wrong with asking about the origin of the universe? If we can legitimately ask about the nature of particular things, and of classes of particular things, why can't we ask about the nature of all particular things? Why should the notion of world-cause be any less objectionable than the notion of world, or universe, or all-encompassing reality? Wouldn't the same objection apply here? Couldn't someone argue that just because some things include others within the realm of ordinary experience we have no reason to assume that there is something that includes everything, so the very idea of a universe is meaningless? But this is ridiculous. In the final analysis, insisting that the notion of world-cause makes no sense is nothing more than a refusal to grant the question of the universe's origin.

What about the idea that it begs the question of God's existence to ask about the ultimate cause of things? We must grant that there is a large-scale circularity involved in questions of ultimate reality. Asking a question about anything presupposes that the questioner has some concept of what an acceptable answer would be. On the level of factual inquiry, we avoid circularity because an intelligible question can clearly have more than one intelligible answer. The situation is different, however, when we ask about the nature of reality as a whole. Is there meaning in the universe? Is there an ultimate explanation for things? These questions make sense only if the answer is yes. So, the very enterprise of asking questions about the universe presupposes certain views of reality. If the universe were utterly unintelligible, it would be impossible even to ask about it. But the circularity involved in questions of this type—metaphysical questions, to be precise—is not a vicious circularity. On the surface, certainly, the claim that God exists is by no means just as controversial as the claim that the universe has an explanation. It is not apparent at the outset that the ultimate explanation for things is a self-existent being identifiable as God. So the cosmological argument satisfies the criterion mentioned above that good arguments must use premises that are less controversial than their conclusions.

The Teleological Argument

The teleological argument, or the argument from design, is far and away the most popular argument for the existence of God.[33] Of all the classical proofs, it is the one most likely to appear in sermons or literature for the general public. Ordinary believers who offer evidence for their belief in God will almost certainly provide some version of it. In fact, expressions of the argument from design have even been set to music.[34]

Like the cosmological argument, the teleological argument begins with a pervasive feature of the world around us. The cosmological argument, as we just saw, begins with the perception that everything in the realm of ordinary experience depends on something else; its existence requires an explanation beyond itself. In the case of the teleological argument, however, it is not the dependent nature of things, but the order and design we find in things that provides the starting point. While the cosmological argument springs ultimately from a sense of wonder that there is anything rather than nothing, the teleological argument arises from admiration for the intricacy and complexity we find throughout the universe. The splendor of the starry sky, the immense variety of animal life, the unique behavior of each organism, and the sophistication of our own physical and mental processes—these are the sort of things that have suggested this argument.

From the observation of order or design in the natural world the teleological argument infers that there must exist a supreme designer who planned and created it all. The argument turns on the claim that nothing as complicated as the things we see, or the world we live in, could possibly be the product of mindless forces. In the words of a popular religious song, "the odds are too great." The only explanation for the intricate structure and sophisticated operations of nature is the existence of a supreme intelligence or master designer. To give the argument a simple formulation: (1) the world contains order; (2) order presupposes an orderer; (3) consequently, there must be a world orderer, or cosmic designer, who is God. Let us look at some of the better known formulations and criticisms of this theistic proof.

William Paley, an eighteenth century British clergyman, developed a famous version of the argument.[35] He observed that the discovery of a watch lying on the ground would lead us to conclude that there must be a watchmaker. Among other things, the fact that its various different parts are put together for a purpose, which requires just this arrangment, makes the inference inevitable that "the watch must have had a maker; that there must have existed . . . an artificer or artificers who formed it for the purpose which we find it actually to answer; who comprehended its construction, and designed its use."[36]

Paley applies this to the question of God's existence by asserting that "every indication of contrivance, every manifestation of design, which existed in the watch, exists in the works of nature." Indeed, "the contrivances of nature surpass the contrivances of art, in the complexity, subtilty, and curiosity of the mechanism," as well as in number and variety.[37] Consequently, just as the watch points to the existence of the watchmaker, the various contrivances of nature point to an intelligent designer.

This familiar version of the teleological argument is clearly an analogy. It turns on the comparison between the world and a watch. A watch points to the existence of a watchmaker; the world is like a watch; so the world points to the existence of a cosmic designer, namely, God.[38] The problem with this line of thought is that analogies tend to break down somewhere, and the most vigorous attacks on the argument, like those of David Hume, have pressed just this point.[39] No theistic argument has accumulated a longer list of objections than this one, so we will confine our attention to a few of the better known.

One objection is that evidence of intelligent design within the world does not mean that the world as a whole is the product of intelligent design. We have no right to attribute to the whole something characteristic of its parts. Each human being has a mother and a father, for example, but that doesn't mean that the human race as a whole has one mother and one father. A second difficulty with the teleological argument is the incomparability of the universe. If the universe is by definition unique, then it bears no comparison to other things. There is only one universe, period. Even if the universe is not in principle unique, we have no way to compare it to other universes. We cannot look at ten different universes, half of them produced by an intelligent designer, the other half not, and calculate the chances that this particular universe is the product of a supreme mind.

A contrasting difficulty with the argument is the possibility that the universe has more in common with other things than with a human artifact. Why should we think of the universe as similar to a watch, a mechanical contrivance, which obviously relies on external manipulation? Why not compare it to an animal or a vegetable, with a capacity for internal regeneration and self-direction? In this connection, the theory of evolution has raised particularly thorny problems for the argument.

In its classic form the teleological argument attributes the adaptation of an organism to its environment to an external ordering power which consciously designed the two for each other. But the theory of evolution offers a different account of their relationship. Instead of appealing to an external ordering principle, it attributes the relation between organism and environment entirely to factors internal to nature, such as survival of the fittest. According to evolution, for example, seals have the fat they need to live in arctic waters, not because God created them with it and put them there, but because they would die without such protection. Cold temperatures kill off or drive away the organisms unable to cope with them, leaving the ones who can. So, it isn't a master designer who accounts for the intricate structure of earth's organisms, but the ruthlessness of nature.

Another criticism of the teleological argument is that it claims more for its conclusion than the evidence warrants. It attributes the origin of the universe to a supreme intelligence, who is infinite and perfect. But this goes far beyond anything the present state of affairs could justify. How can we infer from a universe that is far from perfect that a perfect being created it? The massive presence of evil in the world raises serious questions about its creator. It seems impossible that the creator of this world could have all the qualities that Christianity traditionally attributes to God, such as perfect goodness and power.

In addition, it is not hard to think of other ways to account for the creation of the world. For all we know, the maker of this world botched several previous attempts and has yet to produce a really first-rate universe. Perhaps he is more of an apprentice than a master designer and has better projects in mind for the future. Then, too, how do we know that the world isn't the product of a committee? Evidence for design doesn't always point to a single designer. Why should we conclude that a single cosmic intelligence created the world?

The list of objections goes on, but you get the idea. Many thinkers have serious reservations about the attempt to infer God's existence from the characteristics of natural phenomena.

In spite of all the questions it raises, the teleological argument has remarkable appeal. Even Immanuel Kant, who dismantled the traditional theistic arguments, respected it, calling it of all the proofs "the oldest, the clearest, and the most accordant with the common reason of mankind."[40] More recent versions of the argument do not appeal to specific phenomena within the world, but call attention instead to the orderly character of the world as a whole. According to F. R. Tennant, for example, "The forcibleness of Nature's suggestion that she is the outcome of intelligent design lies not in particular cases of adaptedness in the world, nor even in the multiplicity of them." Instead, it lies in "the conspiration of innumerable causes to produce, by their united and reciprocal action, and to maintain, a general order of Nature." We can make a much stronger case, he believes, for this "wider teleology" than we can for the "narrower teleology" of specific natural phenomena.[41]

Similarly, Charles Hartshorne expands the notion of order to the widest dimensions possible, treating it as a metaphysical necessity rather than a natural phenomenon.[42] As Hartshorne sees it, the presence of order in the world is not something we detect by examining the features of our specific environment. Instead, it is a necessary condition for all reality and all knowledge. The very concept of world involves the notion of order, as the Greek word "cosmos" indicates. An unordered world could not exist and it would certainly be unknowable, because knowledge involves ordering the mind to reality.

Shifting our attention from the nature of this particular world to the essential characteristics that any world must have recasts the central issue of the teleological argument. What needs to be accounted for is not the specific order we find in the features of this particular world, but the order necessary for there to be any world at all. Hartshorne maintains that the universe does not require perfect harmony, but only enough harmony to allow its inhabitants to exist and to exercise a minimal amount of freedom. The corresponding idea of a world orderer is not that of a being who could impose any pattern it chose on things, but that of a being who keeps the amount of discord within tolerable limits. Hartshorne argues that the best candidate for such an agent is a personal being. After all, the order with which we are most familiar is the order which we bring as conscious, personal agents to our own experience.

Transposing the argument as Hartshorne does from an empirical to a metaphysical key gives it greater probative power and leaves it less vulnerable to criticism. The question which the teleological argument poses, therefore, is not whether we can find enough order in the world around us to support the claim that God exists. It is whether the very concept of world makes sense unless there is a supreme ordering principle.

The Problem of Evil

The problem of evil figures in every discussion of God's existence, and it often arises in connection with the teleological argument. We need to consider it in order to assess the rational case for theism.

The massive discord we find in the world seems incompatible with the qualities religious faith characteristically attributes to God. If there is a being who is perfect in power and love, it seems, then evil could not exist. As David Hume succinctly asked,"Is he willing to prevent evil, but not able? then is he impotent. Is he able, but not willing? then is he malevolent. Is be both able and willing? whence then is evil?"[43]

Philosophers have responded to the problem of evil in many different ways. For some, evil represents a necessary ingredient in a world designed to promote character development. Painful though it is, suffering provides indispensable material for soul-making. God created a world where his creatures would rebel against him for a time, but the good that eventually results from their difficulties will more than make up for their negative experiences.[44]

Other thinkers treat evil as a "pseudo-problem," or a "so-called problem." For them, there is no incompatibility whatever between the reality of God and the presence of suffering in the world. God is in no position to prevent evil, they argue, because what we call evil is nothing but the inevitable consequence of creaturely freedom. God is not the only one who has an influence on the course of events. There are billions of creatures who make decisions, too, non-human as well as human. And when a universe contains a multiplicity of agents, some of their decisions are bound to come in conflict. What we call "evil" is actually nothing more than the unavoidable unpleasantness that occurs when creaturely decisions conflict with each other. To affirm creaturely freedom is to deny that God is directly responsible for everything that happens. Properly understood, therefore, what we typically call evil poses no problem for belief in God.[45]

The most influential and, I believe, the most helpful response to the problem of evil is the well-known "free will defense." In its classic formulation, it affirms that God created the world and populated it with beings who had the capacity to respond freely to God's love for them. There was a risk involved in bringing such beings into existence, however, because freedom to accept God's love is also freedom to reject it. And this, tragically, is what the creatures did. Through no fault of God's, they misused their freedom to rebel against divine sovereignty, and this is how evil entered the universe.[46]

Evil thus originated in the misuse of creaturely freedom. It is not something for which God is responsible. God could have guaranteed the prevention of evil only by excluding freedom, but as a loving creator he was unwilling to do this. Unlike the responses to the problem of evil just mentioned, the free will defense does not give a "reason" for the existence of evil. Indeed, it insists that there is no reason or justification for it at all. Evil entered the universe as a violation of God's will and contrary to his purposes. According to traditional Christian faith, God is presently working in the world to mitigate the consequences of evil, and eventually he will succeed in removing it from the universe. But it was never part of his original plan that creatures should suffer.

Over the centuries the presence of evil has been the most formidable obstacle to belief in God, both intellectually and personally. No matter what we accomplish on the level of philosophical reflection, the pain of our own sufferings will always present a challenge to personal faith in God. When philosophers and theologians respond to the problem, their objective is not to explain why specific instances of suffering occur. Instead, they seek to show that the presence of evil is not logically incompatible with the reality of God. Granted, they argue, it poses an obstacle to belief in God, but it is not inconceivable that evil should exist in a world which God created.[47] We can acknowledge the reality of evil without having to abandon belief in God.

The Moral Argument

We mentioned earlier that philosophers have found evidence for the reality of God both in the nature of the world at large and in various aspects of human behavior. Among the latter, the phenomenon of morality has probably received more attention than any other. The moral argument for the existence of God moves from the pervasiveness of moral experience to the conclusion that God is the ultimate source of our moral requirements and the supreme object of moral obligation. Here is a brief statement of the argument: (1) moral experience is universal; (2) moral obligations are objectively valid; (3) there exists a supreme lawgiver, a supreme object of moral responsibility.

The initial premise is that moral obligation is universal. All human beings have a sense of right and wrong—a deep conviction that our behavior matters and that some forms of behavior are preferable to others. We instinctively reject "moral nihilism," the view that there is no significant difference between good and evil, love and hate, compassion and cruelty. Whatever our theories about morality may be, our behavior on a practical, personal level will reveal our inner sense of moral obligation. We simply cannot avoid approving and disapproving of the way people act, including ourselves. For example, we expect people to keep their promises to us, as C. S. Lewis observes, whether or not we believe in a real Right or Wrong.[48]

Significantly, no one has ever been able to live as a consistent moral nihilist, not even in fiction. The central character in Albert

Camus' novel *The Stranger* responds to everything that happens to him with utter indifference, insisting that it all comes to the same thing.[49] But eventually he feels superior to those who fail to recognize this, so knowing that nothing matters turns out to be better than not knowing it. But this is self-contradictory. If nothing makes any difference, how can it make a difference to know that nothing makes a difference? In the end, Camus' story confirms the very point he set out to refute—that it is impossible for human beings to live without a degree of moral sensitivity. A sense of moral obligation is inescapable.

It is important to note that moral sensitivity is not the same as moral behavior. It is one thing to feel a responsibility to do something, and quite another to fulfill that responsibility. As a matter of fact, nobody meets all their obligations. Sooner or later we all do things that we regret. That's why an uneasy conscience is universal among human beings, too. But this phenomenon supports the point we are making. It shows that moral sensitivity permeates human experience.

In addition to a universal sense of moral obligation, some proponents of the moral argument maintain that certain obligations are universally accepted as well. They say that human beings everywhere believe that it is wrong to kill, that people ought to tell the truth, and so on. This claim is much more difficult to support. The obvious objection is that standards of acceptable conduct vary widely from one culture to another. Stealing is unthinkable in one culture; in another it is virtually a way of life. One culture strongly forbids the taking of human life. In another, killing someone is a right of passage to manhood. One society permits the sexual behavior that others find outrageous. And so it goes. It is difficult to specify any particular moral requirement that humans everywhere accept.

The task is less formidable if we state moral obligations abstractly. Even where taking human life is acceptable, for example, it is wrong to take life indiscriminately. Who gets killed is still important. One culture may not prohibit the sexual behavior which another proscribes, but it will still insist on some boundaries for sexual activity. There are certain areas of human life where "right" and "wrong" always apply, even though the specific application varies from one culture to another. Whether this is convincing or not, it is safer for proponents of the moral argument to appeal to the prevalence of moral sensitivity alone, and not try to argue that certain specific obligations are universally binding.

The second premise of the moral argument may be more problematic than the first. Not only do we all have a sense of moral obligation, it holds, but we feel that these obligations are objectively valid. In other words, our moral sensitivity is nothing less than an awareness of objective moral law. "Right" and "wrong" refer to something in reality, not just to our experience. A familiar criticism of this step in the argument is that moral rules are the product of social conditioning or the projection of certain psychological needs and desires, or possibly both. They reflect our backgrounds and personalities, but they do not correspond to anything "out there."

There are two responses to this "psycho-sociological" objection to the idea of an objective moral law. For one thing, it doesn't square with our actual experience. People who condemn such things as the torture of infants do so because they believe that these activities are inherently wrong. Saying, "Murder is wrong," is not the same sort of thing as saying, "I don't like yogurt," or "Let's agree not to kill each other, OK?" Moral obligations are not merely social or human conventions. They are not just "rules of the game," arbitrarily devised in order to keep the wheels of society running smoothly. When I condemn the mass extermination of Jews in Europe, I am not simply expressing a personal preference or projecting my individual psychological needs or reflecting the influence of my particular background. I am making a claim about "the way things are." A moral judgment makes an assertion about objective reality.

In the second place, there is no conflict between the "objective" status of our moral obligations and the fact that these moral obligations correspond to our personal psychological needs and/or the constraints of society. As students of elementary logic know, the acquisition of a belief has nothing to do with its truth or falsity. As a matter of fact, we acquire most of our beliefs under the influence of other people, and it never occurs to us to question them. After all, what is education for? We didn't invent the multiplication table, we learned it in elementary school. But the fact that I came to believe that nine times eight is seventy-two because Mrs. Walker told me so thirty-five years ago doesn't lead me to doubt its validity. So, it does not detract from the objective status of moral obligation to grant that our moral sensitivity reflects various social and psychological influences.

The moral argument infers that the ultimate source and object of our moral obligation must be a supreme personal reality. Several things support this conclusion. One is the fact that we feel naturally responsible to persons, not to things. Although we speak of the "law of gravity," for example, we don't view gravity as something we are accountable to. If we disregard this law, we may experience pain and embarrassment, but we don't feel guilt. Our experience is different when it comes to things like telling the truth and keeping our promises. Here we feel accountable for our behavior, and we experience guilt when we disregard these obligations. Furthermore, our sense of accountability often goes beyond the persons who are directly affected by our speaking and acting, and we feel the force of certain obligations whether or not other human beings are involved at all. But if we always feel accountable *to* someone, who is it to whom we are accountable? The best answer is, a supreme personal being.

We also need to affirm a supreme personal being in order to account for the conviction that our actions and decisions "make a difference." We sense that it is better to tell the truth than to lie, to preserve life than to end it, and so on. But it is not clear just what this "better" means. There are times when it seems to make no difference at all whether we lie or tell the truth. There are even times when the consequences of doing the right thing seem to be negative. Being truthful can often be costly. In what sense, then, is it better to do the right thing? How does it make a positive difference in reality?

Moral experience attributes a value to our actions which no finite scheme of things can adequately account for. It assumes that the ultimate consequences of doing right are positive, whether or not the immediate consequences are. But human beings do not have the power to guarantee such fulfillment, because every human achievement is vulnerable to destruction. Consequently, in order to justify our confidence that the positive results of moral actions will be realized, there must exist some transcendent force which guides events toward a positive end. Moreover, such a power must be personal. As one philosopher put it, "The course of events must itself be governed by the same Mind which is the source of our moral ideas."[50]

To summarize the argument, moral experience requires us to view our actions in relation to a transcendent source and guarantor of meaning, and only God, a supreme personal being, can provide such a source.

The Ontological Argument

The most famous argument for the existence of God is also the most controversial. Unlike all other theistic proofs, it appeals neither to some aspect of human behavior, such as morality or religion, nor to some characteristic of the world, such as dependence or order. Instead, it begins with the idea of God itself. The ontological argument, as it is called, derives the conclusion that God exists from the concept of God as a perfect being.

Let us paraphrase the reasoning of Anselm, the medieval theologian who gave the argument its classic formulation in the eleventh century.[51] It begins by identifying God as the greatest conceivable being, a being "than which a greater cannot be thought." For Anselm God's greatness consists in the fact that he is not only superior to everything else that exists, but so great that it is not possible even to think of anything greater. In other words, he is not only the greatest actual being, but the greatest conceivable being—"not conceivably surpassable." As the greatest being imaginable, God must exhibit every good quality to the highest possible degree. If there were any positive quality which God failed to possess, then we could imagine a being which did possess it, and this being would be greater than "the greatest conceivable being," which is clearly contradictory.

The next step in the argument concerns the nature of existence. Anselm asserts that it is better to exist in reality as well as in the mind than to exist in the mind alone. It is clear that God exists in the mind, he argues, because even those who deny God, like the biblical fool, must have some concept of what they are rejecting. Consequently, he must exist in reality as well. The very idea of a perfect being thus requires us to affirm that being's existence.

Objections to the argument arose immediately, and they have continued ever since. Many of them express our instinctive suspicion of any attempt to move from thought to reality. We know that it is impossible to think things into existence. Gaunilo, a contemporary of Anselm, tried to expose the absurdity of the argument by demonstrating that one could use the very same logic to posit the existence of practically anything. Imagine, for example, a greatest conceivable island. If such an object exists only in the mind, it is possible to think of an even greater island, one that exists in reality as well. So the greatest conceivable island must exist.

Immanuel Kant is responsible for the most famous criticism of the ontological argument. It concerns the way Anselm uses "existence."[52] He treats it as a predicate or an attribute, a quality just like other qualities we employ to describe something. Kant maintains that this is mistaken. When we say that something exists, he argues, we do not add another quality to our description of it; we merely posit it. We assert that there is something in reality which corresponds to our description.

Most scholars believe that Kant was right. It doesn't make sense to treat existence as a predicate. As they see it, we cannot enrich the concept of something by adding existence to a list of its qualities. If two bachelors are arguing over the qualities in an ideal wife, for example, one can't turn to the other and say, "My concept is better than yours, because my ideal wife not only has looks, talent, education, and personality. She also has existence." If a teacher tells arithmetic students to calculate the sum of two hundred dollars and three hundred dollars, it would make no sense for them to ask whether the dollars are real or imaginary. Five hundred real dollars is exactly the same sum as five hundred imaginary ones.

Although almost everyone agrees that it is wrong to treat existence as a predicate, several contemporary philosophers detect another version of the ontological argument in Anselm's writings which is not guilty of this error.[53] In his reply to Gaunilo's criticism Anselm speaks of the greatest conceivable being as existing "so truly that it it cannot be conceived not to exist." Instead of comparing real beings with imaginary ones, this time Anselm compares "a being which cannot be conceived not to exist" with "one which can be conceived not to exist." He argues that the former is greater, and concludes that a being than which nothing greater can be conceived cannot even be thought of as not existing.

Moreover, he insists, this is true only of God. Anything else we might think of—islands, wives, dollars, etc.—we can think of as either existing or not existing. But we can think of God only as existing. What makes God unique is the kind of existence, indeed, the only kind of existence, we can attribute to him. To quote Norman Malcolm, "What Anselm has proved is that the notion of contingent existence or of contingent non-existence cannot have any application to God. His existence must either be logically necessary or logically impossible."[54]

Malcolm's point is not difficult to grasp. Things that exist contingently might not have existed, and they may cease to exist at some time in the future. This includes cars, houses, the United States of America, the planet earth, you and me, etc. Things whose non-existence is contingent might have existed, or they may yet exist. It depends on whether certain conditions are fulfilled. These include Gary Hart's presidency, the Confederate States of America, Carl Lewis' fifteenth Olympic medal. Now, it is obvious that God does not belong to either of these categories. As the greatest conceivable being, God must be more powerful than anything else. If such a being exists, then nothing could terminate his existence, for nothing is as powerful as he is. So, he doesn't fit the first category. And if he doesn't exist, nothing could bring him into existence, for it would have to be as great as he is to do so, and then he would not be the greatest imaginable being. Consequently, God doesn't fit the second category, either. We cannot apply either contingent existence or contingent non-existence to God.

This leaves just two other options—necessary existence and necessary non-existence. The class of things that do not and cannot exist would include married bachelors, square circles, etc.—things that are inherently contradictory. They don't exist because they are logically inconceivable, not because someone hasn't discovered or invented them yet. The class of things that cannot not-exist is either empty, or includes one member, namely God. Consequently, we must view God in one of only two ways. Either we cannot even form a coherent concept of God, because the very idea makes no more sense than that of a four-sided triangle. Or we must conceive of God as existing—existing without the possibility of not-existing. In other words, God's existence is either necessary, or it is impossible.

For the most part, contemporary supporters of the ontological argument do not claim that it establishes the reality of God. Its real accomplishment, they believe, is to demonstrate the status of the idea of God. The only kind of existence that could apply to God is necessary existence, so if God is logically conceivable, then he necessarily exists. To quote Norman Malcolm, "The only intelligible way of rejecting Anselm's claim that God's existence is necessary is to maintain that the concept of God . . . is self-contradictory or nonsensical."[55] A student of mine put it this way: "If he *can* exist, then he *must* exist."

What the Proofs for God Accomplish

The four theistic arguments we have described are but a few of the many that have been formulated over the centuries, but they are among the most famous. At the very least they show that the question of God's existence has received careful philosophical attention. Some of the greatest minds in history have wrestled with it, and no single issue in the history of Western thought has been the subject of more extensive discussion. The crucial question, of course, is what these proofs accomplish. Do they demonstrate that God exists, or not? To address this question, we need to step back and look at the proofs as a whole.[56] Let us review their basic strategy and see what happens when we put them all together.

We noted earlier that the essential strategy of each argument is to link up belief in God with one or another of the various beliefs which are basic to our cognitive structure. The proofs attempt to show that belief in God is logically implied by a number of our basic beliefs—the fundamental presuppositions of all our thought and experience. With the exception of the ontological argument, all the proofs appeal to certain elements in common human experience perceptible to any reflective person. The cosmological argument begins with our awareness of the dependent or contingent nature of things. The teleological argument begins with the order we find around us. The moral argument begins with moral sensitivity, our inherent sense of obligation. Each theistic argument concludes that God, a supreme personal being, provides the best explanation for the belief in question. The proofs thus present God as the objective ground in reality which accounts for our deepest intuitions about the nature of things. They show that the fundamental features of thought and experience point to the reality of God.

The number and variety of theistic proofs that have developed over the centuries comprise a case for theism that we can describe as complex, coherent and comprehensive. To begin with, the philosophical case for God that emerges from the proofs has more to it than a series of individual arguments. If we look closely at the different proofs we find that they join together to form a powerful network of evidence for theism. Critics of theistic arguments typically follow a strategy of divide and conquer. They tear into them one at a time, expose their individual weaknesses, and discard the lot as ineffective. The resulting impression is that the proofs for God are successive failures in a misguided attempt that was doomed at the outset, like a series of ill-conceived assaults on Mt. Everest.

Critics have also argued that the proofs are connected in such a way that a significant weakness in one affects the others, too—a little like a spreading computer virus. Kant believed that the basic weakness of the ontological argument invalidates the cosmological argument as well, since the latter "owes any cogency which it may have to the ontological proof from mere concepts."[57] As we saw, Kant rejects the ontological argument because it erroneously uses "existence" as a predicate and concludes that the idea of a "necessary being" is incoherent. He then rejects the cosmological argument on the grounds that it, too, involves the concept of a "necessary being." This approach suggests that different theistic proofs are like links in a chain. If one of them has weaknesses, it undermines the others.

The proofs do have individual weaknesses; and they are interdependent, as Kant recognized. But careful examination reveals that the proofs have complementary and compensating strengths. Certain proofs are strong precisely where others are weak. For example, the ontological argument demonstrates that the concept of God is unique. It shows that the idea of a perfect being is such that we must either dismiss it as impossible, or conceive of it as existing necessarily. But this argument does not decide between these alternatives. So, it establishes the inference, "If the idea of God is coherently conceivable, then God must exist"—if possible, then actual—but it leaves open the question of whether the idea is conceivable.

In contrast, the other arguments we reviewed indicate that the idea of God makes sense, but they do not establish its uniqueness. The cosmological argument shows that a self-existent being explains the existence of a contingent world. The teleological argument reveals that a cosmic designer accounts for the order we find in reality. And the moral argument reveals that the concept of a supreme personal being provides an explanation for our moral experience. These arguments show that the idea of God makes sense because it provides a reasonable explanation for some fundamental aspects of reality. But they do not demonstrate that God's existence is the only way to explain these things. As critics are fond of pointing out, these features of reality allow for other explanations, too. So, these arguments show that the idea of God is intelligible, but they do not demonstrate that it is unique.

As we just noted, however, this is precisely what the ontological argument does. It shows that the concept of a perfect being—and only this concept—requires the quality of necessary existence. God cannot be *merely* possible; if he is possible at all, he must be actual, too. This means that the ontological argument is strong precisely where the others are weak, and the other proofs are strong just where the ontological argument is weak. The ontological argument shows that the idea of God is unique, but does not establish its intelligibility. Other arguments show that the idea of God is intelligible, but do not establish its uniqueness.

Suppose we put these different arguments together, so the strength of one compensates for the weakness of the other(s). The result is a powerful case for theism which shows that the idea of God is both unique and meaningful. We can formulate this comprehensive argument this way: (1) If the idea of God is conceivable, then God must exist (ontological argument). (2) The idea of God is conceivable (the other arguments). Therefore, (3) God exists. Instead of dragging each other down, then, the different proofs strengthen each other. They are less like links in a chain than strands in a cable. Their collective strength compensates for individual weaknesses.

As the cable analogy suggests, the philosophical case for theism is cumulative as well as complex. It is not a single argument, but a variety of arguments. As we have seen, the theistic proofs draw from a wide range of human experience, and their combined effect is to show that theism provides us with a comprehensive perspective on life and reality. The idea of God does not explain one small feature of the universe, or resolve some esoteric logical problem. It illuminates the whole of our existence. Charles Hartshorne makes the point in these words: "All the arguments are phases of one 'global' argument, that the properly formulated theistically religious view of life and reality is the most intelligible, self-consistent, and satisfactory one that can be conceived."[58] Gary Gutting appeals to the explanatory breadth of the proofs in a somewhat different way. He rejects the quest for a "single master argument," a single chain of reasoning which ultimately depends on a few well-defined premises. Instead, he says, effective theistic arguments are "multi-dimensional." They appeal to "a large, diverse, and indefinitely extendible body of data, pointing as a whole to its conclusion."[59] But for both thinkers, the illuminating power of the proofs, the broad scope of experience they draw from, constitutes a strong case for theism.

Theism is also attractive to many thinkers because of a quality logicians refer to as elegance. It is related to a venerable philosophical principle known as "Ockham's razor,"[60] which holds that an explanation should be economical; it should not employ any more factors than necessary. In home construction, an experienced framer drives nails with one or two strokes of the hammer, while a do-it-yourselfer takes a dozen. In chess, a grandmaster can checkmate in two or three moves where a novice might need twenty. Similarly, in philosophy, an elegant theory can accomplish with a few concepts what less helpful ones require many to do.

One of the most impressive things about theism is its capacity to illuminate vast ranges of experience with a minimum of explanation. The single idea of God provides the basis for an integrated and coherent view of all of life and reality. On the other hand, discard the idea of God, and we have nothing left but "piece-meal" explanations for important features of reality, or no explanation at all. This is what we meant when we said earlier that theistic proofs put a price tag on the rejection of God. If we reject the reasoning of the cosmological argument, we are forced to say that the world is simply there—a brute fact with no explanation. If we reject the teleological argument, we have no explanation for the order essential to reality. It, too, is simply there—the result of blind chance. And if we reject the argument that morality has its basis in a supreme personal being, we have no answer to the question, Why be moral? We have no rational basis for condoning or condemning different forms of human behavior.

By thus showing what it costs to reject the idea of God, theistic arguments highlight the difference between theism and alternative views of reality. It is true that theism has its difficulties. The problem of evil, in particular, will always be a source of perplexity for those who believe in God. But other world views have their difficulties, too, and the true value of theism emerges only in comparison to the alternatives. For many who believe in God, theism deserves to be accepted not because it is the only position available, nor because it is free of difficulties, but because it is superior to the alternatives. It provides the most coherent and comprehensive interpretation of life and reality available to us. As Richard Purtill says, "The difficulties of accepting and understanding the theistic view may be formidable, but the difficulties of rejecting it are insurmountable."[61]

Are the proofs for God successful? This all depends on what is expected of them. If they are supposed to persuade everyone that God exists, then they obviously fail. Many people read the proofs and remain unconvinced that there is a God. But it is not appropriate, as we noted earlier, to make persuasiveness a standard for philosophical arguments. The purpose of such endeavors is to establish logical connections, not to achieve personal convictions. In fact, if the inability to convince all comers invalidates a proof, then virtually all philosophical arguments, not merely theistic proofs, are doomed. It is impossible to construct an argument for anything significant that only a blockhead could deny.

All right, then, are the proofs for God effective philosophical arguments? Do they constitute a rational case for theism? Here again, the answer depends on our criterion of rationality. We can distinguish at least five different categories of belief: beliefs which are theoretically certain, beliefs which are practically certain, probable beliefs, plausible beliefs, and beliefs which are merely theoretically possible. A belief is plainly rational if it falls within one of the first three categories; that is, when there is no conceivable evidence against it; when the evidence for it is overwhelming; or when it enjoys a clear preponderance of evidence. Such a belief satisfies the rational ideal we described in Chapter 2. However, we also found that the rational ideal is too restrictive. Under certain conditions one is entitled to beliefs for which the evidence is inconclusive.

In view of these cagetories, then, what do theistic proofs accomplish? Do the proofs for God demonstrate that God's existence is an absolute theoretical certainty, beyond all possibility of doubt? Do they establish God's existence beyond a reasonable doubt? Do they show that it is probable, that it enjoys a preponderance of evidence? Do they show that it is plausible, that at least the evidence on the question is divided? Or, do they show that it is only theoretically possible that God exists, but unlikely since nearly all the evidence goes against it?

It is fairly clear that theistic proofs do not establish God's existence beyond all doubt. Conclusive demonstration is possible only in matters of logic and mathematics, not where the issues are more concrete. Nor do the proofs establish God's existence beyond a reasonable doubt. On the other hand, it also seems that the proofs do more than show that God's existence is a mere possibility. This leaves us with two remaining categories, plausibility and probability, and opinions vary as to whether the proofs show that God's existence is probable, or merely plausible.

A number of thinkers take the position that whether or not the proofs accomplish what they ostensibly set out to do, namely, demonstrate that God exists, they do show that it is reasonable to believe in God. Gary Gutting, for example, maintains that the effect of theistic arguments is not to force us logically to admit their conclusion, but to put us in a position to judge that the conclusion is true.[62] And William L. Rowe concludes that while the arguments fail to prove that God exists, they may nevertheless show that the existence of God is a "plausible hypothesis by which we might account for the world and our experience." They provide us with reasons for defending belief in God as *rational* and therefore have a significant role in the intellectual defense of theism.[63]

At the very least, I believe, the various arguments for God establish theism as an intellectually responsible position. As we have seen, they present a case for God's existence that is complex, cumulative, coherent and comprehensive, as well as elegant. So, belief in God is not restricted to people with diminished mental capacity. Our common experience as human beings provides significant support for it.

Many thinkers also believe that the arguments demonstrate that it is not only plausible, but probable that God exists. The weight of evidence may not be overwhelming, but on balance, it favors the reality of God. This is Richard Swinburne's contention in *The Existence of God*. He considers the existence of the universe, its conformity to order, the existence of animals and humans, the pattern of history, the presence of evidence for miracles, and the occurrences of religious experiences. He concludes that we have more reason to expect such things if there is a God than we do if there isn't. For Swinburne, the evidence of religious experience tips the scale decisively in favor of theism, but only because evidence from other sources contributes to its probability. "The experience of so many men in their moments of religious vision corroborates what nature and history shows to be quite likely—that there is a God who made and sustains man and the universe."[64]

According to a more generous assessment of their effect, theistic arguments do more than demonstrate that it is reasonable for human beings to believe in God, they also show that it is unavoidable. In other words, they demonstrate that some sort of belief in God is universal. The strategy of the proofs, remember, is to link up belief in God with various basic beliefs—fundamental convictions we all have about experience and reality. If the inferences which the arguments make are logically valid—that is, if our basic beliefs really do imply the existence of God—then every human being has an awareness of God, even if it is only vague and imprecise. An accurate analysis of human experience would therefore reveal an elemental experience of God apart from any specific religious perspective. For if God is the ultimate explanatory power, then God is a factor in everyone's experience, whether or not we explicitly recognize his existence. To quote Charles Hartshorne again, "All proofs for God... are merely ways of making clear that we already and once for all believe in God, though not always with clearness and consistency."[65]

The issue between the theist and the atheist involves the interpretation of their common humanity. Consequently, one or the other is mistaken about the nature of his or her own existence. For either everyone experiences God in one way or another, or else no one does. If believers are right, then atheists have an experience of God which they fail to recognize as such. The purpose of the proofs is to elevate this awareness to the level of reflective consciousness. Consequently, instead of introducing God into someone's experience for the first time, the effect of theistic arguments is to make people aware of something that has been a part of their experience all along.

In one of his essays, Paul Tillich compares two types of philosophy of religion, the ontological and the cosmological, to two ways of approaching God, the way of overcoming estrangement and the way of meeting a stranger.[66] Our conclusions here resemble the ontological type. As we have seen, the Bible portrays God the creator as a factor in the experience of every person, and the arguments for God show that belief in God is implied in the most basic aspects of our thought and experience. Rather than introduce God into our experience, the proofs reveal that God is always a part of our experience, whether or not he is perceived and understood. The effect of the proofs, then, is not to convince us that God exists, but to show us that we already believe in him.[67]

We have explored the philosophical case for God at considerable length in order to determine whether the contents of faith are accessible from the perspective of common human experience. Our conclusion is affirmative. There is public evidence to support the religious belief in God. As we have seen, philosophers disagree as to the strength of this evidence. For a few it is conclusive. For some, it only shows that God's existence is theoretically possible. And for others, its effect is somewhere in between. But whether or not the evidence for God satisfies the rational ideal we described in Chapter 2, it does show, I believe, that theism is a responsible belief.

The Limits of Philosophical Theology

If philosophy says something about God, how does this compare to what religion says about him? As we just saw, reason and faith agree that God exists. Beyond that, however, there are striking differences between their respective ideas of God. In fact, many people, especially believers, react negatively to arguments for God's existence because they find so little in common between the object of personal religious devotion and the "God" referred to in these philosophical exercises. For them this bare philosophical abstraction is hopelessly inadequate to the powerful personal presence they experience day by day, who sustains and comforts them with his love. They join with Pascal in sharply separating the God of Abraham, Isaac, and Jacob from the God of the philosophers. [68]

There is no question that important factors distinguish the "God of religion" from the "God of philosophy." Religion, after all, has much more to say about God than philosophy does, and the language it characteristically uses is quite different. But it does not follow that the two ideas of God are contradictory or incompatible. Instead, they represent descriptions of the same being, or person, as seen from different perspectives. My wife's driver's license, for example, lists her height, weight, date of birth, address, and so on. The information is accurate as far as it goes, but it is woefully inadequate as a description of the woman I love. It conveys nothing of her charm, her intelligence, her many talents. The expressions I would use to describe her are quite different from those on her driver's license. But even though the two descriptions are different, they are not incompatible. They refer to the same person. My personal description may well include the information on her license, but it would certainly contain a great deal more as well. I would recognize the woman referred to by her driver's license as my wife, despite the paucity of information it provides. So, the license is not adequate as an account of her significance to me, but it suffices as a means of identification.

The God of philosophy—the God of theistic proofs—and the God of religion are a little like these two descriptions of my wife. Philosophy views God in light of his most basic features, or defining characteristics. The God of philosophy is anybody's God, or everybody's God. In contrast, the God of religion is the portrait of God developed by a community of faith over a long period of time. It is a portrait rich in details drawn from the manifestations and apprehensions of God within the community's history. Compared to the content of revelation, natural or philosophical knowledge of God is limited and abstract. All that reason alone can learn of God, it seems, is the mere fact of his existence, and certain fundamental qualities, such as intelligence, power and personness. It has little to say about his disposition toward the finite world or his involvement in creaturely affairs. Rational theism, then, pales next to the fullness of revelation. The God of the philosophers is infinitely less interesting and religiously satisfying than the God of Abraham, Isaac, and Jacob. Nonetheless, the two views of God refer to the same ultimate reality. Reason may not say a great deal about God, but what it does say agrees with religion.

In fact, many thinkers believe that reason can anticipate the contents of revelation. From an analysis of publicly accessible evidence, reason leads to the conclusion that God is personal. Now a personal being is one who can, if it chooses, communicate to another person. Indeed, it must do so in order to form a personal relationship. Consequently, by showing that God is personal, reason establishes the possibility of divine revelation. The fact of revelation, however—whether God has revealed himself, how he reveals himself, and what the contents of this revelation are—is not something that a rational analysis of public evidence can determine. These belong to the contents of faith. By reason, then, we learn that God can reveal himself; by faith we affirm that God has revealed himself.

This conclusion respects both the continuities and the discontinuities between faith and reason. It recognizes that what we can know of God by reason is neither exhaustive of, nor irrelevant to, the claims of faith. To summarize, there are continuities between reason and the contents of faith, but the scope of these continuities is very limited. Are these continuities religiously important in spite of their limitations? This is our question in Part 3.

---

[1]*Summa Contra Gentiles*, 1, 9, n. 4; quoted in James F. Ross, *Philosophical Theology* (Indianapolis and New York: The Bobbs-Merrill Company, Inc., 1969), p. iii.

[2]From *theos*, the Greek word for "god."

[3]*The Many-faced Argument: Recent Studies on the Ontological Argument for the Existence of God*, ed. John H. Hick and Arthur C. McGill (New York: The Macmillan Company, 1967).

[4]Charles Hartshorne, "Ten Ontological or Modal Proofs For God's Existence," in *The Logic of Perfection and Other Essays in Neoclassical Metaphysics* (LaSalle, IL: Open Court Publishing Company, 1962), pp. 28-117.

[5]See, for example, the title of Charles Hartshorne's work, *Anselm's Discovery: A Reexamination of the Ontological Proof for God's Existence* (LaSalle, IL: Open Court Publishing

Company, 1965).

⁶Ronald W. Hepburn finds versions of it in Plato and Aristotle ("Cosmological Argument for the Existence of God," in *The Encyclopedia of Philosophy*, ed. Paul A. Edwards [New York: The Macmillan Company, Inc. & The Free Press, 1967], 2:232-33).

⁷John Hick gives a helpful description of the difference. "An *a posteriori* argument is one which relies on a premise derived from (hence after, or posterior to) experience. ... An *a priori* argument on the other hand operates from a basis which is logically prior to and independent of experience. It rests upon purely logical considerations . . . ." (Introduction to *The Existence of God*, ed. John Hick [New York: Macmillan Publishing Company, 1964], p. 3).

⁸*Dialogues Concerning Natural Religion*, Part ix, in *The English Philosophers From Bacon to Mill*, ed. Edwin A. Burtt (New York: The Modern Library, 1939), p. 733.

⁹Willam L. Rowe, *The Cosmological Argument* (Princeton: Princeton University Press, 1975), p. 3; see also Willam L. Rowe, *Philosophy of Religion: An Introduction* (Belmont, CA: Wadsworth Publishing Company, 1978), pp. 16-17.

¹⁰Hartshorne labels the "supposed distinction between the 'a priori' ontological argument and the 'a posteriori' cosmological and design arguments" as "unclear and essentially erroneous" (*A Natural Theology for Our Time* [LaSalle, IL: The Open Court Publishing Co., 1967], pp. 66-67).

¹¹Cited in Frederick Ferre, *Basic Modern Philosophy of Religion* (New York: Charles Scribner's Sons, 1967), p. 152.

¹²*Immanuel Kant's Critique of Pure Reason*, trans. Norman Kemp Smith (New York: St. Martin's Press, 1965), p. 510.

¹³Charles Hartshorne, *Creative Synthesis and Philosophic Method* (LaSalle, IL: Open Court Publishing Company, 1970), p. 276.

¹⁴"This proof always deserves to be mentioned with respect," writes Kant. "It is the oldest, the clearest, and the most accordant with the common reason of mankind" (*Critique of Pure Reason*, p. 520).

¹⁵My friend Fritz Guy attributes this description to Langdon Gilkey.

¹⁶Hartshorne, *Anselm's Discovery*, p. ix.

¹⁷"Modernizing the Case for God," *Time*, April 7, 1980, pp. 65-68.

¹⁸A couple of recent examples are William L. Rowe, *The Cosmological Argument*, and Ronald M. Green, *Religious Reason: The Rational and Moral Basis of Religious Belief* (New York: Oxford University Press, 1978).

¹⁹Introduction to *The Existence of God*, pp. 5, 7.

²⁰Ross, p. 4.

²¹Ibid., pp. 11, 33, 18.

²²See p. 46 above.

²³Ross, pp. 20-21.

²⁴Ibid., pp. 27, 26.

²⁵Antony Kenny, *Faith and Reason* (New York: Columbia University Press, 1983), pp. 18, 20.

²⁶"Noetic" comes from *nous*, the Greek word for "mind."

²⁷See Charles Hartshorne, "Why There Cannot Be Empirical Proofs," in *A Natural Theology For Our Time,*, pp. 66-89.

²⁸*The Existence of God*, p. 169.

²⁹Mortimer Adler, *How to Think About God: A Guide for the 20th-Century Pagan* (New York: Macmillan, 1980), pp. 144-45.

³⁰*The Existence of God*, p. 175.

³¹Ibid.

³²Ibid., pp. 6-7.

³³A number of philosophers differentiate between the cosmological argument and

164 Reason and the Contours of Faith

the argument from design, but for our purposes we can put them in the same category.

[34] See, for example, "Master Designer," in Ralph Carmichael and Kurt Kaiser, *Tell It Like It Is: A Folk Musical* (Waco, TX: Lexicon Music, Inc., 1969).

[35] Paley's work, *Natural Theology, or Evidences of the Existence and Attributes of the Deity collected from the Appearances of Nature*, appeared in 1802, twenty-three years, ironically, after the publication of David Hume's classic critique of the teleological argument in *Dialogues Concerning Natural Religion*.

[36] Quoted in *The Existence of God*, p. 100.

[37] Ibid., p. 103.

[38] Actually, Paley does not compare the world as a whole to a watch, but specific phenomena within the world, each of which, as we noted, could serve as the basis for a theistic proof.

[39] See Hume's famous *Dialogues Concerning Natural Religion*, in *The English Philosophers From Bacon to Mill*, pp. 690-764.

[40] *Critique of Pure Reason*, p. 520.

[41] Quoted in *The Existence of God*, p. 121.

[42] See *Creative Synthesis and Philosophic Method*, pp. 284-85. Hartshorne, remember, insists that all theistic proofs are properly *a priori*.

[43] *Dialogues Concerning Natural Religion*, Part X, *The English Philosophers From Bacon to Mill*, p. 741.

[44] The most influential presentation of a soul-making theodicy in recent years is John Hick's book, *Evil and the God of Love* (rev. ed.; New York: Harper & Row, Publishers, 1966).

[45] Process philosophy is well-known for taking this approach to the question of evil. See, for example, Charles Hartshorne, "A New Look at the Problem of Evil," in *Current Philosophical Issues: Essays in Honor of Curt John Ducasse*, ed. Frederick C. Dommeyer (Springfield, IL: Charles C. Thomas, 1966), pp. 201-212.

[46] Alvin Plantinga presents a particularly cogent version of the free will defense in *God, Freedom, and Evil* (New York: Harper & Row, Publishers, 1974).

[47] The word "theodicy" refers to a philosophical response to the problem which seeks to show that evil is not an insurmountable obstacle to faith in God. As the roots of the word indicate, its purpose is to defend God from the challenge which evil represents.

[48] C. S. Lewis, *Mere Christianity* (New York: The Macmillan Company, 1960), p. 5.

[49] Albert Camus, *The Stranger*, trans. Stuart Gilbert (New York: Vintage Books, 1946), p. 72.

[50] Hasting Rashdall, in *The Existence of God*, p. 151. Immanuel Kant gave the moral argument its classic formulation. In the best possible world, he argued, happiness is perfectively proportioned to morality. But there is nothing in morality which supports this connection. The only thing with the requisite power to guarantee such a connection is an independent cause of nature, that is, a being of intelligence and will, and such a being is God. According to Kant, then, "it is morally necessary to assume the existence of God" (quoted in *The Existence of God*, pp. 138-139).

[51] Anselm's argument appears in virtually every book of readings in philosophy of religion. See, for example, Baruch A. Brody, ed., *Readings in the Philosophy of Religion: An Analytic Approach* (Englewood Cliffs, NJ: Prentice-Hall, Inc., 1974), pp. 12-28.

[52] See Alvin Plantinga, "Kant's Objection to the Ontological Argument," in Brody, pp. 28-36.

[53] There is no indication that Anselm believed that he was formulating two different arguments.

[54] In *The Ontological Argument From St. Anselm to Contemporary Philosophers*, ed. Alvin Plantinga (Garden City, NY: Anchor Books, 1965), p. 145.

[55] Ibid.

[56] I am deeply indebted to the work of Charles Hartshorne for my understanding the

Natural Theology: The Philosophical Question 165

proofs, both individually and collectively. Three of his books are particularly important for developing the comprehensive case for theism described in this section: *A Natural Theology For Our Time, Creative Synthesis and Philosophic Method, Man's Vision of God and the Logic of Theism* (Chicago: Willett, Clark and Co., 1941; reprinted, Hamden, CN: Archon Books, 1964).

[57]*Critique of Pure Reason*, p. 510.

[58]*Creative Synthesis and Philosophic Method*, p. 277.

[59]Gary Gutting, *Religious Belief and Religious Skepticism* (Notre Dame, IN: University of Notre Dame Press, 1982), p. 110.

[60]Named for the medieval philosopher William of Ockham (c. 1285-1349), who evidently did not use the principle in its most familiar form: "Entities are not to be multiplied beyond necessity" (Ernest A. Moody, "William of Ockham," in *The Encyclopedia of Philosophy*, 8:307).

[61]Richard L. Purtill, *Reason to Believe* (Grand Rapids, MI: William B. Eerdmans Publishing Co., 1974), pp. 111-112.

[62]Gutting, p. 110.

[63]Rowe, *Philosophy of Religion*, p. 57.

[64]Richard Swinburne, *The Existence of God* (Oxford: Clarendon Press, 1979), pp. 277, 291.

[65]*Man's Vision of God and the Logic of Theism*, p. 274.

[66]Paul Tillich, "Two Types of Philosophy of Religion" in *Theology of Culture*, ed. Robert C. Kimball (London: Oxford University Press, 1959), p. 10.

[67]Cf. John Baillie's comment: "For though we may not try to prove either to ourselves or to others that God exists, we may do something to persuade both ourselves and others *that we already believe in Him*. . . . Such is the only legitimate kind of theistic proof" (*Our Knowledge of God* [New York: Charles Scribner's Sons, 1959], p. 240; italics his).

[68]Of his dramatic conversion, Pascal wrote in his *Memorial*, "God of Abraham, God of Isaac, God of Jacob, not of the philosophers and of the learned" (quoted in Richard H. Popkin, "Pascal, Blaise," in *The Encyclopedia of Philosophy*, 6:52).

6
NATURAL THEOLOGY: THE THEOLOGICAL QUESTION

This chapter will conclude our examination of the relation of reason to the contents of faith. It deals with the contribution of reason to the task of Christian theology and thus returns us to the general concern of Chapter 3. The question which occupies us here, however, is different and presupposes our discussion in all of the three preceding chapters. The topic of Chapter 3 was the application of reason to the contents of faith from a perspective which presupposes that these contents are true. We examined Christian theology, defined as the enterprise which seeks to give logical, systematic expression to the beliefs of the Christian community.

In Chapter 4 we turned to the question of general revelation. We asked if the contents of faith include anything to indicate that they might be perceptible from the perspective of common human experience, apart from participation in the Christian community, the special light of revelation, or the standpoint of personal Christian commitment. Our answer was affirmative. The contents of revelation support the conclusion that there is publicly accessible evidence for some of what Christians believe.

In Chapter 5 we examined philosophy of religion. As traditionally conceived, philosophy is the quest for universal principles, ideas which can be applied without restriction to human experience and reality. Accordingly, philosophy of religion concerns the extent to which religion illuminates human experience in general. It surveys the broad range of religious phenomena—beliefs, practices, and theories—looking for ideas which apply to our common human experience as well. It selects concepts that appear to be capable of universal application, carefully analyzes their meaning, and assesses their truth.

Our review of public evidence for God discovered an impressive philosophical case for theism. It consists of a number of related arguments developed from aspects of our common human experience. So, our answer to the philosophical question of natural theology was positive. There is evidence to support this central Christian belief which does not presuppose the vantage point of faith.

This chapter addresses the question of natural theology in its theological, as distinct from its philosophical, form. Theology, in the sense of Christian theology, seeks to interpret the contents of Christian faith. Its primary concern is a particular religious tradition, rather than human experience in general. But an important issue theology must consider is the relation between Christian beliefs and publicly accessible evidence. Does an examination of common human experience help us to understand Christian beliefs? Can public evidence help in its endeavor to interpret the contents of faith? So, the *philosophical* question of natural theology concerns the existence of public evidence for religious belief; the *theological* question concerns the role of such evidence in the interpretation of faith.

Chapters 4, 5, and 6, then, address these questions, respectively: Do the contents of faith point to any continuities between faith and reason? Does a rational examination of religious belief discover such continuities? Do these continuities contribute to our understanding of faith? We have answered the first two questions affirmatively. Now we must address the third.

Framing the Question of Natural Theology

Though it sounds simple enough, the theological question of natural theology is actually rather complicated. It involves several levels of inquiry leading to increasingly narrow differentiations. On one level it asks if theology has any use for public evidence, or philosophical reflection, as it seeks to interpret the contents of Christian faith. If the answer is yes, further questions arise. One concerns the specific role of philosophical reflection in relation to theology. Is it largely preparatory to theology proper, or does it have an integral part in theological discussion?

Another question concerns the philosophical sources which theology should employ. Should theologians do their own philosophical work, or should they rely on the philosophical reflections of others? Are there specific philosophers or schools of thought which a theologian simply cannot ignore? Can theologians use a variety of philosophical positions, or should they confine themselves to one point of view? A third question is the extent to which theology should rely on these sources. Are they helpful here and there in the course of theological reflection, say, to shore up the case for the reality of God? Or should they figure in the development of the entire theological system?

The second and third questions overlap. If theology needs to make use of philosophy throughout, should it rely on one philosophical resource, such as the system of Aristotle or that of Alfred North Whitehead? Or should it turn to different sources, depending on their relative value for the specific topic under discussion? Perhaps one philosophical viewpoint, such as process philosophy, will prove to be especially helpful in developing a doctrine of God, while another, such as existentialism, has more to contribute to a Christian understanding of humanity.

As we work toward a position of our own on these issues, it will be helpful to see how different theologians have answered these questions. The field is too broad for us to attempt anything like a survey of theological methods, nor will we be able to describe the views of any one thinker in detail. But a brief description of some representative positions will give us a good idea of what the options are.

Natural Theology as Apologetics

Many Christian thinkers view the philosophical evaluation of religious beliefs as external or adjunctive to theology. They approve of the enterprise, but they see it as something quite distinct from theology. On the model of "Christian apologetics," the task of relating the contents of faith to general human experience is subsequent to that of theology. The essential task of theology is to expound the contents of faith in a systematic, logical way, drawing from the accepted authorities of the Christian community. For people outside the community, the claims of faith may raise a number of questions, however. So, once theology has done its work, there remains the task of responding to these questions and criticisms. This is the business of apologetics. It seeks to show that Christian beliefs make sense to any thinking person, not just those who accept them on the basis of religious authority. To do this, apologetics appeals to evidence provided by our common human experience.

As the word suggests, apologetics is essentially a defensive maneuver. One writer defines it as "the positive declaration of this Gospel in the face of the facts and circumstances with which it is confronted and by which it is often opposed."[1] The challenges to faith vary from age to age, so the agenda which apologetics faces is constantly changing. Although apologetics is typically directed to those outside the Christian community, attacks on the faith can come from inside the church as well, so apologetics seeks to expose heresy and protect the faith from internal ruin, too.

Apologetics has a long history in the church. In fact, some of the earliest Christian theologians, such as Justin and Tertullian, are known as apologists, since the burden of much of their work was to correct the mistaken impressions people had of the Christian religion and to defend it from attack. Some of the most popular religious literature in our own time is apologetic in nature. C. S. Lewis' books are no doubt the best example. Lewis defended the central teachings of Christianity, especially its more controversial beliefs, in a number of writings, including *Screwtape Letters, Mere Christianity, Miracles,* and *The Problem of Pain,* to mention a few.

As Lewis' writings reveals, apologetics presupposes a well-defined concept of Christianity and a settled commitment to it. Its purpose is not to establish the claims of faith, but to defend them once they are already in place. Lewis never gives the impression that the outcome of his discussion is in doubt, or that the truth of Christianity hangs in the balance, depending on the success of his arguments. The truth is settled in his mind. The only question is whether his readers will see it and accept it, and he wants to help them along by answering their questions.

Apologists are often laymen, as Lewis was, rather than trained academic theologians. And many of them, again like Lewis, are converts to Christianity rather than life-long members of the church.[2] Consequently, they often focus on what they take to be the basic issues of Christianity, those most likely to concern people who are not Christians, and avoid getting involved in intricate theological matters.[3]

Natural Theology as Theological Foundation

A second answer to the question of natural theology shares two characteristics with apologetics. It views the contents of faith and the results of rational inquiry as two distinct areas, and it sees a positive relation between them. But it differs from apologetics in reversing their priority. For apologetics, as we just saw, an appeal to public evidence logically follows an exposition of the contents of faith. It presupposes a well-developed body of belief derived from revelation. For this approach, however, an appeal to public evidence logically precedes a statement of faith's contents. Instead of defending a body of knowledge which is established independently, reason provides a basis, a foundation drawn from public evidence, on which the contents of faith can firmly rest.

This position makes a sharp distinction between two spheres of religious knowledge. Natural theology consists of religious truths which can be developed by reason alone. Revealed theology contains truths of a supernatural nature—truths which we could never know apart from divine revelation. Natural theology serves as a basis for the claims of faith, which are derived from revelation. It plays a preparatory, or propaedeutic role.

This view of faith and reason is typically associated with Roman Catholic thought. Official Catholic doctrine affirms the possibility of knowing God through reason alone and distinguishes between truths of reason and truths of revelation. Here is a statement from one of the documents of Vatican II, which quotes extensively from Vatican I:

> Through divine revelation, God chose to show forth and communicate Himself and the eternal decisions of His will regarding the salvation of men. That is to say, He chose "to share those divine treasures which totally transcend the understanding of the human mind." This sacred Synod affirms, "God the beginning and end of all things, can be known with certainty from created reality by the light of human reason" (cf. Rom. 1:20); but the Synod teaches that it is through His revelation "that those religious truths which are by their nature accessible to human reason can be known by all men with ease, with solid certitude, and with no trace of error, even in the present state of the human race."[4]

The writings of Thomas Aquinas are authoritative for the Catholic position. Aquinas identifies two different kinds of theology, or two sciences concerned with "divine beings." The kind of knowledge acquired through natural reason is "divine science," or "philosophical theology." The knowledge of divine beings attained from their self-revelation constitutes "sacred doctrine," or "the theology of the Sacred Scripture."[5] These two theologies differ in content as well as source. Divine science knows nothing of divine beings themselves. It can only examine their effects on the world. From the fact that the things we experience through our senses are effects dependent upon a cause we can infer that God exists and that he exists in a manner radically different from our own.[6]

Aquinas' famous "five ways" contain examples of the cosmological type of argument for God we encountered in the previous chapter. Each of the first three ways begins with something we experience through our senses, such as change, and concludes that we cannot understand the phenomenon unless its ultimate cause is something whose mode of existence is radically different from its effects. Taken together, these arguments provide a composite description of the world we experience as pointing toward the existence of a transcendent source and ground which we can identify as "God." What Aquinas' ways demonstrate, then—indeed, all that reason by itself can ever know of God—is the mere fact of God's existence. To learn anything else about God we must turn to revelation.

Following Aquinas, Thomist philosophy assures us that God exists and reason can infer certain truths about the divine reality from our common human experience. But only divine revelation can acquaint us with other important truths, such as the doctrines of the Trinity, the Incarnation and the Atonement.[7] The basic distinction between natural and revealed knowledge of God lies behind the two-storied concept view of Christian theology proper, developed from the contents of revelation, resting on a base provided by reason.

Such a view of natural and revealed theology has received severe criticism. One evangelical theologian regards this two-stage theory of truth as the beginning of a long decline in Western culture which ultimately results in a complete loss of rational meaning. According to Francis Schaeffer, Aquinas' distinction between nature and grace leads to a dualism which splits our lives into separate parts like the upper and lower stories of a house. Reason operates in the lower story, the sphere of nature, but it has no access to the upper story, the sphere of grace and freedom. As a result, ultimate meaning is something reason can never attain. It is non-rational and non-logical. In order to achieve personal meaning, therefore, to fulfill our existence as free creatures, we must take a leap of faith into the irrational.[8]

Schaeffer traces the decline of Western culture, as he sees it, directly to this bifurcated view of reality. The upper-lower story split between grace and nature becomes a split between faith and rationality. The two are separated by "a line of despair," since ultimate meaning is not accessible to reason. One by one over the course of time various enterprises moved upstairs to the sphere of the irrational. The first was philosophy, then came art, music, and general culture. The last to be relegated to the upper story was theology.[9] As a result of this process, modern human beings have no hope that reason can ever achieve meaning and value.[10]

Schaeffer's simplistic account of Western civilization rests on a rather common misperception of Aquinas, and fairness to the great doctor requires us to correct it. Like Schaeffer, many people attribute the two-story view outlined above to Thomas Aquinas, and numerous Catholic thinkers view natural and revealed theology on the model of foundation and superstructure. But this was not Aquinas' own position. True, he does distinguish two types of knowledge of God, but he does not regard them as discrete, separate spheres of inquiry. For him, natural theology is not an independent enterprise which constructs a foundation for revealed theology on its own. It is clear from the context of the famous five ways that Aquinas sees natural theology as an integral part of revealed theology, not separated from it.[11]

Although Aquinas himself did not view natural theology as an independent foundation for revealed theology, there are theologians who see this as the role of reason in relation to faith. For them, a rational examination of public evidence provides an indispensable basis for the contents of revelation. The full-fledged exposition of Christian faith is thus a two-level construction, with the truths of reason below and the truths of revelation above.

Philosophy of Religion as Natural Theology

For other theologians, too, an appeal to public evidence is both distinct from and important to theology, but these thinkers do not regard it as a rational foundation on which the truths of revelation rest. Like the concept of natural theology just mentioned, their appeal to public evidence is introductory or preparatory to the task of theology proper. But instead of proving the contents of faith, its purpose is to show that the concerns of theology are related to an essential aspect of human existence and are therefore worthy of intellectual inquiry.[12] Such an endeavor represents a "prolegomenon" to theology, but it is not a foundation for it.

The introduction to Friedrich Schleiermacher's major work, *The Christian Faith*, is the best example of this approach to the problem. It excludes from theology attempts to prove the contents of faith and proposes something else to take their place. According to Schleiermacher, the essence of Christianity is a particular way of being conscious of God, and the task of theology is to explicate the contents of the Christian religious self-consciousness. Christian doctrines are therefore "expressions of inward experiences,"[13] or "accounts of the Christian religious affections set forth in speech." They have their only basis "in the emotions of the religious self-consciousness."[14] Insisting on religious experience as the basis for Christian doctrine gives theology a strongly, in fact, an exclusively, ecclesiastical character. Because the Christian religious self-consciousness arises only out of the Christian community, the primary object of theological reflection is the Christian Church.[15] Consequently, only what originates with the corporate experience of the Christian community—and nothing else—really belongs to a theology.[16]

As Schleiermacher defines theology, philosophical reflection is theologically irrelevant. If theology is concerned exclusively with the self-consciousness of a specific religious community, then speculative philosophy, or rational theology, has nothing to do with it. It provides theology with the terminology it needs, but it contributes nothing to the actual content of Christian doctrine.[17] Schleiermacher does not discredit speculative philosophy or rational theology, he only denies that it has a place in Christian theology. What "human reason in itself" can say about God or humanity does not originate within the Christian church, so any attempt to establish a doctrine of God on a foundation of general principles or to prove that the content of Christian faith is consonant with reason, must be excluded.[18]

Schleiermacher particularly objects to the idea that proofs for the existence of God provide a rational basis for Christian doctrine. He rejects any two-story arrangement like the one described above, in which a suprarational theology, valid only within Christianity, rests on a purely rational natural theology which is valid outside as well as inside the church.[19] The starting point for theology, he insists, is not a rational demonstration of its contents, but the sheer givenness of its object, namely, Christian religious self-consciousness.

Although he opposes the practice of "inflating doctrine with rational proofs and criticism," Schleiermacher's major theological work includes something which fulfills a similar purpose—something which "entirely takes the place, for the system of doctrine, of all the so-called proofs for the existence of God." This alternative to theistic proofs is a description of the feeling of absolute dependence as a universal element of human life.[20]

Schleiermacher identifies Christian religious self-consciousness as a particular species of a universal human phenomenon he calls "piety." Piety belongs to the sphere of feeling, as distinct from knowing or doing—the other two divisions of human experience—but it is different from ordinary feelings in several ways. In piety we have a feeling of dependence that is absolute; we are totally dependent on the object. Moreover, this feeling does not exist in a single moment of experience, but instead it accompanies our whole existence. And, third, this feeling consists in "the consciousness that the whole of our spontaneous activity comes from a source outside us."[21] Since the feeling of dependence is absolute, it cannot be anything other than God; its object cannot be something within the world, nor even the world as a whole. And since the feeling of absolute dependence is universal, we must conclude that the consciousness of God is a permanent element in all our experience.[22]

Because there is nothing specifically Christian about this feeling of absolute dependence, Schleiermacher insists that it is not really a matter of concern for Christian theology. So, he does not view his discussion of piety as an attempt to prove that Christianity is true or to give the contents of Christian faith a basis in reason. Nevertheless, the way in which Schleiermacher deals with the topic strongly implies that it has theological value. After all, his analysis of the feeling of absolute dependence appears in the Introduction to his dogmatic system, and he even describes it as replacing the proofs for the existence of God. We therefore conclude that this discussion of the feeling of absolute dependence plays a role in Schleiermacher's theological project which is analogous to the role of natural theology in more traditional proposals. Its purpose is to connect the distinctive contents of Christian faith with our common human experience. It shows that theology is concerned with things that are related to a basic dimension of our existence.

In more recent times, other theologians have taken a similar approach to the question of natural theology. They reject anything like the traditional arguments for the existence of God, or attempts to prove the truth of Christianity; then they put something in their place which serves a comparable purpose. They try to show that the contents of Christian faith are related to certain aspects of our common experience as human beings. Langdon Gilkey's work, *Naming the Whirlwind*, fits this description.[23]

Gilkey describes his book as a "prolegomenon" to theology. It does not expound the contents of Christian faith in the manner of traditional systematic theology, nor does it construct proofs for the existence of God in the manner of traditional natural theology. Instead, it seeks to justify the use of religious language by delineating a dimension of general human experience in which the objective referent of this language appears. In other words, it represents a quest for dimensions of the sacred within ordinary secular experience.

We need an enterprise of this nature, Gilkey argues, because contemporary secularism poses such a radical challenge to Christian faith. The secularist attitude prevails inside as well as outside the Christian community, and it calls into question not merely the truth but the very meaning of religious language.[24] To meet this challenge, theology must reflect upon its own foundations, and its "first order of business" must be to establish the meaning of religious language.[25] This seems to call for something just like the traditional task of natural theology, but the peculiar nature of the secularist challenge makes natural theology just as problematic as theology itself.

As we have seen, the classic proofs for the existence of God argue from some universally experienced aspect of things to God as its sole intelligible ground or cause.[26] They seek to show that the nature of reality is such that only God can account for its coherence and intelligibility. The problem with such arguments, according to Gilkey, is the fact that they always move within the framework of a given metaphysical system. Presupposing that reality has a coherent structure and that our minds can apprehend it, they proceed to the conclusion that God provides the best explanation for certain aspects of our experience. Gilkey insists that this approach cannot meet the contemporary challenge to religious language, because its rationalistic assumptions are just as alien to the prevalent secular mood as explicitly religious language is. If natural theology itself needs help in order to establish its intelligibility, it is in no position to give assistance to theology proper.[27]

Instead of metaphysics, then, Gilkey turns to language analysis and phenomenology in order to formulate a prolegomenon to theology.[28] His strategy is to show that the basic symbols of religion, the fundamental statements of theology, are relevant to concrete secular experience because they thematize some significant area of our common ordinary lives.[29] With careful examination, he argues, we can identify the essential structures of human existence. We see that qualities such as contingency, relativity, temporality, and freedom are permanent aspects in our experience. We may sense them more vividly at certain times than at others, but they are never absent. Careful examination also reveals that these basic structures point beyond themselves to a dimension or context of "ultimacy" or "unconditionedness." Accordingly, this dimension is always present in human life as its source, ground, horizon, and limit, and is thus the presupposition of all we are and do.[30] The dimension of reality to which religious language refers is thus a dimension that emerges, not just in religion, but in all human experience, our common or secular experience included. For this reason, religious language must be meaningful.[31]

Gilkey carefully limits the scope of his conclusion. He insists that his proposal deals with the meaningfulness but not the truth of God-language.[32] So, the careful description of ultimacy or transcendence he provides does not constitute a doctrine of God. In fact, it does not even explicitly speak of God. Like Schleiermacher in his Introduction to *The Christian Faith*, Gilkey insists that his prolegomenon to theology is neither a systematic nor natural theology. All the same, in certain respects the purpose of his proposal is similar to that of natural theology. It, too, shows how the contents of faith are related to human experience in general.

The Rejection of Natural Theology

Another response to the question of natural theology contrasts sharply with the positions we have examined so far. The most influential Christian theologians during the first half of the twentieth century, in particular, Karl Barth and Emil Brunner, insisted that philosophical reflection is utterly irrelevant to the work of theology. As they describe it, the task of theology is to elaborate the contents of Christian revelation by means of concepts which revelation itself provides, not to build bridges between revelation and the results of human speculation. Consequently, there is no place in theology for appeals to anything which lies outside the framework of revelation and faith. The purpose of theology is not to make faith palatable to the unconverted mind. In a famous statement attributed to Karl Barth, "Belief cannot argue with unbelief: it can only preach to it!"[33]

This does not necessarily mean that the enterprise of apologetics is invalid. Emil Brunner, for example—next to Barth the greatest neo-orthodox theologian—describes apologetics as a necessary task for the church.[34] Nor does it mean that theology has absolutely nothing to do with philosophy. As Bernard Ramm argues, Barth allows philosophy a limited role in theology.[35] What it means is that we cannot allow anything outside revelation to establish the truth of revelation or to determine its contents. Revelation cannot be dependent on anything other than itself. Consequently, Christian faith must not begin the attempt to understand its contents through a dialogue with human thought in general. To quote Brunner, "Discussion with non-Christian thought cannot be the basis and the starting-point of dogmatics itself."[36] Accordingly, philosophy may assist us in expressing the contents of faith, but it has nothing to contribute to these contents.

The neo-orthodox rejection of any foundational role for public evidence in theology stems from the distinctive concepts of revelation and faith we noted in our discussion of general revelation in Chapter 4. For neo-orthodox theology, revelation is an event in which the transcendent personal God imparts himself to human beings, confronting them with a demand to respond.[37] Revelation thus has the nature of a gift from God, so its intellectual contents are unattainable through any other means. It involves "a knowledge that is unexpected, something that has not [been] gained by our own efforts but, in one way or another, is always a gift, a 'disclosure,' which we could not have expected."[38] For Brunner, "God and revelation are so intimately connected that there is no other revelation than that which comes to us from God, and there is no other knowledge of God than that which is given to us in revelation."[39]

In *Church Dogmatics* Barth finds God's "knowability in the readiness of God Himself." Consequently, "a theology which makes a great show of guaranteeing the knowability of God apart from grace and therefore from faith . . . —in other words, a 'natural' theology—is quite impossible within the Church and . . . cannot be discussed even in principle."[40] Barth bases his opposition to natural theology on the unity of the divine nature. Because God is both Creator and Redeemer, not separately, but at one and the same time, there can be no knowledge of God as Creator—the sort of knowledge natural theology represents—independent of knowledge of God as Redeemer.[41]

For neo-orthodoxy, faith and revelation are strictly correlated.[42] There is no revelation without faith, and there is no faith apart from revelation. This correlation has important consequences. Because its source is revelation, knowing God is never a matter of mere cognition, a neutral possession of information. It always involves a dynamic personal relationship to God. And because God has revealed himself specifically in Jesus Christ, this relationship is wholly determined by the unique content of the Christian Gospel. Consequently, faith is not just one among many manifestations of some generic religious experience characteristic of humankind. It is a gift that becomes available only in connection with revelation.

The distinctive nature of revelation and faith means that reason is opposed to true religious understanding. Outside faith, human beings are not merely neutral toward God, they are in a state of rebellion.[43] So reason is not an independent cognitive faculty standing outside the opposition between belief and unbelief; it is a manifestation of unbelief. For if revelation is indeed the only source of a true knowledge of God, then any other supposed source of knowledge can only be a delusion, a manifestation of our sinful desire to assert ourselves against God's sovereignty.

The very concept of revelation thus excludes the possibility of rational knowledge of God. If knowledge of God comes only through revelation, then reason provides no basis for achieving it. Brunner's words on this point are worth quoting here:

> To wish to argue for revelation in rational terms means that we have not begun to understand what revelation is. That which can be based on rational grounds is, by its very nature, not revelation but rational truth. The truth of reason is that which we as rational beings can tell ourselves; the truth of revelation is that which, by its very nature we could not tell ourselves. ... Anything a human being can verify or deduce for himself by any process of argument, investigation, or proof, cannot possibly be revelation, and, vice versa, that which is revelation cannot be verified by any such process.[44]

For neo-orthodox theology, then, reason provides no basis for a knowledge of God independent of or prior to revelation. It does not form a bridge from common human experience to the unique experience of God. Nor does it represent a standard we can use to evaluate the contents of revelation. Most emphatically, then, it is not the task of reason to justify or validate the contents of faith. We must accept revelation on its own terms in response to its own inherent power.

This approach discredits the central enterprise of philosophical theology, the attempt to formulate arguments for the reality of God. "A theology that allows itself to be drawn into producing proofs for its claim to revelation has already thrown up the sponge," Brunner insists. "Either faith or proof; you cannot have both."[45] Theistic proofs are not only irrelevant to the contents of faith, but the supreme being whose existence they support is nothing more than an idol. Like all idols, Barth says, it springs from our "natural" human capacity "to persuade [ourselves] and others of a higher and divine being." To identify this intellectual construct with the God of revelation is nothing short of "an attempt to unite Yahweh with Baal."[46]

History will probably judge neo-orthodoxy to be the most important theological development of this century, even though its influence has waned somewhat during the past twenty-five years. Its polemic against natural theology is the negative side of a permanent theological achievement. Its most important theme, certainly, is the emphasis on revelation. The contents of Christian faith as expressed in the Bible cannot be reduced to anything else. We cannot ignore the distinctive truth-claims of Christianity without doing violence to the faith. And we must allow the Gospel to speak against us, to judge us in every aspect of our existence, including our thinking.

Neo-orthodoxy therefore provides a helpful critique of a prevalent theological tendency to read current thought-forms into the Christian message, so, instead of Gospel, we hear only the echo of our presuppositions. As one thinker puts it, neo-orthodoxy widened and deepened the conception of the theological task to include "criteria of appropriateness" to the central meanings of the Christian faith.[47] Besides divine transcendence and the importance of revelation, neo-orthodoxy also deserves credit for recalling the biblical emphasis on the negative aspects of human existence. It revitalized sin as an important theological category.

Neo-orthodoxy demands that we resist the easy assimilation of philosophy with religion. When philosophers speak of God, they have a tendency to view God's worldly, or cosmic, functions as the essence of divinity. As a result, God becomes a metaphysical principle rather than a living personal being. Aristotle's philosophy contains a familiar example. Aristotle's unmoved mover explains the existence of the universe, but it is not "available for religious purposes," to use one scholar's expression.[48] The caveat of neo-orthodoxy on this point is well-taken. We can never identify the ultimate reality which is God with our human conceptions of God. We must allow God to speak in freedom against all our preconceptions.

At the same time, we cannot accept neo-orthodoxy's relentless disparagement of natural theology. While it forcefully reminds us of the important discontinuities between faith and reason, this approach obscures the fact that important continuities also exist. Indeed, if revelation itself points to such continuities, as numerous biblical passages indicate, then a theology that takes revelation seriously should support the effort to look for them. But neo-orthodoxy, for all its emphasis on the contents of the Bible, slights the biblical indications of continuity between our common human experience and the experience of faith.

Neo-orthodoxy is guilty of inconsistency as well as overstatement. Neo-orthodox theologians consulted the Bible extensively and made impressive use of biblical categories in developing their theological positions. But they did not accept the biblical view of reality over the modern, scientific one. Instead, neo-orthodox theologians fused these two perspectives together, or tried to, and this uneasy amalgam of antiquity and modernity produced enormous tensions.

Langdon Gilkey analyzed this flaw in neo-orthodoxy a quarter of a century ago in his well-known article "Cosmology, Ontology, and the Travail of Biblical Language,"[49] and later in the book we examined above, *Naming the Whirlwind*.[50] As Gilkey describes it, neo-orthodoxy repudiated the closed worldview of liberalism, which excluded anything like transcendent revelation or specific divine acts in history. But it did not reject the scientific view of reality as a closed causal continuum of space-time experience.[51] Consequently, neo-orthodox theologians dramatically referred to the mighty acts of God in history and insisted that they were actual historical events, but they did not take the biblical descriptions of such events literally. Instead, they viewed these accounts as expressions of profound religious faith on the part of the biblical authors. To describe something à la neo-orthodoxy as "an act of God," therefore, is not to provide an objective account of its occurrence in the phenomenal world, but to speak of the event as it is viewed from the perspective of faith. It is interpretation, not explanation.

There has been a resurgence of interest in neo-orthodox theology in the past few years, but a more widespread view is that it collapsed as a movement years ago because of the inner tension we have described. As Gilkey puts it, "The union of these two worldviews, one modern and one ancient, proved more difficult than at first it promised to be; the secular elements warred against the Biblical one, and the result was the ultimate breakup on the intellectual level of neo-orthodox theology."[52]

A related problem with neo-orthodoxy is the enormous emphasis it places on inner experience. Revelation is an event which takes place entirely within oneself; there is nothing outside the experience to corroborate it. In fact, it is the very idea of corroboration that neo-orthodoxy condemns. The motive of this privatizing emphasis is to safeguard the contents of faith from intellectual erosion, but instead of rendering faith invulnerable, such a move leaves it defenseless. Without some demonstrable tie to common human experience, faith loses intelligibility and ultimately its relevance to lived experience.

Finally, there is the point that publicness is an important characteristic of all rational discourse, including theology. Exaggerating the uniqueness of faith and refusing to relate its contents to public evidence has brought not only criticism but ridicule on neo-orthodoxy. According to one philosopher, it has "glorified absurdity with the claim that God was above logic."[53] Another reacts to Barth's claim that faith cannot argue with unbelief in this way:

> To concede such a claim would be to despair not only of reason but of human solidarity. It would be to accept a sort of religious racism; in which the saved and the damned are, at least in this most crucial respect, different kinds of creatures. It would be to recognize a cold war of the mind; in which there can be no room for genuine and fruitful dialogue between the enlightened and the unenlightened.[54]

Natural Theology as Part of the Theological System

In sharp contrast to neo-orthodoxy, many theologians believe that the task of interpreting the contents of faith must incorporate an appeal to public evidence within theology itself. In fact, it is probably safe to generalize that over the centuries most Christian theologians agree that common human experience is important for the attempt to explain the contents of Christian faith, and many definitions of theology include a reference to philosophy. As a recent publication observes, "The two main sources of Christian theology are the Bible and hellenic culture, especially Greek philosophy."[55]

On this model of theology, philosophical reflection functions as an integral aspect of the theological task. It is not dismissed as irrelevant to Christian faith, nor treated as a secondary, adjunctive discipline alongside theology, nor viewed as something which precedes theology. Theologians who take this approach do not all agree as to just what role philosophical reflection should play in theology, and there are many differences concerning the appropriate resources for such reflection. But they share the view that theology has a responsibility to demonstrate that its contents are related to our common human experience.

Among theologians who accept the importance of philosophy, some do their own philosophical thinking and incorporate the results within their theology. Such theologians pursue philosophical reflection as an aspect of their theological endeavors. Their interest in theological questions leads them to engage in philosophical inquiry. Certain theologians are just as well-known for their philosophical as for their theological work, and some of the most influential philosophical writings in Western thought are the work of theologians. Anselm's argument for the existence of God is a good example. The writings of Thomas Aquinas contain many others.

Although it is possible for theologians to develop their own philosophical positions, most of them make use of the philosophical work of others, often drawing from widely accepted philosophical sources.[56] Many early Christian writers relied on Platonic and neoplatonic writings. Augustine made extensive use of neoplatonic ideas. Later on theologians relied heavily on the works of Aristotle. Here, of course, Thomas Aquinas is the outstanding figure. Occasionally Aquinas wrote on Aristotle's work from a purely philosophical perspective.[57] But he is certainly best known for the way and the extent to which he incorporates Aristotelian philosophy within his theological system. In fact, his work is often described as a monumental synthesis of Christian faith and Aristotelian philosophy.

In our own time as well, theologians make frequent use of specific philosophical positions, or schools of thought, as they endeavor to interpret the contents of Christian faith. Along with Rudolf Bultmann, who is famous for his call to "demythologize" the New Testament, many theologians have employed the insights of existentialist philosophy.[58] And a number of British and American theologians find the writings of Alfred North Whitehead helpful in expressing the Christian faith today—so much so that "process theology" is now an influential movement in contemporary theology. A widely discussed issue in recent years has been the use of Marxist philosophy as a resource for Christian theology. Many liberation theologians believe that a Marxist analysis of human society is indispensable to an interpretation of the Christian message that is responsive to the social and political situation confronting the church today.[59]

While some theologians depend rather heavily on the work of one particular philosopher, or one school of thought, such as existentialism or process philosophy, other theologians draw on a variety of philosophical sources. Schubert M. Ogden proposes a combination of the insights of process philosophy and existentialism.[60] In his complex "revisionist model for contemporary theology," David Tracy draws on linguistic analysis, phenomenology and transcendental Thomism.[61]

Theologians not only rely on different philosophical resources, they employ these resources in different ways. Some assign philosophy a rather limited role in their theological program. They appeal to philosophy in selected spots as they explain Christian beliefs, and once the specific need is met, they move on. No doubt the most widespread use theologians make of philosophy is to help formulate the doctrine of God. Traditional approaches to this doctrine include a discussion of God's existence which describes or advances various philosophical arguments.[62] Some theologians treat the existence of God as a philosophical matter entirely.[63] They make it the one theological point where philosophy has the last word.

In contrast to occasional use of this sort, other thinkers give philosophy a much broader theological role. In fact, some believe that theology should be carried out in continuous conversation with philosophy. For them, philosophy is a major theological tributary, along with the Bible and historic expressions of Christian faith. And the question of the right philosophy is not just one of several questions for theological method, it is the most important methodological question of all. Let us note the work of two theologians who incorporate extensive philosophical reflection within their theological projects.

No contemporary theologian is better known for integrating theology and philosophy than Paul Tillich. Tillich describes theology as the attempt to "penetrate the meaning" of the biblical symbols which are basic to Christian faith by using philosophical and psychological concepts.[64] Theology therefore has a twofold character. It seeks to express the eternal truth of the Christian message within a temporal situation comprising many different cultural forms. To achieve this goal Tillich proposes a "method of correlation," which brings the two essential elements in theology—message and situation—together in a constructive relationship.[65]

Tillich rejects the approaches to natural theology we described earlier. He objects to the older theological practice of providing a section on natural theology as a preamble to a theology of revelation. And he rejects theological proposals like Schleiermacher's, in which a general philosophy of religion serves the same purpose. He also objects to the neo-orthodox demand that theology be based exclusively on the contents of revelation. His "apologetic theology" is superior to all of them, he believes, because it brings philosophy directly into the theological program and gives it an integral role to play.

Following the method of correlation, Tillich divides each major part of his theological system into two sections. The titles of the parts reflect this scheme: "Reason and Revelation," "Being and God," "Existence and the Christ," "Life and the Spirit," and "History and the Kingdom of God." The sections are correlated in a question-answer arrangement. The first section of each part develops a question by carefully analyzing the human situation. The second formulates an answer to this question out of the contents of Christian revelation. As the word "correlation" implies, the two sections are intimately related. According to Tillich, the question is asked under the impact of the answer, and the answer is formulated under the guidance of the question.[66]

Philosophy plays an important role in this procedure. According to Tillich, the first section of each part, the analysis of human existence, is the work of philosophy. And philosophy contributes to the second, or answering, phase of each part, too, inasmuch as an answer always depends to some degree on its question. As Tillich says, "man cannot receive answers to questions he never has asked." Although the form of the answers depends on philosophy, their content derives solely from revelation. They would not be genuine answers unless they were "spoken" to human existence from beyond it.[67] The role of philosophy, then, is to analyze the human situation and determine the essential questions it raises, and in so doing, to prepare us to receive the message which revelation provides.

Tillich's nuanced view of the role of philosophy in theology leads to an interesting assessment of the most important part of traditional natural theology—the arguments for the existence of God. It is exactly what we would expect, given the role assigned to philosophy by the method of correlation. According to Tillich, the proofs help to formulate the question of God, but they do not represent an answer to it. In his words, "The arguments for the existence of God neither are arguments nor are they proof of the existence of God. They are expressions of the *question* of God which is implied in human finitude."[68]

On the negative side, the arguments have two major problems. In speaking of God's existence, as they do, the various arguments treat God as something which exists within the totality of being, as a being alongside or above other beings. But God is not *a* being, Tillich insists, God is *being-itself*, the very structure of reality. To speak of God as "existing" is therefore to relegate divine being to the status of a finite being. The other difficulty concerns the method of arguing to a conclusion. Every argument derives conclusions about something sought from something that is given. In theistic arguments the world is given and God is sought, so their conclusions about God are derived from the nature of the world. But a God derived from the world cannot transcend the world. Such a God is nothing more than a missing part of the world. Consequently, we cannot move from the special characteristics of the world to the existence of a highest being conceived in terms derived from finite existence.[69]

While they cannot answer it, Tillich maintains, theistic arguments help us immensely as we address the question of God. They reveal that this question is implied in the very structure of being, and they demonstrate both the possibility and the necessity of answering it. The ontological argument shows that an awareness of our own finitude includes an awareness of the infinite, and this makes the question of God possible. The cosmological arguments show that the question of God is necessary. As finite beings, we experience the threat of non-being in the form of anxiety, and this drives us to ask if there is anything in reality that makes it possible for us to overcome this threat. According to Tillich this, too, is the question of God.[70]

For Paul Tillich, then, philosophy is an integral part of Christian theology. Its role is to demonstrate the relevance of the Christian message to the fundamental questions of human existence. Appeals to public evidence therefore do more than prepare the way for theology, or defend its conclusions from criticism. They do not determine the specific contents of the Christian message, but they contribute significantly to its formulation.

If Tillich goes beyond traditional approaches to natural theology and brings philosophy directly into theology, other theologians go even farther. For Schubert M. Ogden, philosophy contributes to the content as well as the expression of Christian beliefs.

Ogden defines Christian theology as "the fully reflective understanding of the Christian witness of faith as decisive for human existence."[71] In other words, theology is the attempt to express the Christian witness of faith, as embodied in the Scriptures, in the most adequate conceptual form possible. From this definition it follows that every theological proposal must satisfy two criteria: it must be at once understandable within the present situation and appropriate to the essential claims of the Bible.[72] In other words, it must be conceptually adequate and biblically faithful.

Ogden maintains that both criteria come directly from faith itself. At the center of Christian faith stands this claim: the only true answer to the question of the ultimate meaning of our existence is the answer re-presented to us in Jesus Christ.[73] But this implies the further claim that it meets the conditions of truth that are given everywhere within experience.[74] Consequently, theology has no basis for any of its claims except our common human experience,[75] and properly makes no assertion that public evidence cannot support.

Ogden believes that the second criterion is implicit in the first. So, a theological proposal which is genuinely faithful to the Bible will also be adequate to human experience. Any attempt to express the claims of Christian faith must therefore examine our common human experience to determine if these claims are corroborated. According to our earlier analysis, however, this is exactly what natural theology involves. So, for Ogden, Christian theology and natural theology are essentially the same thing. Their common task is to assess the contents of Christian faith from the perspective of our common human experience.

Ogden also maintains that Christian theology must establish the truth of theism—another task traditionally assigned to natural theology. His reasoning takes the following steps. Ogden accepts Rudolf Bultmann's call for a "demythologizing" of the New Testament. He believes that the Bible expresses its message in the mythical terms of an outmoded worldview, and this message must be reinterpreted if it is to be intelligible to people today. He also shares Bultmann's conviction that existential philosophy provides helpful categories for achieving this objective. Accordingly, we can understand the "life in faith" of which the Bible speaks as authentic historical existence.[76] Ogden further believes that authentic existence is universally available to human beings, in view of the universal accountability the Bible assigns to them. This, in turn, presupposes that divine revelation is a universal phenomenon, and that God is universally present in human life.[77]

All of Christian theology thus comes down to the single question of God. The reality of God constitutes "the *one* essential point to all authentic faith and witness," and as a result, "the *sole* theme of all valid Christian theology."[78] The central task for theology, then, is to validate the truth of theism, to demonstrate that God is a universal factor in human experience. And to do this, theology must rely on philosophy, because the task of philosophy is to bring the basic presuppositions of human existence to the level of reflective consciousness. Consequently, the question of the "right" philosophy is the most important question theology ever has to answer.[79]

To answer the question of God, Ogden presents a two-stage argument for theism. First, he demonstrates that the idea of God is the most adequate account we can give of certain experiences in which all human beings share. Then he formulates a conception of God designed to do justice to these experiences. Everything we do, Ogden begins, reflects an underlying confidence in the meaning and worth of life, something he calls a "basic existential faith." And the word "God" refers primarily to whatever it is about reality as a whole that calls forth this fundamental trust we have.[80] Consequently, faith in the worthwhileness of life is nothing other than faith in God.

Now, if we identify God as the objective ground of our confidence in the final worth of existence, then our concept of God must correspond to this essential aspect of our experience. The nature of this confidence suggests two essential characteristics which must be applied to God. To provide a basis for our confidence in the worth of life, God must be relative to our life in the world; everything we experience must have a genuine effect on God. In addition, God's relatedness to our life must itself be absolute. Ogden concludes that the only view of God which accounts for both elements in our faith in the worth of life is one which conceives of God as both relative and absolute.[81]

Because the philosophical writings of Alfred North Whitehead and Charles Hartshorne contain precisely such a twofold, or dipolar view of God, Ogden regards their work as an important resource for theology today. Unlike the classical view of God as a being who is utterly absolute, necessary, immutable, and eternal, "neoclassical theism," as Hartshorne calls it, conceives God as both absolute and relative, both changeless and changing, both necessary and contingent, both eternal and temporal. This view of God, Ogden believes, satisfies both criteria incumbent on theology. It is conceptually adequate, and it is faithful to the claims of Scripture.[82]

For Ogden as for Tillich, then, philosophy has an integral role to play in Christian theology. But it has more to do in his proposal than formulate the questions to which Christian faith supplies the answers. For Ogden, the primary objective of theology is to show that the claims of faith have the support of our common human experience. Because the central task of philosophy is to analyze the features of our basic experience, theology must incorporate the task and insights of philosophy in its work.

Our analysis of theological responses to the question of natural theology reveals a wide range of views. At one end of the spectrum we find neo-orthodox thinkers excluding public evidence as irrelevant to theology. At the other end, we find Schubert Ogden claiming that theology not only needs the support of public evidence but may not include anything that does not have it. In between there are several other positions. Some theologians believe that an appeal to public evidence may be helpful in defending Christian faith, *after* its contents are established on the basis of revelation. Others, like Langdon Gilkey, believe that the challenges to religious faith today make such an appeal necessary *before* the contents of faith can be expressed. Somewhere nearby stands the traditional two-story concept which makes natural theology the foundation on which systematic theology rests. With these options before us, we now turn to the task of formulating our own response to the question of natural theology.

The Need for Natural Theology

All the positions we reviewed have important things to tell us, but our own answer to the question of natural theology does not coincide precisely with any of them. To begin with, there seem to be compelling reasons for including appeals to public evidence within theology. One is the existence of strong biblical and historical precedents. As we saw in Chapter 5, the Bible itself contains appeals to public evidence. It identifies phenomena in the natural world and in human experience which point to the reality of the Creator. A faithful exposition of the contents of revelation, therefore, must take account of this evidence. According to the book of Acts, the preaching of the apostles cited general human experience as supporting the reality of God (Acts 14, 17). From the beginning, then, evidence available to reason has played a role in expounding the contents of Christian faith.

Another reason for including appeals to public evidence within theology is the concrete situation in which the church is called to proclaim the Gospel today. While the primary obligation of theology is to interpret faithfully the contents of revelation, it always pursues this task within specific historical circumstances, and it cannot express its beliefs effectively without taking this situation into account. Both liberal and conservative theologians make this point. According to Paul Tillich, we cannot throw the message like a stone at the situation and expect people to understand it.[83] Similarly, Francis Schaeffer declares, "You have to preach the simple gospel so that it is simple to the person to whom you are talking, or it is no longer simple."[84] Wolfhart Pannenberg insists that Christian theology in the modern age must consult the results of contemporary studies of human nature. We have no alternative, he asserts, because "individuals are not free to choose the problematic situation in which they prefer to play a part and make a contribution."[85] In its effort to communicate the claims of faith, then, Christian theology can never avoid the specific form of unbelief confronting it. And to meet this challenge it must find public or rational evidence to support these claims.

Such appeals are particularly important in the social environment of contemporary Western culture. Modern atheism is different from its historic precedents "both in its extent and its cultural establishment." Atheism is a widespread and respected intellectual position today—something that was never the case prior to the nineteenth century. Even more significant, atheism has become a pervasive social phenomenon as well. Schubert Ogden observes that the reality of God is now expressly denied on an unprecedented scale.[86] In the opinion of another scholar, "the rise of a radical godlessness" is "as much a part of the consciousness of millions of ordinary human beings as it is the persuasion of the intellectual."[87]

Another distinctive feature of our current situation is the radical nature of the atheistic challenge to faith. It consists in the view that language about God is, quite literally, non-sense; it fails to satisfy the minimal criteria of cognitive meaning. The secularist response to Christian faith is not to say, "I disagree with you," but, "I don't understand you. It is not that your affirmations of God are erroneous. They are meaningless."

In the face of this challenge, theology must demonstrate the meaningfulness of fundamental Christian claims. People will not be able even to consider what Christianity has to say unless they can understand its language, and in the present climate, we cannot take that for granted. Consequently, theology must explore its basic assumptions about reality as it explicates the contents of Christian faith, and for this purpose appeals to public evidence are indispensable.

The pervasiveness of unbelief today also renders ineffective some recent attempts to avoid the task of defending theism. Over the past ten years or so a number of thinkers have responded to rationalist rejections of belief in God by questioning the premises of foundationalism. As we observed in Chapter 3, anti-foundationalists reject the view that all reasonable beliefs are either self-evident or incorrigible, or else demonstrably derived from beliefs that fall into these categories. Instead, they argue, our noetic structure contains a number of beliefs that are properly basic and do not fit any of these categories. So, in spite of the fact that belief in God is neither self-evident nor incorrigible, nor derivable directly from beliefs that are, there is no reason for us not to regard it as a basic belief, and therefore as reasonable.[88]

Many thinkers find this strategy ineffective in defending theism, even if we do have a number of basic beliefs of the sort just described. In response to anti-foundationalism, Antony Kenny agrees that there are basic beliefs, which do not satisfy the rigid foundationalist criteria of rationality, but he denies that belief in God is one of them. "The proposition that God exists," he observes, "is not one which must be basic to the belief-structure of every rational being."[89] There were times in the history of Western civilization when it seemed to be, but that is manifestly not the case today. So, it will not do to argue that basic beliefs exist and assert that belief in God is one of them, as if that sufficed to establish its rational status.

The change in intellectual climate referred to not only requires Christian theology to make use of public evidence, it alters the theological role such evidence plays. When Thomas Aquinas incorporated the famous five ways for proving that God exists in his *Summa Theologiae*, virtually everyone already believed in God. His objective in developing these arguments was not to offer evidence for God's existence for the benefit of people who doubted it. Instead, he wanted to show just how belief in God's existence fits within the general framework of Christian beliefs. He also wanted to demonstrate that Aristotelian philosophy—the source of these five arguments—was compatible with the contents of faith and represented a valuable resource for Christian thought. So, Aquinas' use of philosophical arguments had intra-theological rather than apologetic motivations.

As we have seen, the intellectual environment surrounding Christians today is radically different, and so is the challenge confronting theology. In the face of pervasive doubt about God's existence, the pressing task confronting theology is not to assemble evidence in favor of a belief in God that people already have. The stakes are higher now. The challenge confronting theology today is to show that it makes sense to believe in God, not just for people who already do, but for people who don't. For contemporary theology, developing evidence for the reality of God is more than a methodological exercise; the viability of Christian faith may depend on it.

Natural theology is important today, not only because the church is in the world, but because the world is also in the church. The current climate of unbelief has effects inside as well as outside the Christian community. Many who participate in the corporate life of the church do so largely for social reasons, not out of confidence in the truth of Christian claims. Indeed, many church members have serious doubts about traditional Christian beliefs. As a result, appeals to public evidence to support the claims of faith are important for those who are within the Christian community. The implications for theology are significant. If we cannot draw a clear line between the church and the world as far as belief is concerned, then we should not try to make a sharp distinction between systematic theology and apologetics—the one for people inside the church, the other for people outside. All theology today must include an apologetic aspect.

The source and nature of our basic perspective on reality provide yet another reason for theology to give careful attention to our common human experience. As we just noted, we cannot evade the explicit challenges to faith that arise within our culture, such as the probing questions modern thinkers ask about God, because they often affect people inside as well as outside the church. But in a larger sense the spirit of our age affects all our thinking. The prevalent ideas and assumptions of our time exert an inevitable influence on our perspective. We use concepts and values that are part of the culture we live in. We acquire the concepts and values of our culture unconsciously, through the natural process of growing up and participating in society. Since they figure in all our thinking, these aspects of our mental outlook inevitably affect our thinking about religion. The work of theologians inevitably rests on what John Cobb describes as "presuppositions that are subject to evaluation in the context of general reflection."[90] In order to give our religious beliefs intellectual expression—to explicate the contents of faith—we must therefore give our basic presuppositions a careful review.

Actually, the real question is not whether we *should* make use of contemporary concepts in our theological endeavors, because they will have an effect on our thinking whether we want them to or not. The real question is whether such concepts will make their way into our theology imperceptibly, or whether they will be carefully analyzed and critically evaluated. If we are not explicitly aware of the contemporary ideas at work in our thinking, the chances increase that they will influence our thinking unduly and distort our understanding of religion. As Bernard Ramm observes, "The more we reflect on our philosophical coloring, the better chance we have of neutralizing it in our theology."[91] As we reflect on the contents of faith, then, we cannot dispense with an analysis of those concepts which we share with all thinking people.

For a number of important reasons, then, a careful account of our common human experience has an important role to play in our theological reflection. To summarize, natural theology is the attempt to demonstrate the relevance of Christian beliefs to general human experience and to show that evidence available to any thoughtful person corroborates the claims of the Christian community. Such efforts assist people in understanding the contents of faith and help to show that faith is intellectually responsible. An expression of Christian faith that hopes to receive a sympathetic hearing in contemporary society, or even to be taken seriously, cannot ignore the questions it raises in people's minds, and appeals to public evidence can be vital in meeting them.

The Role of Natural Theology

It is one thing to assert that philosophical reflection has a role to play in theology. It is much more difficult to specify just what that role should be, and it would take a full-fledged "foundational theology" to spell it out in detail—an endeavor that lies beyond the scope of our efforts here. We will conclude our discussion of reason and the contents of faith by trying to sketch in outline the intra-theological significance of reason.

For Christian faith to be a viable option for thinking people today, we just argued, its claims must make sense to them, and for its claims to be intelligible, they must have the support of public evidence. Consequently, Christian theology should include natural theology. But this endorsement of natural theology leaves some important questions unanswered. First, how much public support do Christian claims need in order for faith to be responsible? Is there a certain amount of evidence, a "critical mass," we might say, that must accumulate before someone is entitled to believe? Second, just where do Christian claims need public support—throughout the entire body of beliefs, or only in certain parts? In other words, how many beliefs need such support? Does each belief require an equal amount of evidence? If *most* of its claims have the support of public evidence would this make faith responsible? Are certain beliefs more important than others and therefore more in need of rational support? If so, which ones?

Not surprisingly, theologians give different answers to questions like these. As we have seen, those who affirm the value of natural theology do not necessarily agree on its theological function. Some feel that appeals to public evidence are appropriate within a limited area of theological inquiry, such as the existence of God; others extend them to the entire doctrinal system. Thomas Aquinas maintains that the scope of our natural knowledge of God is much smaller than the scope of revealed knowledge, while Schubert Ogden insists that the two are essentially identical—that Christians can claim nothing on the basis of revelation which does not have the support of public evidence as well.

My own conviction is that we should affirm but not exaggerate the theological role of natural theology. While we cannot ignore what reason has to say, as we have argued at length, we must also avoid giving reason too much to say. Appeals to public evidence have an important place in the attempt to explicate the contents of Christian faith, yet other things are just as important. As we saw in Chapter 4, faithfulness to Scripture is the primary criterion of theological adequacy. The purpose of natural theology, therefore, is to place reason in the service of faith, not to give it mastery over faith.[92]

As for the place, or places, within a theological system which require public support, several things need to be said. What we might call the Christian doctrinal scheme does not consist of a series of beliefs, lined up like identical beads on a string. Its components are neither independent of each other, nor do they all have equal importance, or—it might be better to say—do they perform the same function. As we observed in our earlier discussion of Christian theology, the claims of faith are not discrete propositional elements, essentially unrelated to one another, but interconnected aspects of an organic whole. Consequently, every belief is important, but some are more vital, or more central, than others—just as a car can run without a muffler, but not without a carburetor (or a fuel injection system), or a human being can live without limbs, but not without lungs.

This "organismic" view of Christian beliefs has implications for our present concern. First, it means that public evidence which supports faith is helpful wherever it becomes available. If essential Christian beliefs are interconnected, then public support anywhere strengthens the overall case for faith everywhere. It is therefore appropriate and important for theologians to appeal to public evidence anytime it can help to illustrate or answer questions about the claims of faith. And as such evidence accumulates throughout the theological system, the case grows stronger for the intellectual responsibility of faith.[93]

Take, for example, the traditional Christian hope for an individual human future beyond death. Such a belief raises questions about the bases of personal identity. Is it possible for human beings to recover or maintain their identity after death? Can the *same* person occupy two radically different and temporally separated stages of existence—our present earthly life and a glorified, immortal life in the future? It takes careful reflection to answer questions like these. Again, with its strong affirmation of human community, the doctrine of the church raises questions about the social dimension of human life. To what extent and in what ways do human beings depend on communities? Is a higher level of fulfillment available to human beings with a strong sense of being together than it is to human beings who have a heightened sense of their separate individuality? Careful reflection on the nature of human relationships can help to answer such questions, and in so doing can render the contents of faith respectable or even attractive to thinking people.

Although they are potentially helpful in relation to all the contents of faith, appeals to common human experience are particularly important in the connection with certain Christian beliefs because they occupy a vital position in the structure of faith. In fact, in some cases such appeals are indispensable. This is true of the doctrine of God, especially the question of God's existence. For one thing, the reality of God is absolutely central to Christian faith. Unless God exists, as we argued earlier, it is next to impossible to make sense out of anything else in Christianity. For another, it is precisely in connection with belief in God that the most fundamental challenges to faith always arise, as the most pressing challenges of our own time testify. Third, and perhaps paradoxically, this particular belief is just where the Bible seems to indicate we should find the strongest public evidence to support the claims of faith. The Bible attests to abundant public evidence for God's creative power. So, in relation to the reality of God rational support for faith is both most needed and most accessible.

In numerous ways, then, throughout a systematic theological program, rational investigation, appeals to public evidence, can assist in explaining and recommending the contents of faith. And at certain points, appeals to public evidence are crucial to establishing the intellectual responsibility of faith. Although public evidence is helpful anywhere, however, it is unrealistic to demand it everywhere. Just as some beliefs are more central or basic to faith than others, some are more accessible than others to rational inquiry and enjoy more public support. For example, the belief that human beings are "fallen," that there is a brokenness or fault that permeates the human condition, has abundant support of the sort that any observant person could recognize. In contrast, the belief that God is three-in-one enjoys far less public evidence, if it has any at all. To demand that every claim of faith have the same amount of public evidence before we can conclude that faith is a responsible commitment ignores the textured nature of Christian beliefs. As we shall see in Part 3, it also ignores the nature of the experience of faith. The things that lead to important personal commitments like faith are factors we can never neatly quantify or calculate, so demands for certain amounts of evidence to support specific beliefs overlook the protean and concrete character of religion.

The textured quality of faith requires us to qualify the theological role of natural theology, or philosophical reflection. There are significant differences between theology and philosophy, and it is important to keep the two enterprises distinct. Not every matter of philosophical concern is necessarily of theological interest. And, as we just noted, not every aspect of Christian faith is accessible to philosophical inquiry. Consequently, we may appeal to common human experience in explicating the contents of faith, but we cannot reduce the contents of faith to what reason alone can establish. The Christian community may affirm a good deal that could never be derived solely from an observation of common human experience. So, there is validity in the time-honored distinction between the truths of reason and the truths of revelation, and the relative content of natural theology will be considerably smaller in scope than that of revealed theology.

It is important to acknowledge the potential liabilities of granting philosophy a significant role in theology. It can be just as damaging to give philosophy too much to say in developing our theology as too little. As Paul Tillich acknowledged, an attempt to express the contents of faith in the terms and concepts of contemporary culture runs the risk of losing the essential message in the process.[94] The sorry death-of-God episode in American theology illustrates the catastrophic effect of applying inappropriate philosophical criteria to religious belief. Its proponents were determined to satisfy narrow empiricist criteria of linguistic meaning and in the process they lost essential elements of the Gospel. So, theology cannot ignore the neo-orthodox caveat against an inappropriate reliance on philosophy. Theologians must select and use their philosophical resources with great care. Two cautionary notes are called for.

First, theologians should be wary of regarding any one philosophical resource as "the" philosophy for Christian thought. Any attempt to express the contents of Christian faith in contemporary thought-forms runs the risk of losing the content of the Gospel, but the risk of forcing the contents of faith artificially into a philosophical mold increases if one particular philosophical position, such as process thought, is regarded as the only viable resource for Christian theology today. There is a danger that those who are deeply committed to one school of thought will read their philosophical concepts into the claims of Christianity, instead of using philosophical concepts to help them express the meaning of Christian faith.[95]

Theologians must also beware of allowing philosophy to determine the course of theological reflection. Christian theology cannot ignore the questions which the claims of faith raise in the minds of thinking people, but it must not allow the world, so to speak, to set its agenda and determine its message. Theologians preoccupied with meeting the demands of the modern mind have occasionally lost sight of the distinctive contents of Christianity. When that happens, instead of becoming more intelligible and therefore more attractive to thinking people, what they have to say becomes much less interesting. Recent writers have issued some strong warnings about this danger.

In *The Flight From Authority*, Jeffrey Stout appeals to the dilemma of modern theology which Alisdair MacIntyre described over twenty years ago. According to MacIntyre, "any presentation of theism which is able to secure a hearing from a secular audience has undergone a transformation that has evacuated it entirely of its theistic content." Stout agrees. The very attempts to make theology more interesting to modern culture, he argues, have actually made it less so. As he sees it, there is irreducible paradox in Christianity. And "to leave the paradoxical features out . . . is to make theistic vocabulary superfluous." Far from rendering Christian faith more attractive, those who seek an alternative to confrontation with the "cultured despisers" of religion only give them "less and less in which to disbelieve."

Stout is relentless. Theologians who try to have it both ways, he insists, to "remain within the secular academy without abandoning the community of faith, have often been reduced to seemingly endless methodological foreplay." They keep talking about what it means to talk about faith and never get around to doing it. As a result, they lose respect on all fronts. They are alienated from both the academy and the community of faith.[96] According to Stout, fidelity to the Christian message and meaningfulness to contemporary culture are incompatible. A theological attempt to gain contemporary intellectual and cultural relevance is an exercise in self-destruction.

Michael J. Buckley reaches similar conclusions from a study of the development of modern atheism. Instead of strengthening confidence in God's reality, various attempts to prove the existence of God have consistently weakened it. History reveals that shifting the strategy of the arguments for God's existence only produced different bases for denying it. In the face of arguments that God is the presupposition or the corollary of nature, natural philosophy eventually disposed of God. When thinkers like

Natural Theology: The Theological Question 203

Kant and Schleiermacher turned from the natural world to human experience as a basis for affirming the reality of God, their efforts led, not to a denial of atheism, but to its transposition into a new key. Eventually the denial of god became an absolute necessity for human existence. So, "the shift in theological foundations evoked, carried, and even shaped its corresponding atheism."[97]

According to Buckley, the origin of atheism in the intellectual culture of the West lies with "the self-alienation of religion itself."[98] Atheism does not arise out of a lack of adequate evidence for the reality of God. It comes from the more fundamental mistake theology made of appealing to philosophy to begin with. Modern atheism resulted from the willingness of theologians to relegate the question of God's existence to the arena of philosophical discourse. Once the question of God's existence became a philosophical rather than a religious question, the triumph of atheism was assured. Religion generated its own denial, then, when theology entrusted itself to philosophy. To quote Buckley, "Religion protested that it could not speak for itself, that only philosophy could argue for it. Philosophy spoke, and its final word was no. In failing to assert its own competence, in commissioning philosophy with its defense, religion shaped its own eventual negation." Atheism "is the secret contradiction within a religion that denies its own abilities to deal cognitively with what is central to its nature."[99]

Buckley is not opposed to philosophical theories of God per se. The problem is allowing such theories to supplant the religious concept of God which is central to Christianity. Nor is Buckley opposed to arguments for the existence of God. The problem is arguments which ignore the sort of evidence which could support a distinctly religious idea of God—namely, the evidence of religious experience and the concrete history of Christianity. "As the question is primarily religious," he states, "so the religious experience of human beings provides evidence that cannot be supplanted by something else."[100] In affirming the reality of God, then, theology must never evacuate the concept of God of its distinctive religious content.

The contentions of Stout and Buckley raise obvious questions for our concern here. They seem to call for an emphatic rejection of anything like natural theology in both concept and method. Stout criticizes the attempt to render the contents of faith accessible to contemporary culture. Buckley criticizes philosophical arguments for theism as inadequate to the Christian concept of God. These concerns are worth taking seriously, but they do not require us to give a negative answer to the question of natural theology. As we noted above, there are important reasons why Christian theology must include an appeal to public evidence, to our common human experience, as it seeks to express the contents of faith. These reasons arise not only from the situation confronting Christians today, but also from the very content of faith itself. Both internal and external considerations require Christians to take the modern mind into account as they interpret their message.

At the same time, we can learn some important things from these critiques of modern theology. One is that every aspect of Christian theology must remain distinctly Christian. No part of the theological system should be subsumed under philosophy, not even the question of God's existence. As we mentioned above, it is appropriate to appeal to publicly accessible evidence at any point in the theological system, but at no time does theology give philosophy the last word or the only word on the subject. So, when theology appeals to common human experience, it does not set aside the distinctive contents of faith and replace them with something else. Instead, it makes use of philosophical terms and concepts in the attempt to explicate and illuminate those contents. Accordingly, a Christian doctrine of God may rely on philosophical reflection in places, but at no point does the doctrine cease being theological and become purely philosophical. Even when it deals with public evidence for the existence of God, theology does so as theology, not as philosophy. Theology never collapses into philosophy, nor abandons its work to philosophy.

Our affirmation of the importance of natural theology leaves us with an important question. What do the applications of reason to the contents of faith respectively described in Chapters

3 and 6 represent? Are they conflicting conceptions of theology—one right and the other wrong? Are they alternative ways of doing theology—each with its distinctive strengths and weaknesses? Are they complementary moments in a comprehensive theological program?

Some theologians maintain that only the first concept of theology is acceptable, while others insist on some version of the second. For neo-orthodox theologians, the formulation of a systematic inventory of the contents of faith which *assumes* their truth rather than *arguing* for it is the only legitimate course theology can take. In contrast, for someone like Schubert M. Ogden such a concept of theology is inadequate. As he defines it, the discipline involves interpreting the contents of faith from the perspective of our contemporary situation, and this requires a philosophical assessment of the truth-claims of faith. For other theologians, these two concepts of theology represent enterprises that are different, but not necessarily competitive. John Macquarrie entitles Parts One and Two of his book *Principles of Christian Theology* "philosophical theology" and "symbolic theology," indicating that the two are distinct but complementary moments of theological reflection.[101]

I think that Macquarrie's position is preferable to the alternatives on this point. It is possible to explore the contents of Christian faith from within the perspective of the Christian community, or on the assumption that these contents are true, and a great deal can thus be learned about the central concepts and symbols of Christianity. At the same time, this interior exposition of the contents of faith does not meet all the obligations which theology faces, particularly in the modern world. An adequate formulation of Christian faith today needs appeals to public evidence to support its basic claims. So, in addition to systematic or "symbolic" theology, there is an important function for philosophical theology, too. As far as organization is concerned, it is possible to pursue these enterprises together within a single theological proposal, rather than relegating them to different sections as Macquarrie does, but it is also important to keep in mind the significant distinctions between them.

Summary

In this section we have seen that there is a close and complex relation between reason and the contents of faith. In Chapter 3 we examined Christian theology as the application of reason to the contents of faith "from inside," that is from within the perspective of the Christian community. It seeks to explore the beliefs of the Christian community from a perspective which assumes the truth of those beliefs. Accordingly, it draws conclusions from the private evidence which the community accepts as authoritative—principally the Bible. It also takes into account the development of Christian doctrines and the beliefs of the living and dynamic community of faith.

Chapters 4, 5 and 6 all dealt with the relation between reason and the contents of faith in light of public evidence—apart from the specific perspective of faith or the special illumination of revelation. The first question was whether the contents of faith would permit such investigation. The second question was whether such an investigation yielded positive results, whether there is any publicly accessible evidence which supports the claims of faith. The third question was whether such evidence has a role to play within the task of Christian theology. Our answer to each question was affirmative. We concluded that revelation points to the presence of demonstrable continuities between faith and reason; that a careful examination of public evidence supports the contents of faith; and that appeals to the results of this endeavor contribute to the work of Christian theology. At the same time, we emphasized the fact that the scope of these continuities is very limited. And, as just noted, theology must not abandon its special perspective on the contents of faith in its appeals to public evidence.

We turn now to the second major aspect of our question. What is the relation of reason to the experience of faith?

---

[1] J. K. S. Reid, *Christian Apologetics* (Grand Rapids, MI: William B. Eerdmans Publishing Co., 1969), p. 13.

[2] G. K. Chesterton, perhaps this century's most famous apologist, was a convert to Catholicism. J. N. D. Anderson, an Anglican layman, is an attorney (see his book, *A Lawyer*

Natural Theology: The Theological Question 207

Among the Theologians [Grand Rapids, MI: William B. Eerdmans Publishing Co., 1973]). The Preface to one of Lewis' books contains these words: "If any real theologian reads these pages he will very easily see that they are the work of a layman and an amateur" (*The Problem of Pain* [New York: The Macmillan Company, 1962], p. 10). Anderson writes, "I make no pretentions to being a theologian and am very conscious that I am venturing to stray into an academic discipline other than my own" (*A Lawyer Among the Theologians*, p. 9).

[3] In the Preface to *Mere Christianity*, C. S. Lewis writes, "Ever since I became a Christian I have thought that the best, perhaps the only, service I could do for my unbelieving neighbors was to explain and defend the belief that has been common to nearly all Christians at all times" (*Mere Christianity* [New York: The Macmillan Company, 1960], p. vi).

[4] "Dogmatic Constitution on Divine Revelation" (*Dei Verbum*), art. 6; *The Documents of Vatican II*, ed. Walter M. Abbott (New York: America Press, 1966), p. 114.

[5] Thomas Aquinas, *The Division and Methods of the Sciences: Questions V and VI of his Commentary on the De Trinitate of Boethius*, trans. Armand Maurer (3rd rev. ed.; Toronto: Pontifical Institute of Medieval Studies, 1963), pp. 41-46; *Summa Theologiae*, ed. Thomas Gilby, O.P. (Garden City, NY: Image Books, 1969), Ia, 1,1 ad 2.

[6] *Summa Theologiae*, Ia, 12,12.

[7] Alan Richardson/John Macquarrie, "Natural Theology," *The Westminster Dictionary of Christian Theology*, ed. Alan Richardson and John Bowden (Philadelphia: The Westminster Press, 1983), p. 393.

[8] Francis A. Schaeffer, *Escape From Reason* (Downers Grove, IL: Inter-Varsity Press, 1968).

[9] *Escape From Reason*, pp. 42-43; cf. *How Should We Then Live? The Rise and Decline of Western Thought and Culture* (Old Tappan, NJ: Fleming H. Revell Company, 1976), p. 55.

[10] According to Schaeffer, "the hallmark of the present generation of humanistic thinking" is "the acceptance of the dichotomy, the separation of optimism about meaning and values from the area of reason" (*How Should We Then Live?*, p. 255).

[11] The setting and the purpose of the five ways are distinctly theological, rather than philosophical. As part of the *Summa Theologiae*, they contribute directly to theological reflection on God's nature. In this context, their function is not to give a philosophical demonstration of God's existence, but to assist theology as it explores the essence of God on the basis of revelation. They show that God's existence can be inferred from his effects in the world, so what little reason can know of God is consistent with the contents of revelation.

[12] A good example of this approach to philosophy in relation to theology is Langdon Gilkey, *Naming the Whirlwind: The Renewal of God-Language* (Indianapolis: The Bobbs-Merrill Company, 1969).

[13] Friedrich Schleiermacher, *The Christian Faith*, ed. H. R. Mackintosh and J. S. Stewart (2nd ed.; Edinburgh: T. & T. Clark, 1928), par. 100.3.

[14] Ibid., pars. 15, 15.2. Accordingly, "all doctrines properly so-called must be extracted from the Christian religious self-consciousness, i.e., the inward experience of Christian people." And, "the whole compass of Christian doctrine" is coextensive with "the facts of religious self-consciousness." "Its only purpose is to describe and elucidate that experience" (Ibid., pars. 64.1, 11, 100.3).

[15] Ibid., par. 24.4.

[16] Ibid., pars. 2, 2.1.

[17] Schleiermacher, *Brief Outline on the Study of Theology*, trans. Terrence N. Tice (Richmond, VA: John Knox Press, 1966), pars. 226, 213, 214, 24.

[18] *The Christian Faith*, par. 2.1.

[19] Ibid., pars. 100.3, 33.3, 13 Postscript.

208 Reason and the Contours of Faith

[20] Ibid., pars. 33.3, 33.
[21] Ibid., pars. 4.1-3, 5.1, 33.
[22] Ibid., pars. 4.4, 4, 6.1.
[23] *Naming the Whirlwind: The Renewal of God-Language* (Indianapolis: Bobbs-Merrill Company, Inc., 1969).
[24] Ibid., pp. 13, 10, 183.
[25] Ibid., p. 181.
[26] Ibid., p. 220.
[27] Ibid., pp. 224-27.
[28] Ibid., pp. 246-47.
[29] Ibid., pp. 19-20, 272.
[30] Ibid., pp. 265, 296-97.
[31] Ibid., pp. 363, 295, 272.
[32] Ibid., pp. 260-62, 282, 412-416.
[33] Quoted in Antony Flew, *God: A Critical Enquiry* (2d. ed.; LaSalle, IL: Open Court Publishing Company, 1965), p. 3.
[34] Emil Brunner, *Revelation and Reason: The Christian Doctrine of Faith and Knowledge*, trans. Olive Wyon (Philadelphia: The Westminster Press, 1946), p. 15.
[35] Bernard Ramm, *After Fundamentalism: The Future of Evangelical Theology* (San Francisco: Harper & Row, Publishers, 1983), pp. 67-70.
[36] Emil Brunner, *The Christian Doctrine of God*, Dogmatics, Vol. 1, trans. Olive Wyon (Philadelphia: The Westminster Press, 1949), p. 101.
[37] Brunner states, "The real content of revelation in the Bible is not 'something,' but God Himself. Revelation is the self-manifestation of God" (*Revelation and Reason*, p. 25).
[38] *Revelation and Reason*, p. 29.
[39] Ibid., p. 23.
[40] Barth, *Church Dogmatics*, II/1, ed. G. W. Bromiley and T. F. Torrance (Edinburgh: T. & T. Clark, 1957), p. 85.
[41] *Church Dogmatics*, II/1, pp. 79, 83.
[42] To quote Brunner once again, "To become aware of the revelation is itself revelation, and this awareness is the act of faith" (*Revelation and Reason*, p. 34).
[43] Brunner argues that "man, simply as man, is the being which is related to God, a 'theonomous' being. Hence the understanding of human nature, the *humanum*, as something 'in itself' apart from its relation to God, is the *proton pseudos* [first lie] of anthropology. It stands in the sharpest opposition to the Bible understanding of man, which knows no other view of man save that which sees him 'before' God, responsible to God" (*Revelation and Reason*, pp. 56-57). A famous dispute between Barth and Brunner concerned the question of a "point of contact" between divine grace and human nature. Barth insisted that there is no such thing. The Holy Ghost "does not stand in need of any point of contact but that which he himself creates" (*Natural Theology: Comprising "Nature and Grace" by Professor Dr. Emil Brunner and the reply "No!" by Dr. Karl Barth*, trans. Peter Fraenkel with an introduction by John Baillie [London: Goeffrey Bles: The Centenary Press, 1946], p. 121). Brunner argues that there is such a point of contact, but it consists of the fact that humans as such are related to God, that is, responsible to God. It does not refer to some innate ability to achieve knowledge of God independent of divine revelation. His point is that "even the unbeliever is still related to God, and therefore that he is responsible, and that this responsibility is not put out of action even by the fullest emphasis upon the generous grace of God . . ." (*Man in Revolt: A Christian Anthropology*, trans. Olive Wyon [Philadelphia: The Westminster Press, 1939], p. 11).
[44] *Revelation and Reason*, p. 207.
[45] Ibid., p. 212.
[46] *Church Dogmatics*, II/1, p. 84.

Natural Theology: The Theological Question 209

[47] David Tracy, *Blessed Rage For Order: The New Pluralism in Theology* (New York: Seabury Press, 1975), p. 29.

[48] See Stephen Ely, *The Religious Availability of Whitehead's God* (Madison: University of Wisconsin Press, 1942).

[49] *The Journal of Religion* 41 (1961): 194-205; reprinted in *God's Activity in the World: The Contemporary Problem*, ed. Owen C. Thomas (AAR Studies in Religion, Number 31 [Chico, CA: Scholars Press, 1983]), pp. 29-43. Page references in this chapter are to the latter publication.

[50] *Naming the Whirlwind: The Renewal of God-Language*.

[51] "Cosmology," p. 31.

[52] *Naming the Whirlwind*, pp. 91-92.

[53] Antony Kenny, *Faith and Reason* (New York: Columbia University Press, 1983), p. 47.

[54] Antony Flew, *God: A Critical Enquiry*, p. 3.

[55] Diogenes Allen, *Philosophy for Understanding Theology* (Atlanta: John Knox Press, 1985), p. 1.

[56] John Cobb, Jr., *A Christian Natural Theology*, pp. 263-64.

[57] See, for example, Thomas Aquinas' *Commentary on the Posterior Analytics of Aristotle* (trans. F. R. Larcher, O.P. [Albany: Magi Books, Inc., 1970]).

[58] See his famous essay, "New Testament and Mythology," in *Kerygma and Myth: A Theological Debate*, ed. Hans Werner Bartsch (New York: Harper & Row, Publishers, 1961), pp. 1-44. John Macquarrie and Schubert M. Ogden have also argued for the theological significance of existentialism.

[59] This is particularly true of Latin American theologians such as Gustavo Gutierrez and Juan Louis Segundo. Helder Camara challenges Christians today to use the writings of Karl Marx just as earlier theologians used the writings of Aristotle ("What Would Saint Thomas Aquinas, the Aristotle Commentator, Do If Faced with Karl Marx?" [*The Journal of Religion*, 58 (1978):S174-182].

[60] "Bultmann's Demythologizing and Hartshorne's Dipolar theism," in *Process and Divinity: The Hartshorne Festschrift*, ed. William L. Reese and Eugene Freeman (LaSalle, IL: Open Court Publishing Co., 1964), pp. 493-513.

[61] *Blessed Rage For Order*, pp. 43-63.

[62] In the first discourse of his classic work, *Discourses upon the Existence and Attributes of God*, entitled "On the Existence of God," Stephen Charnock, for example, offers popular versions of the cosmological and teleological arguments (2 vols.; reprint of 1853 edition; Grand Rapids, MI: Baker Book House, 1979), 1:42-63.

[63] Michael J. Buckley, *At the Origins of Modern Atheism* (New Haven: Yale University Press, 1987), pp. 341-42.

[64] Paul Tillich, *Systematic Theology*, 3 vols. (Chicago: University of Chicago Press, 1951-63), 3:4-5.

[65] Ibid., 1:1-3.

[66] Ibid., 1:61-64.

[67] Ibid., 1:61-65.

[68] Ibid., 1:205 (italics original).

[69] Ibid., 1:204-205, 235, 239.

[70] Ibid., 1:205.

[71] "What Is Theology?" *The Journal of Religion* 52 (January 1972): 22.

[72] *The Reality of God and Other Essays* (New York: Harper & Row, Publishers, 1966), p. 67.

[73] "Faith and Truth," *The Christian Century* 82 (September 1965): 1058.

[74] "What Is Theology?" p. 25.

75 "Present Prospects for Empirical Theology," in *The Future of Empirical Theology*, ed. Bernard E. Meland, Essays in Divinity, Vol. 7 (Chicago: University of Chicago Press, 1969), p. 67.

76 Ogden, *Christ Without Myth: A Study Based on the Theology of Rudolf Bultmann* (New York: Harper & Row, Publishers, 1961), p. 64.

77 "Present Prospects For Empirical Theology," pp. 73-75.

78 *The Reality of God*, p. x.

79 "Bultmann's Demythologizing and Hartshorne's Dipolar Theism," p. 495.

80 *The Reality of God*, pp. 34, 36-37.

81 Ibid., pp. 47-48.

82 Ibid., pp. 66-67.

83 See *Systematic Theology*, 1:7.

84 Francis A. Schaeffer, *He Is There and He Is Not Silent* (Wheaton, IL: Tyndale House Publishers, 1972), p. 11.

85 Wolfhart Pannenberg, *Anthropology in Theological Perspective*, trans. Matthew J. O'Connell (Philadelphia: Westminster Press, 1985), p.15.

86 *The Reality of God*, p. 13.

87 Michael J. Buckley, *At the Origins of Modern Atheism*, p. 28.

88 According to Alvin Plantinga, because some of the beliefs essential to the foundationalists' position themselves fail to satisfy the foundationalists' own criteria, there is no reason why belief in God may not be regarded as foundational just because it does not satisfy them ("Is Belief in God Rational?" in *Rationality and Religious Belief*, ed. C. F. Delaney [Notre Dame: University of Notre Dame Press, 1979], pp. 7-27).

89 Antony Kenny, *Faith and Reason*, p. 23.

90 John B. Cobb, Jr., *A Christian Natural Theology*, p. 262. In his earlier work, *Living Options in Protestant Theology: A Survey of Methods* (Philadelphia: The Westminster Press, 1962), Cobb shows "how, whether recognized or not, theological positions depend systematically on affirmations that are not private to theology" (*A Christian Natural Theology*, p. 262 f.n.).

91 Bernard Ramm, *After Fundamentalism*, p. 69.

92 My friend George L. Goodwin finds two motives in my work. As he describes them—correctly I believe—I want to give reason a place, but not too much of a place, in Christian theology.

93 Philosophical theologians often discuss the cumulative case for theism, with reference to the fact that there several different arguments for the reality of God. I am proposing that a similar case be made for the credibility of Christian faith as a whole, by developing public evidence for the claims of faith wherever possible in explaining the contents of faith.

94 "I am not unaware of the danger that in this way [by using philosophical and psychological concepts and referring to sociological and scientific theories] the substance of the Christian message may be lost" (*Systematic Theology*, 3:4).

95 The extent to which many "process theologians" go in seeking to integrate Christian faith and process philosophy illustrates this problem. One such example is Lewis S. Ford, *The Lure of God: A Biblical Background for Process Theism* (Philadelphia: Fortress Press, 1978).

96 Jeffrey Stout, *The Flight From Authority: Religion, Morality and the Quest for Autonomy* (Notre Dame: University of Notre Dame Press, 1981), 146-147.

97 Michael J. Buckley, *At the Origins of Modern Atheism*, pp. 332-33.

98 Ibid., p. 363.

99 Ibid., pp. 357, 359.

100 Ibid., p. 361.

[101] John Macquarrie, *Principles of Christian Theology* (2d ed.; New York: Charles Scribner's Sons, 1977).

PART THREE

REASON AND THE EXPERIENCE OF FAITH

7
THE RELEVANCE OF REASON TO FAITH

In Part 2 of our discussion we explored the application of reason to the contents, or cognitive claims, of faith. We described Christian theology and philosophy of religion, respectively, as interior and exterior analyses of faith's contents. As we identified them, the central issue in theology is biblical interpretation and the central concern of philosophy of religion is the concept of God. We saw that the contents of Christian faith are open to rational investigation, and we found that it is possible to draw on public evidence to make an impressive case for the existence of a supreme personal being. We also concluded that appeals to public evidence have a role to play in systematic theology. Part 3 concerns the relation of reason to the experience of faith. Our question here is whether rational inquiry has any contribution to make to personal religious commitment. To set the stage for this phase of our work, it will be helpful to review some of our earlier observations.

In Chapter 1, we identified the basic meaning of faith as trust and saw that the experience of faith includes three important dimensions. It is receptive, cognitive, and volitional. These dimensions both require and qualify the relationship of reason to faith. In its cognitive dimension, faith involves knowing something. But it is knowledge that does not rest on proof or demonstration, as our common use of the expression reveals. We "take something on faith" when the evidence we have for it is less than coercive. At the same time, religious faith involves complete certainty. To have faith in God is to trust him implicitly, to have complete confidence in him. Accordingly, the experience of faith manifests a confidence that goes beyond the available evidence. In addition, the exercise of faith is a matter of personal decision as well as cognition, which is why we defined faith as a voluntary act.

In an earlier chapter we also distinguished between broad and narrow uses of reason. In the broad sense, reason involves any cognitive activity. In the narrow sense, reason is reason*ing*—the activity of examining evidence and reaching conclusions. Because faith involves knowing something, reason in the broad sense obviously participates in faith. But there are questions about the relation of faith to reason in the narrow sense. Does the process of examining evidence and reaching conclusions contribute anything to the experience of faith? Is faith in any sense dependent on rational investigation?

The distinction between public and private evidence bears on this question, too. As we have seen, Christian theology examines the contents of faith in light of private evidence—evidence accepted by the community of faith. Philosophy of religion examines these contents in light of public evidence—evidence perceptible to any attentive observer. But does either enterprise play a role in the experience of faith? Does the methodical examination of evidence, public or private, make any contribution to personal religious commitment?

As with every aspect of our topic, this question generates a wide range of answers. We just noted that faith involves both knowing something and having a confidence that goes beyond mere knowledge. Many people tend to emphasize one of these two features at the expense of the other. Thoroughgoing rationalists insist that faith depends entirely on reason, indeed, that faith is the product of careful investigation. Fideists, in contrast, insist that reason is irrelevant to faith. For them, the experience of faith is self-authenticating; it depends on nothing outside itself, particularly not on plodding intellectual inquiry. For rationalists, reason substantiates and dignifies faith; for fideists, reason distorts and ultimately trivializes faith.

Our objective in Part 3 is to develop an alternative to both rationalistic and fideistic views of faith and reason. In contrast to fideism, we shall argue that reason is relevant to the experience of faith, indeed, that reason has an important contribution to make to faith. In contrast to rationalism, however, we shall argue that the contribution of reason to faith is limited. We can never regard faith as an intellectual achievement, as the product of rational investigation. The burden of this chapter is to show that rational inquiry is indeed relevant to the experience of faith. Chapter 8 will examine the ways in which reason contributes to faith and note their limitations.

Support for the Relevance of Reason to Faith

Several factors contribute to a *prima facie* case for the relevance of reason to the experience of faith. One is the comprehensive nature of this experience. Religious commitment involves the whole human person, including our cognitive faculties. We see this in what Jesus called the "first and great commandment" of the law: "You shall love the Lord your God with all your heart, and with all your soul, and with all your mind."[1] What is sometimes referred to as "the intellectual love of God" is therefore an integral aspect of genuine religious commitment.

Another indication that reason is relevant to the experience of faith is the prominence of the *word* in biblical revelation. Familiar texts which emphasize the priority of the word include Deuteronomy 8:3, "Man does not live on bread alone but on every word that proceeds from the mouth of the Lord" (NIV); Isaiah 40:8, "The grass withers, the flower fades; but the word of our God will stand forever"; and John 6:63, "the words that I have spoken to you are spirit and life." The expression "the word of the Lord" appears countless times in the prophetic books of the Old Testament. To be sure, the biblical concept of word includes far more than abstract conceptual formulas. Metaphors, symbols, myths, parables, and stories abound in the Bible, and Jesus himself is identified as "the word" (John 1:1, 14). But, as Carl F. H. Henry remarks, "it is not centrally in symbols and visions, but especially in words, that the Old Testament focuses its account of divine-human relationships."[2] The fact that words are so basic to biblical revelation suggests that biblical religion involves responding to a message that can be apprehended intellectually at least to some degree. Faith may be much more than mere intellectual assent, but it cannot be less.

The history of Christianity points to the same conclusion. The massive accumulation of theological literature over the centuries shows that rational inquiry has figured prominently in the experience of many influential Christians. We see a profound integration of religious commitment and intellectual rigor in the lives of people like Augustine and Anselm. The latter formulates his famous argument for the reality of God within the context of a prayer. "And so, Lord," he begins, "do thou, who dost give understanding to faith, give me, so far as thou knowest it to be profitable, to understand that thou art as we believe; and that thou art that which we believe."[3] Whether or not the most important part of Christianity is its intellectual content, rational inquiry is an essential part of Christian experience. As Joseph Runzo puts it, "human reasoning is not incidental, but foundational, to any human life explicitly following 'the ways of God.'"[4]

It is also significant that Christian proclamation included an apologetic element from the very beginning. Traditionally, Christian faith has always been argued for, not merely asserted as true. The earliest proponents of Christianity maintained that its teachings deserve to be believed. To Jewish audiences, for example, the apostle Paul presented arguments based on the Scriptures to support the claim that Jesus was the Messiah.[5] To Gentile audiences, he appealed to the evidence of their own experience for God's creative power.[6] The first epistle of Peter urged Christians, "Always be prepared to make a defense [*apologia* in Greek] to anyone who calls you to account for the hope that is in you."[7] So, appealing to evidence and formulating arguments—both rational operations—have been important elements in communicating Christianity from its inception.

Yet another indication that reason is relevant to religious experience is the fact that some of the most formidable obstacles to Christian commitment are intellectual in nature. There are many things, of course, that can prevent people from making a religious commitment. Some people fail to do so because religion carries a social stigma or because a religious lifestyle involves personal inconvenience. Others are deterred by unpleasant encounters with religious institutions and presumably religious people. But there are also important intellectual obstacles to religious commitment.

It has always been difficult, for example, to reconcile the reality of God with the massive presence of evil in the world. More recently, the view has emerged in which religious beliefs are simply the product of social conditioning, or the expression of personal psychological needs. Furthermore, many biblical statements appear problematic in light of contemporary science. The worldview of the Bible generally, its description of human origins in particular (Genesis 1-2), and its numerous accounts of miraculous occurrences conflict with the naturalistic view of things which modern science assumes. All of these difficulties pertain to beliefs, or cognitive claims, involved or thought to be involved in Christian commitment, and many thinkers object to religion on the grounds that these claims are not valid. Two who have done so in recent years are Wallace I. Matson and J. L. Mackie.

Matson concludes an extensive analysis of various arguments for and against the existence of God with these trenchant remarks: "Are there any reasons for believing in the existence of a Deity . . .? As far as I can tell, there are none. Is it nevertheless reasonable to believe that there is a Deity . . .? This seems to me very doubtful. Is it, then, reasonable, in any sense at all, to believe that there is a Deity? Apparently it is not."[8] A similar review of arguments for the reality of God and the problem of evil leads Mackie to the same conclusion: "the central doctrines of theism, literally interpreted, cannot be rationally defended." "The balance of probabilities, therefore, comes out strongly against the existence of a god."[9]

Many who reject Christianity, like Matson and Mackie, do so, at least ostensibly, on the grounds that Christian faith involves cognitive claims which are not rationally defensible. But if rational considerations prevent certain people from attaining faith, then rational considerations are also needed in order to make the experience available to certain people. So, the experience of faith needs the support of rational inquiry.

Taken together, the factors we have mentioned form a strong case for the view that reason is relevant to faith. It appears that rational inquiry into the contents of faith has an important contribution to make to religious experience. As we shall see, however, many who are sympathetic to faith do not take this position. There are widely differing answers to the question of reason's relation to the experience of faith.

Various Approaches to Faith and Reason

From very early on Christians, particularly Christians in the West, have felt the force of two obligations. One is to think; the other is to believe, or have faith. Furthermore, Christians have always understood these obligations as both different from and yet related to each other, so there has always been a degree of tension between them. This tension is more strongly felt at certain times, in certain places and by certain individuals than others, but it is always present.

Factors which affect the tension between these obligations include the relative importance and the relative difficulty attached to each of them. For much of Christian history, people felt that it was more important to believe than to understand, and that it was also easier to do so. The value of faith was taken for granted, and the status of reason was problematic. This view prevailed during the Middle Ages, or the Age of Faith, as it is often called.[10] In that era most people believed as a matter of course, and they were suspicious of those like Thomas Aquinas who regarded reason as an avenue to truth and sought to legitimize the use of philosophy within Christian thought.

At some moment in history, however, the burden of proof shifted to the other side. As one of Tom Stoppard's characters puts it, "There is presumably a calendar date—a *moment*—when the onus of proof passed from the atheist to the believer, when, quite suddenly, secretly, the noes had it."[11] Consequently, the importance and the possibility of rational inquiry are generally assumed today, while the status of faith is problematic. It is customary to call faith to account at the bar of reason, rather than the other way around, and if tension between the two becomes intolerable, it is faith that has to give, not reason. The view is widely shared—by supporters as well as critics of religion—that the most important obligation believers face in the modern world is to show that faith is intellectually responsible.

Thinkers sympathetic to faith have reacted to this challenge in a striking diversity of ways. For example, some people argue that faith is compatible with reason because their respective claims agree. According to "rational cognitivists," as we might call them, faith makes truth claims, and reason either supports its claims or says nothing to contradict them. Others who believe that faith involves cognitive claims describe its relation to reason in a notably different way. Instead of arguing that the contents of faith are rationally defensible, they maintain that the experience of faith is rationally responsible because it resembles rational activity in several respects. We come to affirm things by faith, they argue, in the same way we arrive at conclusions generally. So, whether or not we can prove the affirmations of faith, we can show that those who make them are rationally entitled to do so.

In contrast to these two groups, there are those who defend the compatibility of faith and reason by drawing sharp distinctions between them. According to "non-cognitivists," faith and reason are compatible, not because they agree, but because they could not possibly disagree. Religious convictions do not involve cognitive claims, so they cannot conflict with rational inquiry. The two belong to separate dimensions of experience.

For "non-rational cognitivists," too, faith and reason are drastically different, but in another way entirely. They hold that faith involves knowledge, but they insist that both the contents and the experience of faith are utterly unique. Moreover, there is a close connection between them. The contents of faith are apprehended only within the experience of faith, and conversely, the experience of faith is wholly determined by its specific contents. Since faith is thus "self-authenticating," the contents of faith are inaccessible to reason, and the conclusions of rational inquiry are irrelevant to religious commitment.

In Part 2 we argued that the contents of faith are in part accessible to rational inquiry. As we indicated above, our thesis in Part 3 is that such inquiry can make a contribution to the experience of faith. To help us locate this position within the complicated philosophical landscape it occupies and to develop it further, let us examine some of the alternatives more fully and respond to the questions they raise.

1. Reason is irrelevant to faith

Let's start with those who argue in various ways that the nature of faith is such that its contents are not accessible to rational inquiry. These include such diverse figures as the non-cognitivists of the 50's, the death-of-God theologians of the 60's, and the anti-foundationalists of the 80's—all of whom we have referred to earlier in our discussion.

Several participants in the famous "theology and falsification debate" responded to the challenge that God-language is cognitively meaningless by conceding the point. They granted that religious language does not communicate information about reality and assigned it a completely different function. The essential nature of religious language, they argued, is expressive rather than informative. It doesn't tell us anything about the way things are; rather, it expresses the speaker's commitment to view reality a certain way, or to behave in a certain way. R. M. Hare, for example, compared religious language to a pre-cognitive conviction, or "blik," which is incapable of being refuted.[12] It expresses an individual's perspective on reality which discounts all evidence to the contrary.

Richard B. Braithwaite is famous for proposing an empiricist's view of the nature of religious belief, which we mentioned in Chapter 1. As Braithwaite describes it, a religious belief contains two essential elements. One is a moral belief, that is, an intention to behave in a certain way. The other involves entertaining certain stories associated with this belief which reinforce the intention. But religion does not involve belief in its ordinary senses. In Braithwaite's view a believer need not regard the stories which fuel his or her faith as literally true. "A professing Christian," he states, "proposes to live according to Christian moral principles and associates his intention with thinking of Christian stories; but he need not believe that the empirical propositions presented by the stories correspond to empirical fact."[13]

The death-of-God theologians of the 1960s also accepted the positivist critique of religious discourse. They tried to express the content of Christian faith in ways that did not employ the word "God." Instead, they focused on the figure of Jesus and the impact of his life on his followers.

In the past few years anti-foundationalists have taken a completely different tack in addressing the question of faith and reason. In contrast to non-cognitivists, they do not deny that faith includes cognitive claims. Instead, they argue that these claims do not need rational justification because they function as "basic beliefs" within our "noetic structure." Because there is nothing more basic than these beliefs within the framework of our thinking, they do not require the support of anything supposedly more fundamental than they are. For anti-foundationalists the point is not that religious beliefs are incapable of justification, but that they do not need justification. They see no reason for attempts to justify beliefs which we have no occasion to doubt.

2. Faith is prior to reason

A number of important discussions of faith and reason have come from those who maintain that rational inquiry has little to do with personal religious experience. Two of the most influential figures to emphasize the differences between reason and the experience of faith were Blaise Pascal (1623-1662) and Søren Kierkegaard (1813-1855).

Pascal's thoughts on faith and reason are recorded not in a systematic discourse, but in his aphoristic *Pensées*. Here we find the famous statements, "The heart has its reasons, which reason does not know," and "It is the heart which experiences God, and not the reason. Faith is God felt by the heart, not by the reason."[14] In thus contrasting faith and reason, Pascal did not promote the view that faith is irrational. Although the two are radically different, they are complementary, rather than contradictory. The reasons of the heart by which one knows God are similar to our intuitive grasp of first principles such as space, time, motion, and number. "We know truth," Pascal asserts, "not only by the reason, but also by the heart, and it is in this last way that we know first principles."

Moreover, intuitive knowledge is not by any means inferior to the deliverances of reason. The two are simply different. "Principles are intuited; propositions are inferred, all with certainty, though in different ways." Accordingly, "it is as useless and absurd for reason to demand from the heart proofs of her first principles, before admitting them, as it would be for the heart to demand from reason an intuition of all demonstrated propositions before accepting them. This inability ought ... to humble reason ... but not to impugn our certainty, as if only reason were capable of instructing us."[15]

For Pascal the heart by which we know God is not irrational emotion, but, as Hans Küng interprets it, "the personal, spiritual center of man," "the starting point of his dynamic personal relationships with other people." It is the human mind, "as spontaneously present, intuitively sensing, existentially apprehending, totally appreciating."[16] According to Pascal, religion needs both rational and non-rational elements: "If we submit everything to reason, our religion will have no mysterious and supernatural element. If we offend the principle of reason, our religion will be absurd and ridiculous."[17]

It was Pascal who drew the famous contrast between the God of religion and the God of philosophy. The so-called "memorial" recounting his dramatic conversion experience contains these cryptic words: "Fire. God of Abraham, God of Isaac, God of Jacob. Not of the philosophers and the scholars. Certitude. Certitude. Joy. Peace. God of Jesus Christ."[18] For Pascal, faith alone gives us a knowledge of God worth having. In faith we encounter a concrete personal reality, not the abstract impersonal object of philosophical reflection.

In assessing the reasonableness of faith, Pascal introduces the notion of the wager—one of the most extensively discussed elements in his *Pensées*. He rejects philosophical arguments for God as ineffective. "The metaphysical proofs of God are so remote from the reasoning of men, and so complicated," he says, "that they make little impression," and have no lasting benefit. "If they should be of service to some, it would be only during the moment that they see such demonstration; but an hour afterward they fear they have been mistaken."[19] Moreover, the actual effect of appeals to nature as a basis for believing in God, to things like the movement of the moon and planets, is often to strengthen unbelief. They create the impression that "the proofs of our religion are very weak." In the final analysis, "nothing is more calculated to arouse . . . contempt."[20]

Since rational certainty is not possible in religious matters, the reasonable thing to do is make a decision based on probabilities. Consider the options, "God is, or He is not." "According to reason, you can defend neither of the propositions." Ordinarily, if neither of two alternatives is more likely to be true, the prudent course of action is to refuse to wager. But when it comes to the existence of God, this is not an option. "You must wager," Pascal insists. "It is not optional." "Let us weigh the gain and the loss in wagering that God is. . . . If you gain, you gain all; if you lose, you lose nothing. Wager, then, without hesitation that He is."[21] If we believe that God exists and we are right, then we gain everything—"an infinity of an infinitely happy life." On the other hand, if we believe that God exists and we are wrong, we have lost nothing. The odds, then, are as infinity to nothing in favor of belief in God's existence, and the choice to make is clear. So, although rational inquiry cannot determine whether or not God exists, careful reflection can show that, all things considered, it makes sense for us to believe that he does.

Philosophers have discussed Pascal's wager at great length.[22] But for our purposes the important thing is his insistence that faith and reason are radically different and yet compatible, indeed complementary. Reason cannot provide us with a knowledge of God—only faith can do that—but we should not reject reason because of this. There are two extremes to be avoided, "to exclude reason [and] to admit reason only."[23]

3. Faith is superior to reason

Søren Kierkegaard surpasses Pascal in emphasizing the uniqueness of faith. Pascal maintains that faith and reason are distinct, but also complementary. Kierkegaard insists that faith is wholly unlike anything else.

The central concern of Kierkegaard's religious writings is the experience rather than the contents of faith.[24] *Concluding Unscientific Postscript*, for example, his most important book, deals not with the "objective" problem of the truth of Christianity, but with the "subjective" problem of the individual's relationship to Christianity.[25] Its central question is how a single human being who is infinitely interested in eternal salvation can establish a true relation to the message brought by Christianity.[26]

Kierkegaard passionately asserted the decisive uniqueness of faith in reaction to two things, the matter-of-fact, conventional Christianity he found in Denmark in the nineteenth century and the Hegelian philosophy which prevailed in intellectual circles at the time. In opposition to both, Kierkegaard presents the experience of faith as a "leap" which is utterly diverse from the process of rational investigation. Becoming a Christian, he insists, can never be just a natural part of growing up in respectable society. Instead, it is extremely difficult—a crisis, not a social convention.[27] As for Hegelianism, it represents "the greatest possible misunderstanding of Christianity."[28] It distorts the meaning of faith by attempting to incorporate historical events within an all-encompassing rational theory and give the central Christian doctrines a thoroughly logical explanation.

Kierkegaard counters that by logical standards the central aspects of Christianity are doubly absurd.[29] Not only does faith base our eternal happiness on something historical, namely, the life and death of Jesus Christ, but the content of this event—the notion that the eternal God became a human being, lived and died at a specific point in history—defies human reason.[30] Consequently, Christianity could never be absorbed into a rational scheme. To elucidate this concept of faith, Kierkegaard sharply distinguishes subjective from objective thought and describes faith as the culminating sphere, or stage, of human existence. Each of these ideas deserves a brief explanation.

For Kierkegaard, the central human reality is not the thinking self, but the concrete existing self.[31] Or, as he puts it, "The real subject is not the cognitive subject . . .; the real subject is the ethically existing subject."³² This means that the ultimate truth about human life is something we realize in acts of personal decision, not as the conclusion of abstract reflection. As a result, neither historical investigation nor philosophical reflection leads to truth. In fact, as far as faith is concerned, these endeavors form a Catch-22. On the one hand, they only achieve an approximation, never certainty, and an approximation is insufficient as a basis for eternal happiness.³³ On the other hand, if history or philosophy did produce objective certainty, this would interfere with faith because faith depends on passion, and "certainty and passion do not go together." Indeed, "if passion is eliminated, faith no longer exists."³⁴ Intellectual or theoretical certainty is therefore the "most dangerous enemy of faith."

For these reasons Kierkegaard rejects proofs in the area of religion. And if faith does not need proof, then the very quest for proof is a symptom that faith is waning. "[W]hen faith ... begins to lose its passion, when faith begins to cease to be faith, then a proof becomes necessary so as to command respect from the side of unbelief."³⁵ Besides, the whole idea of proving the reality of God makes no sense. "[I]f the God does not exist," he says, "it would ... be impossible to prove it; and if he does exist it would be folly to attempt it."³⁶ For Kierkegaard, then, faith differs radically from rational inquiry in both mental attitude and cognitive content.

The discontinuity between faith and everything else also appears in Kierkegaard's account of the stages of existence, where faith represents the final stage in the process of becoming a person. As we noted, Kierkegaard describes true humanity as subjectivity. It has to do with making choices and involves personal commitment.³⁷

Kierkegaard identifies three ways of choosing which confront us—the aesthetic, the ethical, and the religious. Each of them represents one of the three principal spheres of existence, or stages on life's way.³⁸ People at the aesthetic level do not take choice seriously. They build their existence around the category of the satisfying moment. Their attitude is that "things happen, and my choices have nothing to do with them." In contrast to aesthetic persons, ethical persons do take choice seriously. They live by an ethical code, not by whim or impulse. By emphasizing personal decision, the ethical perspective drives us to affirm that our highest end lies in becoming subjective.

People leave the ethical and enter the religious sphere when they make a passionate commitment to something that cannot be proven. A good example is Socrates, who held fast to the idea of immortality without proof of immortality.[39] Socrates' experience shows that the quality of commitment is what determines truth on the personal level, not the objective status of the belief in question.[40] The highest truth available for an existing individual, therefore, is "an objective uncertainty held fast in an appropriation-process of the most passionate inwardness."

For Kierkegaard, this discrepancy between what is subjectively, passionately affirmed and what is objectively known determines the very meaning of faith. In fact, we can define faith as "the contradiction between the infinite passion of the individual's inwardness and the objective uncertainty." Without this element of risk, then, there is no faith. "If I am capable of grasping God objectively, I do not believe," he asserts, "but precisely because I cannot do this I must believe."[41]

According to Kierkegaard, the transition from one stage of existence to another is a leap, not a natural process of development,[42] so there is no way to introduce someone to the experience of Christian faith or to prepare someone for it by trying to remove the paradox it involves. Since becoming a Christian entails an absolute decision, it is always a qualitative leap.[43]

In summary, Kierkegaard sets religious commitment and rational inquiry in sharp opposition to each other. Since the realization of truth is not an intellectual achievement, but the result of personal decision, intellectual activity not only fails to contribute to the experience, it actually interferes with it. People often misunderstand Kierkegaard, because he makes this distinction so emphatically. In spite of his use of "absurd" and "paradoxical" to describe faith, his point is not that it is irrational to be a Christian. If that were the case, it would hardly make sense for him to write so extensively about the experience. His point is that becoming a Christian can never be viewed as the conclusion of rational inquiry—as a natural, matter-of-fact development.

Such a notion evacuates faith of the wonder, the mystery and the passion that are central to it. To safeguard these qualities, Kierkegaard insists that real faith always has the character of profound personal crisis. It is radically discontinuous with all other experience, and it can never be reduced to anything else.

4. Faith is not belief

Some probing questions to arise more recently concerning the relevance of reason to faith come from the writings of Wilfred Cantwell Smith. In *Faith and Belief* he argues that the two are drastically different, in view of what "belief" has come to mean in modern times. According to Smith, the tendency to regard faith as the act of giving intellectual assent to certain propositions is relatively recent. And a careful study of Buddhist, Islamic and Hindu as well as Christian expressions of faith reveals that faith has never been, and never should be, equated with belief.

Instead, faith is "engagement," a concrete personal response to transcendent reality. Faith is "that quality of or available to humankind by which we are characterized as transcending, or are enabled to transcend, the natural order."[44] It is "an orientation of the personality, to oneself, to one's neighbour, to the universe; a total response."[45]

There are important reasons for keeping faith and belief distinct. For example, it is possible for faith to remain constant while someone's beliefs change and, vice versa, for beliefs to remain constant while someone's faith changes. There are times when beliefs provide an avenue to faith and times when they pose an obstacle for faith.[46] In addition, the members of a given religion will typically exhibit several types of belief, and each person will progress through different stages of faith within a lifetime.

On the larger scale, Smith maintains that the role of belief varies from one religious tradition to another. In Christianity belief is conspicuously important. In fact, western Christians link faith and belief more closely than any other religious group. But other religions have relatively little, if any, theology, and those who do often relegate it to secondary importance. In both Judaism and Islam, for example, law has priority over doctrine.[47]

The most important reason Smith gives for differentiating faith from belief is a major shift in the meaning of the word "belief." Belief as we now think of it has never been the essence of faith, and the tendency to identify the two is a relatively recent development in western thought. In fact, it wasn't until the nineteenth century that people came to regard believing in this sense as the essential thing which religious people do. Originally, "I believe" meant "I hold dear," or "I love."[48] In saying "I believe" someone proclaimed personal commitment to God. But the meaning of the word underwent a series of dramatic transitions.

First, there was a change from a personal to an impersonal object. The object of faith started as a person and ended up as a proposition, a theory, or an idea. Second, statements including "believe" shifted from the first to the third person. People began to use the word to report what someone else believes rather than to affirm their own commitment. And third, the mood of belief changed. In centuries past it expressed one's relation to absolutes, things apprehended as true. Now it typically expresses one's relation to uncertainties. For example, to say, "I believe so," is to say, "I think so, but I'm not sure." As a result, a statement about a person's believing in God now means, "So-and-so reports that the idea of God is part of the furniture of his mind."[49]

As a result of these developments, believing doctrines became the essential content of faith, so that those who believed had faith and those who did not believe did not have it.[50] To the contrary, Smith insists, mentally entertaining an abstract idea or assenting to a proposition is not faith, nor even an essential part of faith. We must not subordinate faith to belief.

Although faith and belief are not at all the same, this does not mean that the two have nothing to do with each other. The point to remember is that belief is one of several religious forms, and like all religious forms, it is secondary to faith, just as faith itself is secondary to "transcendent reality and final truth."[51] Consequently, we should not seek to eliminate beliefs from religion. We cannot set ideas aside, and "let faith wallow innovatingly in sentimental a-rationality." On the other hand, we must avoid absolutizing any particular form of belief. Our ideas are human constructs, but they may serve as windows on the truth beyond them.[52] Third, our concepts should approximate the truth as closely as possible. "It is part of faith," Smith says, "that one's ideas be as true, as valid, as at all one can manage."[53] In the end, Smith's proposal is far less radical than it first appears. As it turns out, beliefs do have a role to play in faith. The important thing is never to reduce faith to an act of mental assent.

5. Reason is essential to faith

The views we have just examined emphasize in varying ways the discontinuities between reason and the experience of faith. Their proponents hold that reason has little or nothing to contribute to religious experience. But there is considerable support for the opposite point of view, too. The work of several scholars within the past few years emphasizes the importance of propositional content to faith and supports the idea that rational inquiry is relevant to the experience of faith.

In *Reason, Relativism and God,* Joseph Runzo argues that the experience of faith not only involves, but provides warrants for knowledge claims about God. The central concern of the book is the "theological dilemma" Runzo finds in the contrast between the certainty of faith and the relativity of truth. To resolve the dilemma, he argues that we can make an absolute commitment to truths which are relative because faith itself warrants knowledge claims about God.[54] "[O]nce believed and then defended and then followed as a life-transforming faith," he states, "our most fundamental beliefs . . . become absolute commitments, though their truth be relative."[55]

Runzo also insists that reasoning about God plays a central role in the religious life.[56] Because all experiential contact with God is mediated by the perspective, and limited by the intellectual capabilities, of the human recipient, human reasoning is "not incidental, but foundational" to religious experience. Indeed, he argues, "without the conceptual resources to understand . . . and experience God, and without the unifying cohesiveness which reason brings to our conceptual resources, an explicitly theistic life is not possible."[57]

Another, quite different, discussion of religion supports a similar conclusion as to the relation between faith and reason. In *Religious Experience,* Wayne Proudfoot rejects theories of religion which assume that it is possible to isolate a level of religious experience that is prior to and independent of concepts and beliefs. Since all students of religion bring certain concepts, beliefs and attitudes with them, every interpretation of religion is "theory-laden," and there is no such thing as a "pure" description of religious phenomena.[58]

Not only is the study of religion incorrigibly conceptual, according to Proudfoot, the same is true of religion itself. Beliefs and concepts are not secondary expressions of religious experience, they are an integral part of the experience. Accordingly, religious language does more than express religious experience. "It also plays a very active and formative role in religious experience."[59] Because religion relies on concepts and language, we cannot isolate it from other aspects of our experience. Says Proudfoot, "The authority of religious doctrine or of the religious form of life cannot be disconnected from other concepts and beliefs." Religious doctrines and experiences "assume concepts and beliefs that are not distinctively religious."[60]

6. Faith and reason are similar

One of the most important thinkers to focus on the experience rather than the contents of faith is John Henry Newman (1801-1890).[61] In his famous *Grammar of Assent,* Newman's strategy is not to assemble rational evidence to support religious beliefs, but to show that those who embrace these ideas are rationally responsible.[62]

The book's central concern arises from this basic contrast between faith and reason: faith involves certainty, but rational inquiry at best can only achieve probability. We saw that Kierkegaard views this difference as something positive. He feels that it safeguards the uniqueness of faith and prevents us from ever reducing it to a piece of speculative philosophy. But for

Newman this discrepancy raises serious questions about the rational integrity of the believer. So, instead of emphasizing the differences between reason and faith, he looks for their similarities.

In doing so, however, Newman takes a different tack from most attempts to show that faith and reason are compatible, for instead of focusing on faith, he concentrates on the nature of reason. His basic point is that our minds operate in the area of religion much as they do in other areas, so rational inquiry is not wholly different from the experience of faith. As Newman carefully describes it, there is much more to human reasoning than developing conclusions through a process of formal inference. Religious faith can therefore be logical in a broad sense of the term, even if its contents are not the product of rational investigation.

The second part of Newman's *Grammar* is important to us here, because it explains how the conditional acceptance of a proposition which inference produces can lead to the unconditional acceptance characteristic of religious knowledge.[63] Or, as one of his contemporaries put it, it shows "that you can believe what you cannot absolutely prove."[64] We will concentrate on two of the major elements in the discussion—the distinction between inference and assent and the claim that concrete rather than formal reasoning is the only route to certainty (or certitude, to use the term he prefers).

Newman describes assent and inference as two ways in which our minds entertain propositions.[65] The major difference between them is the fact that assent is unconditional, while inference is conditional. Accordingly, the strength of inference may vary, proof may increase or decrease, but "assent either exists or does not exist."[66] "There is no medium," he says, "between assenting and not assenting."[67]

Several factors require us to distinguish assent from inference. There are times when we assent to things after we have forgotten the reasons that led us to affirm them in the first place.[68] There are times when we no longer assent, even though the reasons which first led us to do so are still present. And there are times when we never give our assent to things which have admittedly strong arguments in their favor.[69] So, even though we never assent without some sort of evidence, assent is not the product of an inferential process.[70]

Another indication that the two are different is the fact that we assent unconditionally to many things for which the actual evidence is far less than demonstrative.[71] We believe that we exist, for example, that the external world we experience is real, that the past affects the future, that we have a sense of right and wrong, that we had parents, that we cannot live without food, and that we will eventually die. Our inability to provide conclusive proof for such propositions does not detract in the slightest from our confidence that they are true. In fact, one of the laws of human nature is "this absolute reception of propositions as true, which lie outside the narrow range of conclusions to which logic, formal or virtual, is tethered."[72]

If it is natural for us to assent to things we cannot prove, it is also natural for us to look for evidence which supports the ideas we assent to.[73] In the course of religious development, our first assents are often little more than prejudices, and the reasonings which precede and accompany them are not commensurate with their importance. But as time goes by, we gradually begin to modify the notions to which we assent. The process may be formal or informal, and the results are likewise varied. Sometimes we lose our original assent, but sometimes our original affirmation emerges stronger than ever. When this happens, the new assent acquires "the strength of explicitness and deliberation." It now represents "what is commonly called a conviction."[74]

Like assent and inference, certitude is also a natural aspect of human behavior.[75] Newman defines it as a conviction about a proposition that is absolutely true.[76] Those who have certitude not only say, "I know," but, "I know that I know." They are both right and conscious of being right.[77] Moreover, such people reject the possibility that their belief could change.[78] They do not feel compelled to review the reasons for it, to go over all the arguments by which they first came to believe.[79] For them, the matter is settled. "Once certitude, always certitude," Newman says.[80]

When he turns from assent to inference, Newman distinguishes between formal and concrete forms of inference and reverses a popular conception of the two. People often assume that the highest levels of thought are the most technical. They feel that our most important rational activities are ones which employ refined methods of inquiry and the highest types of arguments are expressed in abstract formulas. Newman disagrees. As he sees it, formal inference is inferior and reasoning at its highest level is informal or concrete. "[M]ere skill in argumentative science," he asserts, is inferior to the "higher logic" of "ratiocination as the exercise of a living faculty in the individual intellect."[81]

The fact is that formal inference is too crude to express the way our minds actually work. Its methodical processes, "useful as they are, as far as they go, are only instruments of the mind," and instruments by themselves are not very helpful. "Real ratiocination" acts through them and "reaches to conclusions beyond and above them."[82] It seems clear that we come to our strongest convictions by a process more subtle than that of formal investigation.[83] Consider the belief that we shall eventually die. It is not the conclusion of careful, formal inquiry resulting in logical demonstration, but the outcome of a much more subtle process of observation and common sense. Yet the resultant conviction is stronger than a conclusion of formal inference could ever be. "What logic cannot do," therefore, "my own living personal reasoning, my good sense . . . which cannot adequately express itself in words, does for me." It produces "the most precise, absolute, masterful certitude."[84]

How then does concrete reasoning proceed? What course does it follow? According to Newman, we reach conclusions in concrete matters through the "cumulation of probabilities" which arise independently of each other.[85] When a number of premises all converge toward a conclusion, their combined force provides a convincing case, even though it falls short of strict logical demonstration. We can thus foresee and predict the outcome of a process of concrete reasoning without attaining it. So this is how we pass "from conditional inference to unconditional assent": beginning with "merely probable antecedents," we develop "the sufficient proof of a fact or a truth" and move "after the proof, to an act of certitude about it."[86]

Can we ever be sure that we have reasoned correctly and that our certitude is rightly placed? Is there some criterion for determining the accuracy of our inferences? There is, according to Newman, but it does not consist in some external requirement, some mechanical logical model. "It is the mind that reasons, and that controls its own reasoning, not any technical apparatus of words and propositions."[87] Consequently, "there is no ultimate test of truth besides the testimony born to truth by the mind itself."[88] Like good taste in artistic matters and common sense in everyday matters, the only criterion of valid inference is the good judgment of the thinker, and this can never be reduced to logical terms and formulas.[89]

For Newman, then, the relevance of reason to faith consists in the similarity of the experiences. Faith makes affirmations that we cannot prove, but careful examination reveals that reason does exactly the same thing. In fact, the most important, most deeply held beliefs we have are not the product of formal, discursive reasoning. We reach them through diverse and subtle operations which are never transparent to rational analysis.

Conclusion

The numerous approaches to the question of faith and reason show how varied opinions are on the issue. Let us examine some of these views in light of our conviction that rational inquiry can contribute to religious experience.

The idea that reason is irrelevant to religious commitment is a good place to begin. A number have taken this position in recent years out of a desire to protect religion from the objection that its claims cannot withstand rational scrutiny. But instead of arguing that reason supports the contents of faith, they respond that religion doesn't make cognitive claims in the first place. This tactic is flawed in several ways. On the practical level, it typically fails to earn any respect from those who reject religion. Critics of theism like Matson and Mackie are particularly hard on the assertion that faith is "above" reason. They see it as the last, desperate move of people who are unwilling to admit that they are beaten and take the consequences.

Besides arguing that the existence of God is rationally indefensible, both philosophers insist that the absence of a convincing case for theism ought to make a real difference in our personal beliefs. Matson insists that someone who refuses "to play the rational game" is "in no position to claim access to a 'higher truth.' The rules of the rational game, vague and imperfect as they may be, are the only procedures we have to get at the truth." Consequently, people who say they don't care if their belief in God is irrational may be immune to rational criticism, but their belief can never be anything more than a private conviction. They have "no warrant to recommend it to anyone else on grounds of truth."[90] In the same vein, Mackie rejects both "belief without reason" and "religion without belief," as well as attempts to replace traditional theism with alternative conceptions of God. "There is ... no easy way of defending religion," he insists, "once it is admitted that the literal, factual, claim that there is a god cannot be rationally sustained."[91]

We must beware of allowing atheists to define the terms in which theism is discussed, but these objections lend support to the conviction that rational considerations are relevant if not essential to faith. If all the rational evidence that bears on the question of God's existence points to a negative conclusion, then theism is in terrible shape. And if religion is only available to people who refuse to think about it—in other words, if believers cannot be thinkers, too, and apply their reason to faith—then religion has little to recommend it. Consequently, believers must not abandon the field of rational discussion to those who deny the existence of God. There is nothing to be gained, and much to be lost, if they do.

This argument obliges us to respond to the views of Pascal and Kierkegaard, who are famous for sharply distinguishing faith from reason. A look at the full range of Pascal's statements on the topic reveals that he is not opposed to reason, or even to giving reason some role to play in religious experience. As we have seen, he warns against extremes which would separate the two entirely or make faith appear irrational, and one could even argue that his notion of the wager is an attempt to show that it makes sense to have faith. Instead, Pascal's vigorous objections seem to focus on the kind of move that would make faith directly dependent on reason or reduce faith to some sort of rational procedure. So, notwithstanding his central contention that faith and reason are radically different, Pascal leaves the door open, or at least ajar, to the possibility of a positive if minimal relationship between them. A careful reading of Kierkegaard leads to similar conclusions.

Kierkegaard is famous for removing faith from the arena of rational inquiry and relegating it to the private sphere of individual decision. The most prevalent criticism of this view of faith is that it leads to radical relativism. As one scholar puts it, "every man is the measure of his own religiosity. Though Kierkegaard insisted that the believer's leap of faith 'puts him in an absolute relation to the absolute,' the only available criterion of judging whether he has in fact achieved this relation is his own private feeling."[92] In the words of another commentator, "If what we believe depends on the believer's own ultimate choice of rational criteria, then surely all beliefs have an equal moment, or rather equal lack of moment, for claiming objective truth."[93] Less kindly, still another accuses Kierkegaard of advocating "a sort of intellectual Russian roulette,"[94] with his emphasis on indefensible and apparently unmotivated choice. Kierkegaard seems to allow us to affirm any view whatever, as long as our degree of conviction reaches sufficient intensity.

To reply, it is significant that Kierkegaard does not hold that the truth of Christianity is unimportant to the experience of faith. He does not say that you can believe in anything at all and have faith, so long as you believe strongly enough. His point, instead, is that the truth of Christianity can only be apprehended from within this experience. To safeguard the unique experience of faith he rejects attempts to find rational justification for the contents of faith. It is not that such attempts fail on rational grounds, but that they are fraught with religious liabilities.

Kierkegaard seems to be saying something like this. From the outside, many aspects of faith appear to be continuous with other experiences. After all, Christians make claims of a historical and metaphysical nature that are ostensibly accessible to those modes of inquiry. But from the inside, everything looks different. For the genuine believer, faith represents an earth-shaking experience, a profound personal crisis, something utterly incomparable to anything else. Consequently, from the perspective of someone who has faith, nothing could be more misguided than the suggestion that the experience depends on rational investigation, or that philosophical proofs could somehow produce it, or that intellectual inquiry could prepare for it. No, the experience is *sui generis*, and attempts to give it rational explanation only obscure its essential character.

The claim that Kierkegaard separates theism, or Christianity, from "the only sorts of inquiry that could determine its truth," as one critic puts it,[95] begs precisely the point of his argument. It assumes that truth can be reached only through rational investigation, and this is the very position that Kierkegaard rejects. Truth, he insists, is subjectivity. Faith represents an apprehension of truth that cannot be reduced to rational investigation.

Kierkegaard does not seek to place the contents of faith under quarantine for fear that they could not survive rational scrutiny. Instead, his point is that the results of such inquiry, even if positive, would not be relevant to faith, because faith consists of a quite different way of knowing God.

We can learn a great deal from Kierkegaard's emphasis on the uniqueness of faith, but it is a mistake to overemphasize its discontinuities with other human experience. In order to avoid making faith the matter-of-fact conclusion of philosophical or historical inquiry, Kierkegaard removes it completely from the sphere of rational thought. And thus relegating faith entirely to the private sphere creates the impression that one could have faith in virtually anything. We can do justice to Kierkegaard's basic concern, I believe, without falling into subjectivism by maintaining that faith is indeed unique, but not discontinuous with all other experience. We can even draw on Kierkegaard's own insights to make this point.

Kierkegaard's objection to speculative philosophy is its failure to acknowledge the reality of the concrete existential subject who engages in thinking. By the same token, we might observe, the concrete personal subject who has faith, the believer, is also a being capable of, and incorrigibly inclined, to rational thought. As James Collins puts it, "Man is a being who knows in part and believes in part.... He has a native tendency to unify the truths to which he assents, bringing the deliverances of faith to bear upon the life of reason and, conversely, exploring the groundwork of faith with the aid of reason."[96] If the thinker is also a person, as Kierkegaard insistently reminds us, it is equally true that the person is also a thinker, and the concrete experience of faith cannot be separated from this aspect of human reality. Consequently, the important fact that we must not reduce faith to reason does not mean that reason is irrelevant to faith.

We also need to respond to some of the important points raised by Wilfred Cantwell Smith. Smith's analysis of several religious traditions shows that faith is an essential quality of human existence. And his central contention that faith is not belief, that is, that propositions do not constitute the object of faith, is an important caveat against all intellectual distortions of faith. At the same time, Smith's rigorous critique of belief as assent to propositional truth challenges the relevance of reason to faith, as we have described it. It casts doubt on the value of any attempt to show that religious claims satisfy general criteria of intelligibility. The attempt to find public evidence to support the claims of faith presupposes that faith involves intellectual assent to propositions which are problematic (or they would need no justification), and this is precisely the view of faith that Smith opposes. It seems to equate religion with the act of accepting various doctrines.

There are two questions involved here. One is whether an appeal to public evidence to support religious claims necessarily involves the propositional view of faith to which Smith strongly objects. The other is whether Smith is correct in dividing faith and belief so sharply. Smith is correct in objecting to a propositional view of faith, in the sense that faith must never be reduced to mere mental assent. As we argued earlier, true faith always involves the whole person. It has a volitional as well as a cognitive or intellectual dimension. So, Smith is right to call for an expanded concept of the intellectual dimension of faith. He is also correct in subordinating belief to faith, and faith to reality and truth. And he is right to suggest that all our concepts are at best approximations of the truth and therefore not to be absolutized. But none of this requires the conclusion that belief in the modern sense is irrelevant to faith.

Smith overstates things when he insists that propositional assent is not involved in faith. While faith is certainly more than belief, it is just as certainly never less. In fact, faith presupposes cognitive truth, even on Smith's account. He defines faith as insight and response to the transcendent dimension of reality, and this presupposes the truth of at least two propositions—(1) the transcendent is real and (2) the transcendent is humanly accessible. So, the exercise of faith involves affirming propositions, whether or not it takes the form of explicit, verbal acknowledgment.

In a cultural context which challenges the very presuppositions of faith, the task of accounting for its cognitive contents becomes unavoidable. Smith calls us to appreciate the continuities within the experience of faith which cut across varying religious traditions and diverse historical and cultural situations, but it is also important for us to be sensitive to our specific situation. The circumstances facing many Christians today pose formidable obstacles to faith, and these obstacles must be dealt with if faith is to be available to us now. In fact, in our present situation it is just as important to demonstrate that faith is possible as it is to avoid distorting its essential nature. So, even if the propositional component of faith was less prominent at earlier times in Christian history, and may be less prominent in other religious traditions today, this does not diminish its pressing importance for contemporary Christians. Responsible faith must address the challenges confronting it, no matter where they come from.

The other positions reviewed are generally supportive of our proposal here. Joseph Runzo defends the importance of the cognitive or intellectual dimension of faith. Religious experience is human experience, he argues, and all human experience has a cognitive dimension. It is therefore impossible to relegate faith to a sphere that lies beyond the reach of cognition, because no such sphere exists. Undeniably, our experience includes elements other than intellectual ones, but it always includes a cognitive or intellectual dimension, too.

Wayne Proudfoot's observations also support our position though somewhat less directly. His careful study shows that faith, the essential religious experience, is intrinsically related to experience in general. It draws on our common experience as human beings and on our larger conceptual and linguistic world. If this is so, as I believe it is, then we cannot divorce faith from reason. We cannot isolate the experience of faith from the rational examination of public evidence.

Newman's reflections on the nature of reason also have an important bearing on the question of this chapter, both because of his central thesis and because of the underlying assumption of his work. His careful analyses show that the way of knowing characteristic of faith is similar to human knowledge in general. Proof in the sense of logical demonstration is unavailable for the most fundamental beliefs we hold. We come to believe in ways that cannot be reduced to tidy formulas. Certitude in religious belief is therefore intellectually responsible, because we achieve it through the same process by which we achieve certitude in other matters. So, even if there is a discrepancy between what faith affirms and what reason can support in the way of logical formulas, faith is nevertheless intellectually responsible; it is still rational in the broad sense of the term.

Newman's work supports the position on faith and reason we have taken here. There may be contrasts and tensions between faith and reason, but the two are not wholly dissimilar. They are fundamentally compatible because they involve similar intellectual operations.

Let us summarize the course of our discussion. In Part 2 we sought to show that there are continuities between reason and the contents of faith. In this chapter we have argued that there are continuities between reason and the experience of faith. This claim has a basis in the connection between knowledge and faith we find in the Bible and throughout Christian history. It also reflects the mandate for intellectual responsibility that has exerted such influence in Western civilization. Since all experience

The Relevance of Reason to Faith 243

involves cognitive experience, we cannot exempt religion from rational inquiry without truncating and distorting it. And since the modern world presents serious challenges to the traditional claims of faith, the availability of religion to thinking people today may depend on successful rational investigation. Moreover, on close inspection, the most memorable efforts to distinguish faith and reason, those of Pascal and Kierkegaard, do not deny its rational elements, but strive to preserve its uniqueness and integrity. So, in view of its intrinsic cognitive aspects, and particularly in view of the cultural situation confronting religion today, we must acknowledge the role of reason in faith. Faith, as Christians conceive it, is inseparable from reason.

In saying that reason is relevant to the experience of faith, however, we must beware of exaggerating its significance. As we shall see in our final chapter, even though reason has an important role to play in faith, the scope of its contribution is small indeed.

---

[1] Matthew 22:38, 37. Ellen G. White interprets this as laying upon Christians "the obligation of developing the intellect to its fullest capacity, that with all the mind we may know and love our Creator" (*Christ's Object Lessons* [Mountain View, CA: Pacific Press Publishing Association, 1900], p. 333).

[2] *God, Revelation and Authority* (6 vols.; Waco, TX: Word Books, Publisher, 1976-1983), 6:50.

[3] *Proslogium*, 2, in *St. Anselm: Basic Writings*, trans. S. N. Deane (2d ed.; LaSalle, IL: The Open Court Publishing Co., 1962), p. 7.

[4] Joseph Runzo, *Reason, Relativism and God* (New York: St. Martin's Press, 1986), p. 235.

[5] Acts 17:2-3.

[6] Acts 17:22-29.

[7] 1 Peter 3:15.

[8] Wallace I. Matson, *The Existence of God* (Ithaca, NY: Cornell University Press, 1965), p. 239.

[9] J. L. Mackie, *The Miracle of Theism: Arguments For and Against the Existence of God* (Oxford: Clarendon Press, 1982), pp. 199, 253.

[10] See, for example, Etienne Gilson, *Reason and Revelation in the Middle Ages* (New York: Charles Scribner's Sons, 1938).

[11] Tom Stoppard, *Jumpers* (New York: Grove Press, Inc., 1972), p. 25.

[12] In "Theology and Falsification," in *New Essays in Philosophical Theology*, ed. Antony Flew and Alasdair MacIntyre (New York: The Macmillan Company, 1955), pp. 99-103.

[13] Richard B. Braithwaite, "An Empiricist's View of the Nature of Religious Belief," in *The Logic of God: Theology and Verification*, ed. Malcolm L. Diamond and Thomas V. Litzenburg, Jr. (Indianapolis: The Bobbs-Merrill Company, Inc., 1975), pp. 146, 143.

[14] *Pensées*, 277, 278 (in Blaise Pascal, *Pensées. Thoughts on Religion and other subjects,*

trans. William Finlayson Trotter, ed. H. S. Thayer [New York: Washington Square Press, Inc., 1965]; the numbering follows Leon Brunschvicq's authoritative edition).

[15] Ibid., 282.

[16] Hans Kung, *Does God Exist? An Answer for Today*, trans. Edward Quinn (New York: Vintage Books, 1981), p. 49.

[17] *Pensées*, 273.

[18] Ibid., p. 285.

[19] Ibid., 543.

[20] Ibid., 242.

[21] Ibid., 233.

[22] One recent discussion is James Cargile, "Pascal's Wager," in *Contemporary Philosophy of Religion*, ed. Steven M. Cahn and David Shatz (New York: Oxford University Press, 1982), pp. 229-236.

[23] *Pensées*, 253.

[24] C. Stephen Evans, *Subjectivity and Religious Belief: An Historical, Critical Study* (Washington, D.C.: University Press of America, Inc., 1982), p. 93. Evans cites Kierkegaard's own statement in *The Point of View for My Work as an Author*, trans. Walter Lowrie, ed. Benjamin Nelson (New York: Harper and Row, 1962), pp. 5-6.

[25] *Concluding Unscientific Postscript to the Philosophical Fragments*, trans. David F. Swenson and Walter Lowrie (Princeton, NJ: Princeton University Press, 1941), pp. 18-20.

[26] Niels Thulstrup, *Commentary on Kierkegaard's Concluding Unscientific Postscript With a New Introduction*, trans. Robert J. Widenmann (Princeton, NJ: Princeton University Press, 1984), p. 109.

[27] Kierkegaard says he wrote the *Postscript* to show just how difficult it is to become a Christian (*Postscript*, p. 520).

[28] Ibid., p. 507.

[29] In Kierkegaard's [Johannes Climacus'] words, "there are two dialectical contradictions, first, the basing of one's eternal happiness upon the relation to something historical, and then the fact that this historical datum is compounded in a way contradictory to all thinking" (Ibid., p. 513).

[30] "The absurd is—that the eternal truth has come into being in time, that God has come into being, has been born, has grown up, and so forth, precisely like any other individual human being, quite indistinguishable from other individuals" (Ibid., p. 188).

[31] "Existence," Kierkegaard states, "constitutes the highest interest of the existing individual, and his interest in his existence constitutes his reality" (Ibid., p. 279).

[32] Ibid., pp. 280-81.

[33] Ibid., pp. 25, 26. Indeed, "it is a self-contradiction . . . to be infinitely interested in that which in its maximum still always remains an approximation" (Ibid., p. 32).

[34] Ibid., p. 30.

[35] Ibid., p. 31.

[36] *Philosophical Fragments, or A Fragment of Philosophy*, trans. F. Swenson (rev. ed.; Princeton, NJ: Princeton University Press, 1962), p. 49.

[37] W. T. Jones, *Kant and the Nineteenth Century*; vol. 4 in "A History of Western Philosophy" (2d ed., rev.; New York: Harcourt Brace Jovanovich, Inc., 1975), p. 219.

[38] According to James Collins, this threefold description of human existence is the most influential aspect of Kierkegaard's thought (*The Mind of Kierkegaard* [Princeton, NJ: Princeton University Press, 1983], p. 42). It is also the most comprehensive, since its detailed exposition encompasses all his most important books (see Kierkegaard's account of his earlier works in *Postscript*, pp. 225-266).

[39] In fact, the very absence of proof contributed to the passion of Socrates' commitment (*Postscript*, p. 180).

[40] Kierkegaard says, "The objective accent falls on WHAT is said, the subjective

accent on HOW it is said" (Ibid., p. 181).

[41] Ibid., p. 182. Kierkegaard makes a further distinction between Religiousness A, as he calls it, and "paradoxical religiousness," or Religiousness B. Both involve a passionate commitment to something that cannot be proved, but the object of commitment in Religiousness B is not an idea, like the concept of immortality, but a person, specifically, the God who has existed in time (Evans, p. 104). With its affirmation of two contradictions, paradoxical inwardness in Religiousness B is the greatest possible. It bases eternal happiness on the relation to something historical, and it construes this historical element as the identification of the eternal with something which exists in time (*Postscript*, pp. 507, 513).

[42] This is particularly important in the case of the final transition to paradoxical religiousness, or Christianity.

[43] Ibid., p. 343.

[44] Wilfred Cantwell Smith, *Faith and Belief* (Princeton, NJ: Princeton University Press, 1979), p. 142.

[45] Ibid., p. 12.

[46] Ibid., p. viii.

[47] Ibid. pp. 13-14, 15.

[48] Ibid., p. 105.

[49] Ibid., pp. 118-20.

[50] Ibid., pp. 122-23.

[51] Ibid., p. 125.

[52] Ibid., p. 167.

[53] Ibid., p. 169.

[54] Runzo, *Reason, Relativism and God*, p. 165.

[55] Ibid., p. 264.

[56] Ibid., pp. 183, 258.

[57] Ibid., pp. 234-35.

[58] Wayne Proudfoot, *Religious Experience* (Berkeley and Los Angeles, CA: University of California Press, 1965), p. xv.

[59] Ibid., p. 40.

[60] Ibid., p. 236.

[61] Strictly speaking, it is religious belief rather than faith that occupies Newman in *Grammar of Assent* (M. Jamie Ferreira, *Doubt and Religious Commitment: The Role of the Will in Newman's Thought* [Oxford: Clarendon Press, 1980], p. 130).

[62] John Henry Newman, *An Essay in Aid of A Grammar of Assent,* with an introduction by Nicholas Lash (Notre Dame: University of Notre Dame Press, 1979).

[63] Ibid., p. 137.

[64] Nicholas Lash, "Introduction," Ibid., p. 12.

[65] He identifies doubt as a third.

[66] Newman, *Grammar of Assent,* p. 143.

[67] Ibid., p. 148.

[68] Ibid., p. 141.

[69] Ibid., pp. 142-43.

[70] Cf. Ibid., p. 145.

[71] Ibid., p. 148.

[72] Ibid., p. 150.

[73] Ibid., p. 161.

[74] Ibid., pp. 161-62.

[75] Ibid., pp. 186-87.

[76] It is "the perception of a truth with the perception that it is a truth, or the consciousness of knowing" (Ibid.).

[77] Ibid., p. 182. A special feeling accompanies certitude which Newman calls a "triumphant repose of the mind after a struggle" (Ibid., pp. 168-69).

[78] Ibid., p. 164.

[79] Ibid., p. 167.

[80] "It is a law of the mind," Newman states, "to seal up the conclusions to which ratiocination has brought me," by the formal assent of certitude (Ibid., p. 181).

[81] Ibid., p. 240.

[82] Ibid., pp. 250-251.

[83] "The processes of reasoning which legitimately lead to assent, to action, to certitude, are in fact too multiform, subtle, omnigenous, too implicit, to allow of being measured by rule" (Ibid., p. 240).

[84] Ibid., p. 239.

[85] Ibid., p. 230.

[86] Ibid., p. 260.

[87] Ibid., p. 276.

[88] Ibid., p. 275.

[89] Newman calls this the "illative sense" (Ibid., p. 281).

[90] Matson, *The Existence of God*, pp. 243-44.

[91] Mackie, *The Miracle of Theism*, p. 253.

[92] Jones, *Kant and the Nineteenth Century*, p. 228.

[93] Alisdair MacIntyre, "Kierkegaard, Søren Aabye," in *The Encyclopedia of Philosophy*, ed. Paul Edwards (8 vols.; New York: Macmillan Publishing Co., Inc. & The Free Press, 1967); 4:339.

[94] J. L. Mackie, *The Miracle of Theism*, p. 216.

[95] Ibid.

[96] *The Mind of Kierkegaard*, p. 265.

8
THE CONTRIBUTION OF REASON TO FAITH

In the previous chapter we reviewed a number of factors which indicate that reason is relevant to the experience of faith as Christians perceive it. They included the presence of a cognitive dimension in religious experience, the prominence of the word in biblical revelation, the role which serious reflection has played throughout the history of the church, and the existence of intellectual obstacles to Christian commitment. We also examined several approaches to the relation between faith and reason which question or qualify this view. In spite of the complexities which surround the issue, we returned to our original conclusion. Rational inquiry—in particular, the examination of the contents of faith in light of public evidence—can make a contribution to religious experience.

The purpose of this chapter is to determine what this contribution is. If reason is indeed relevant to the experience of faith, then how, precisely, are the two related? Just how does reason affect personal religious commitment? The question is complicated by a number of things. One is considerable variation in the meaning of both faith and reason. As we have seen, reason can refer to intellectual operations in general, or to specific forms of discursive inquiry. Moreover, such inquiry may be directed to the evidence provided by a particular religious tradition or by one's personal religious experience, or it may focus on the evidence provided by human experience in general. Our interest in the following discussion concerns the significance of discursive reason for personal religious experience, but we will need to take both public and private evidence into account.

Something else which greatly complicates our task is the enormous diversity of religious experience. The way, or ways, in which reason can contribute to faith depends heavily on the dynamics of individual religious experience. In order to determine the contribution of reason to faith, we therefore need to review some of the important variables in religious experience and note their likely effect on the contribution of reason to faith.

Variables Affecting Faith and Reason

The most important variable affecting the relation of rational inquiry to the experience of faith is the presence or absence of conscious religious commitment. Whether or not someone has undergone religious conversion will make a big difference in the way that person thinks about religion. There will be a wide contrast, for example, between both the scope and the kind of evidence available to committed believers and those available to non-believers. Believers have access to the evidence of their own religious experience. It will be more vivid and more extensive than the evidence provided by the sort of experiences which human beings have in common. At the same time, it will be intensely personal and therefore private—not the sort of thing that provides a basis for public arguments. In contrast, unbelievers are likely to insist that arguments concerning religion must appeal to public evidence in order to steer clear of personal prejudice or delusion.

In addition to the nature and scope of acceptable evidence, those who are religiously committed and those who are not may also differ in their attitudes toward the importance of deliberate rational inquiry. We might expect believers to be more interested in religious questions than non-believers. As a matter of fact, however, the rational investigation of religious issues is something that non-believers often find more interesting than believers do. Perhaps non-believers feel that this is the only approach to religious matters available to them, while believers enjoy a religious experience which has many different facets. Or perhaps the most familiar rational arguments relating to religion, such as theistic proofs, touch on issues that believers have completely settled in their minds. For example, a believer may find it difficult to work up an interest in arguments for the reality of

God, when God's existence is one of the most obvious features of daily experience. Or perhaps the non-believer feels that religious faith is possible only if it can be supported by solid rational arguments, while the believer feels no need for such support. Whatever the precise nature and the causes of the differences between believers and non-believers in their attitude toward rational inquiry, it is apparent that such differences exist.

The romantic analogy is helpful in thinking about the "before" and "after" questions relating to religious commitment. A man in the process of trying to decide whether he should marry a certain woman may spend weeks sorting out the pros and cons of such an action. But once his mind is made up, he no longer finds such activity necessary or appealing. Ordinarily, happily married people do not spend a lot of time trying to justify their choice of life partners. And if a couple did, we would probably suspect that something was wrong with their relationship. Similarly, perhaps, committed believers do not find it either necessary or appealing to work out logical reasons for their religious convictions.

Another variable which greatly affects the role of reason within the experience of faith is the level of religious development a person has attained. The phenomenon of faith development has received a good deal of attention in recent years. The scholarly consensus is that our religious growth follows a series of predictable stages, just like the development of other aspects of our lives. The religious experience of a five-year-old will differ from that of a 15-year-old, and this in turn will differ from that of someone who is 25, or 45, or 65. Moreover, there are predictable correlations between religious development and physical, mental and emotional development. So, the role reason plays in someone's religious experience depends to a significant degree on the level of that person's cognitive or intellectual development.

Everyone accepts the fact that religious faith is easier in early life than it is later on. Certainly, discursive reasoning is far less prominent in a child's experience than it is in a mature person. In contrast to older humans, children seem to accept religious beliefs with the same ease with which they entertain their other beliefs about reality. As Reinhold Niebuhr observes, "Life is a battle between faith and reason in which each feeds upon the other, drawing sustenance from it and destroying it. Nature has wisely ordained that faith shall have an early advantage in the life of the child to compensate for its later difficulties."[1]

Bailey Gillespie prefers to speak of "faith situations," rather than "stages of faith," in his study of religious experience.[2] He states that reason always participates in the faith experience to some degree, "because reason is indispensable in providing information and intellectual content to the religious life."[3] At the same time, he observes that the relative importance attached to deliberate rational inquiry varies from one faith situation to another. For example, "knowing" is particularly important during the faith experience of older youth, when "the cognitive understandings of faith are beginning to be formulated, organized, and established."[4]

Other variables also affect the role of reason in the experience of faith. They include an individual's level of intelligence and personality type. Some people are naturally reflective. They are inclined to think things through carefully and consider a wide range of data before making a decision or taking a certain course of action. Other people depend more on instincts and intuitions. They do what feels right without subjecting their choices to careful analysis. Naturally, rational inquiry will play a more prominent role in the religious experience of the former group. We would also expect people with high intelligence to give greater thought to religious matters than those less gifted, but this is not always the case. Not all reflective people are intellectually gifted, and not all highly intelligent people are inclined to be reflective.

Even within the experience of faith, there are often variations in the level of personal commitment. In an important sense, of course, faith is either present or not; one either trusts in God or one does not. But at certain times believers find it more difficult to maintain their confidence in God than at others. The Bible records the experiences of many devout people whose faith was severely tested, and who found it hard to keep trusting in God. Even the greatest prophets became discouraged. Elijah asked God to end his life, and John the Baptist began to wonder while imprisoned if Jesus was indeed the Messiah, in spite of the strong testimony he himself had borne earlier. Job's faith had to survive a series of personal disasters. And in the Bible's most famous challenge to faith, Abraham confronted the prospect of putting to death his promised son Isaac at God's command. We regard such figures as outstanding examples of religious devotion, yet with all of them confidence in God seemed to waver, even though their fundamental commitment to God apparently remained intact. These are exceptional cases, but similar variations in confidence in God occur in the lives of virtually all religious people. We would expect the role which rational inquiry plays in a person's life to vary with the changing course of his or her religious experience. At times what reason has to say about religious issues may seem to be indispensable, and at other times, entirely unnecessary.

Influences of a social nature can also affect the role of reason in someone's religious experience. Certain religious communities place a high priority on belief. Christians, for example, attach more importance to doctrine than do adherents of any other major religion. For other religions, deed is more important than creed. On a visit to Israel, I spoke with a Jewish rabbi who described the essence of Judaism as belonging to a historic community, rather than assenting to certain propositions. We can expect the relative importance people attach to rational inquiry within their religious experience to reflect the emphasis which their religious community places on belief.

Religious communities not only vary in the degree of importance they attach to beliefs, they also differ in the degree of importance they attach to the activity of reflecting on these beliefs. In some religious communities, giving assent to a creed or a statement of beliefs is more or less all that members are expected to do. In others, understanding what one assents to is held to be important too. Members of this second type of community are likely to give rational reflection a more prominent role in their personal religious experience.

The larger social environment also affects people's attitude toward the place of rational inquiry in religious experience. In an age of belief, where the cultural consensus supports religious claims, rational inquiry may seem to be unnecessary for personal faith. It may even be regarded as a threat to it. But in an age of reason, where the cultural consensus includes great confidence in human intellectual powers and requires every important truth claim to undergo rational investigation, the exercise of reason may seem to be indispensable to faith. In such a climate, faith may not be possible for people unless it can survive careful scrutiny.

The list of variables that affect the relation of rational inquiry to religious experience goes on and on, and the situation is further complicated by the possibility of cross-combinations among them. Consider, for example, the first two variables we mentioned—the presence or absence of explicit religious commitment and the existence of various levels of personal faith development. Viewing these together we can see that the time in life when religious commitment begins will have a major impact on the role which reason plays in the experience. For people with a strong religious upbringing intellectual inquiry typically takes the form of attempting to understand what they already accept as true. For people who encounter religious claims as adults, the role of reason may be to determine whether these claims represent a genuine option for serious thinkers. The Catholic theologian Karl Rahner describes his religious development as a process of accepting a tradition that he already belonged to. "I find myself a believer and have not come upon any good reason for not believing. I was baptized and brought up in the faith, and so the faith that is my inheritance has also become the faith of my own deliberate choice, a real, personal faith."[5] But in the experience of people like C. S. Lewis, who moved from atheism to Christianity as a well-educated adult, reason helps to meet the questions which religion raises for serious, sophisticated thinkers. It is not coincidental that Lewis is one of the twentieth century's most widely read Christian apologists.[6]

The number and complexity of the variables surrounding reason and faith make it impossible for us to provide a comprehensive analysis of their relationship here. We will have to settle for an account of the most important distinctions. Our first task will be to examine the role of rational inquiry in the experience of someone who has already made a conscious religious commitment. How does reason operate *within* the religious life? Then we will explore the function of reason in someone's experience before he or she makes a conscious religious commitment. We will try to determine if reason can help to prepare the way for faith. As we shall see, reason can make a positive contribution to religious experience in several ways, but fundamental trust in God, or saving faith, is never the *product* of rational investigation.

The Role of Reason Within Faith

Once faith is present, reason can contribute to religious experience in several different ways. Rational inquiry into the contents of faith increases knowledge and understanding and these, in turn, can deepen religious commitment. Just as love for another human being creates a desire to learn more about the person, love for God awakens a desire to know more about God, to discover new facets of truth.

Various passages of Scripture describe growth in knowledge as an important element in the Christian life. The letter of 2 Peter, for example, exhorts its readers to "make every effort to supplement your faith with virtue, and virtue with knowledge, and knowledge with self-control, and self-control with steadfastness, and steadfastness with godliness, and godliness with brotherly affection, and brotherly affection with love."[7] Acts of the Apostles praises the Jews of Beroea, "for they received the word with all eagerness, examining the scriptures daily to see if these things were so."[8] In Philippians Paul prays that his readers' love "may abound more and more, with knowledge and all discernment."[9] The letter to the Colossians contains the similar prayer that its readers will "be filled with the knowledge of [God's] will in all spiritual wisdom and understanding, to lead a life worthy of the Lord, ... bearing fruit in every good work and increasing in the knowledge of God."[10]

The biblical concepts of understanding and knowledge include much more than intellectual perception, as this last reference indicates. They also involve the notions of submission to the will of God and a life of commitment to his service.[11] But the intellectual element is always present to some degree.

There are also passages which take Christians to task for inadequate intellectual development. The letter to the Hebrews, for example, bemoans its readers' apparent failure to advance beyond a rudimentary grasp of God's word, and urges them to go on to maturity.[12] Similarly, Paul refers to the Christians in Corinth as "babes in Christ," because they are still of the flesh and therefore unready for solid food.[13]

The New Testament also contains several indications as to what the role of understanding should be in the Christian life. According to one of the passages we have cited, it leads to a life of fruitful activity. It also contributes to the general upbuilding of the Christian community.[14] Most significantly for our purposes, it strengthens faith. Intellectual activity increases comprehension, and increased comprehension deepens religious commitment. One passage in particular links together the ideas of knowledge, understanding and conviction—Colossians 2:2. As the New English Bible translates it, this verse expresses the hope that its readers may "come to the full wealth of conviction which understanding brings."

The idea that careful inquiry contributes to faith figures prominently in the thought of many Christian writers. The venerable tradition of "faith seeking understanding" associated with figures like Augustine and Anselm rests on the assumption that rational inquiry can enhance the quality of religious devotion. As we noticed in an earlier chapter, Anselm sets his famous "ontological" argument for the existence of God within the context of prayer and introduces it by expressing the desire that his reason should grasp what he already affirms by faith.

Ellen G. White, the most influential writer in my own religious community, the Seventh-day Adventist Church, urges a careful examination of the contents of faith as a means of deepening one's own spiritual confidence, and enabling one to meet opposition and criticism. Indeed, she insists that this is the only way to keep pace with the advancement of truth itself. "We must not think," she admonishes, "'Well, we have all the truth, we understand the main pillars of our faith, and we may rest on this knowledge.' The truth is an advancing truth, and we must walk in the increasing light."[15] She even speaks of heaven as a school where education will continue for eternity, since there will continually arise "new truths to comprehend."[16] She emphasizes the value of carefully formulated arguments in the presentation of religious truth: "It is important that in defending the doctrines which we consider fundamental articles of faith, we should never allow ourselves to employ arguments that are not wholly sound."[17] In her view, then, the careful examination of truth, the rigorous application of reason to the contents of faith, has an important role to play in the developing experience of the committed Christian.

Reason enhances personal religious commitment in another way, too. Besides increasing believers' comprehension of the contents of faith, intellectual activity can also answer questions or resolve doubts about their beliefs. As students of spiritual formation remind us, the typical course faith follows is not one of smooth, uninterrupted growth in confidence. There are hills and valleys in the terrain of religious experience. Sooner or later, we all encounter trials and obstacles which raise questions in our minds and test our confidence in God. When this happens, reason can help us to overcome our doubts and formulate responses to criticism. The discovery that it is possible to develop effective answers to difficult questions about our beliefs can strengthen our confidence in God.

Significantly, reason can appeal to both private and public evidence in this capacity. People with an extensive religious history often have a rich store of private evidence on which to draw. Someone facing tragedy and tempted to wonder if God still cares may find reassurance in the memory of times when God's presence seemed especially vivid. Previous blessings represent a source of private evidence. On the other hand, the same person may be helped by some solid philosophical reflection on the age-old problem of evil which appeals solely to our common human experience. It can be encouraging to discover that there are impressive arguments to support the claims of faith.

In fact, certain writings on spirituality suggest that responding to doubt is the most important contribution reason can make to religious experience. For example, in her book *Steps to Christ*, Ellen G. White discusses the role of reason in Christian experience in a chapter entitled, "What to Do With Doubt." She begins by observing that "Many, especially those who are young in the Christian life, are at times troubled with the suggestions of skepticism," which unsettle their faith in the Scriptures as a revelation from God. Then she encourages those facing this problem with a strong affirmation of the support which reason gives to faith: "God never asks us to believe, without giving sufficient evidence upon which to base our faith. His existence, His character, the truthfulness of His word, are all established by testimony that appeals to our reason; and this testimony is abundant."[18]

As she goes on to describe it, the evidence which thus supports belief in the divine authority of the Bible is both public and private in nature. On the public side, we find that the truth of the Bible is perfectly adapted to the needs and longings of the human heart. On the private side, the most readily available evidence of all is that of personal experience. Those who act on the Bible's promises, she claims, will discover just how reliable they are.[19] So, reason can help to overcome doubt by finding evidence to corroborate some of the basic claims of faith.

Besides increasing personal commitment and responding to doubt, reason also has an effect on the configuration of belief. According to one model of its role, reason undergirds the contents of faith, or strengthens their foundation, by finding evidence to support them. This presupposes that these beliefs are already firmly in place and reasonably well-established, so that all reason has to do is add bulk to their foundation. In actuality, however, it is seldom the case that reason simply supports views which are already fixed within the overall framework of belief. The typical effects of rational inquiry are much more extensive. Examining the contents of faith can change the relationships among our various beliefs. As a result of rational inquiry, the perceived importance of certain beliefs may increase or decrease. Beliefs assumed to have been central to faith may move to the periphery, and beliefs first thought to be secondary may assume primary importance. Not only that, but confidence in certain beliefs can change under the impact of rational scrutiny. Believers may discover that some of their long held ideas are not as well-founded as they earlier thought. On the other hand, they may find that the evidence which supports certain ideas is more impressive than it first appeared.

Rational inquiry may also discover that traditional arguments for certain beliefs are entirely inadequate. This can result in a loss of confidence in these beliefs, but it can also lead to the discovery of other arguments which place them on more secure footings than ever. It is also possible that the entire dimension of belief may assume greater or less importance within the religious life in general as a consequence of rational inquiry. After examining their beliefs, for example, people may discover that cultivating relationships with others, participating in the life of the religious community, is more important than entertaining various ideas.

These variations in the effects of rational inquiry indicate that there is an element of risk involved in exercising reason within the experience of faith. There is no way to determine in advance just what the outcome of rational activity will be. A careful examination of faith can develop answers to questions, discover further evidence to support beliefs, increase understanding and deepen commitment. But the same activity can also expose inadequate arguments, raise further questions, introduce doubt and weaken confidence.

In view of the potential liabilities of rational inquiry, some people feel that its benefits are not worth the risk, so they try to avoid it themselves and discourage it in others. They believe that we must safeguard faith by refusing to entertain questions about our beliefs. As attractive as many people find it and as effective as it sometimes is, however, this protective strategy is unacceptable. For one thing, even if suppressing rational inquiry is effective as a temporary expedient, in the long run it inevitably fails. Sooner or later, truth will out, as they say, difficult questions will arise. And if these questions emerge on the heels of attempts to stifle the process of inquiry, the threat to faith can be greater than ever. The problems of people who finally start asking questions are compounded by the suspicion that those who discouraged them from doing so were deliberately trying to hide something. This suspicion alone can make people doubtful about religious beliefs. So, whatever the risks of subjecting our beliefs to serious inquiry, the risks of refusing to do so are greater.

Besides the fact that it will not work—not in the long run, anyway—there is a more fundamental reason to reject a protective strategy in matters of faith. A reluctance or a refusal to examine one's beliefs is incompatible with the inherent confidence of faith. Faith involves absolute certainty, the confidence that you can stake your life on the object of your trust. Strong believers may not feel a special burden to formulate an intellectual defense of their faith. After all, when matters are settled in your mind, you don't feel a need to keep inquiring into their truth. At the same time, mature believers will not be reluctant to examine their beliefs if the situation calls for it and will certainly not discourage others from inquiring into them. People who refuse to reflect on their religious convictions, or who are unable or unwilling to offer reasons for their beliefs, convey the impression that they are either not clear as to what they believe or that the confidence they profess to have in their beliefs really is not there.

The Role of Reason Prior to Faith

The quest for evidence to support religious beliefs ordinarily takes place where religious commitment is already present. This is true of appeals to public as well as private evidence. As Bernard Lonergan observes, "with regard to the actual order in which we live, . . . normally religious conversion precedes the effort to work out rigorous proofs for the existence of God."[20] The history of the best known theistic arguments bears this out. As we have noted, Anselm formulated the so-called "ontological" argument in the eleventh century, not in the effort somehow to achieve faith in God, but as an attempt to express and understand what he already believed. "For I do not seek to understand that I may believe," he stated, "but I believe in order to understand."[21] Thomas Aquinas included several versions of the cosmological argument as part of the doctrine of God in his *Summa Theologiae*.

And the most famous presentation of the teleological argument appears in the writings of William Paley, an eighteenth century British churchman.

Rational inquiry also takes place, however, when personal religious commitment is apparently absent, and this raises one of the most important questions about our topic. Does reason contribute to the origin as well as the development of faith? Can rational inquiry help to generate faith, as well as contribute to it once a conscious religious commitment is already present? The answer is a qualified yes; there are times when a rational examination of religious beliefs can prepare the way for personal religious commitment. But most people view them as exceptions rather than the rule. Lonergan, for example, says, "I do not think it impossible that [theistic] proofs might be a factor facilitating religious conversion so that, by way of exception, certain knowledge of God's existence should precede the acceptance of God's love."[22] We will try to describe this function and then assess its limitations.

In Chapter 5 we examined the results of analyzing religious belief in the light of publicly accessible evidence. The best-known examples of this endeavor are the classical arguments for the existence of God. They support the conclusion that there is a supreme personal being who could reach out to us, if he chose to, and invite us into a personal relationship with him. Beyond affirming the mere existence of such a being, however, reason has next to nothing to say about God. So there seems to be very little that we can learn by examining the contents of faith in light of publicly accessible evidence.

In spite of their limitations, the results of this inquiry can provide an important preparation for conscious religious commitment. The demonstration that there is evidence to support the reality of God within our common human experience refutes the familiar objection that religion is merely a matter of private prejudice, which no responsible person could accept, or purely a matter of personal intuition, in which case you either have it or you do not, and there is nothing you can do to acquire it. Reason thus serves as a "clearing house for faith." By removing some of the intellectual obstacles that prevent people from respecting religion, it can establish religious commitment as a viable option for the thinking person. So, even though the continuities between rational inquiry and the contents of faith may be extremely limited, they are nonetheless highly significant.

This "clearing house" effect of reason's inquiry into faith can be helpful to people from religious as well as non-religious backgrounds. It is sometimes more difficult for people who are familiar with religion to look at faith with an open mind than for people who are not. As Kierkegaard says, "It is easier to become a Christian when I am not a Christian than to become a Christian when I am one."[23] People who come from a strong religious background are sometimes inclined to attribute all religious commitment, including their own in earlier life, entirely to social and psychological influences. Had they been raised under different conditions, they suspect, they might never have given religion serious consideration. The availability of evidence which derives from common human experience and therefore cannot be attributed solely to private religious inclination may oblige such people to give greater respect to the claims of faith.

The Limitations of Reason in Relation to Faith

In their eagerness to show that religious commitment is reasonable in the modern world, believers occasionally speak of faith as if it were the natural result of logical investigation. This is understandable in light of the contemporary challenges to religion. For many people, only the results of careful investigation constitute truth, and what is not rationally demonstrable is not worthy of belief. But it is a mistake to exaggerate the importance of reason in relation to faith. Doing so can make religious commitment appear to be simply the matter-of-fact result of rational inquiry, or the necessary conclusion of an argument, and this distorts faith's essential character. Rational inquiry alone can never lead us step by step from unbelief to the point where trust in God is the only logical move to make next. Reason can help to prepare the way for faith, but personal trust in God is not merely a product of rational inquiry. The role of reason once faith is established is also limited. It can contribute to an ongoing religious experience, as we have seen, but it is never the most prominent feature.

A number of factors oblige us to conclude that the role which reason plays in the emergence of faith is so limited. First of all, the origins of faith are notoriously obscure. The facts of experience indicate that people seldom if ever come to faith through a process of rational investigation. It is doubtful that the ontological, cosmological and teleological arguments for God's existence have ever converted anybody.[24] In fact, deliberate, methodical reflection on questions of an intellectual nature plays a noticeable role in the religious experience of very few people, and even when present its impact is typically slight. It never operates alone, and the things which accompany it are much more influential. Instead of logical evidence, clearly accessible to rational assessment, the factors which lead to faith are largely non-rational in character. They may be vague, imperceptible impressions, unconsciously assimilated and responded to, such as the attitudes of other persons, or the particular emotions that accompany certain experiences.

These observations comport with the biblical account of conversion. In a famous passage describing the new birth, the transformation required in order to enter the kingdom of God, Jesus compares the experience to the wind, whose origin and destination are imperceptible. "The wind blows where it wills, and you hear the sound of it, but you do not know whence it comes or whither it goes; so it is with every one who is born of the Spirit."[25] If conversion came about through a process of rational investigation, we would be able to provide a clear, step-by-step account of its arrival. But we never can. We can chart the general course of faith development and observe the characteristics it exhibits in different situations and stages of life, but the actual emergence of faith is inscrutable. It always has an element of mystery. No one moves from unbelief to faith through rational inquiry alone.

Something else which shows that the influence of reason is limited is the fact that the quality of faith, or the depth of personal religious commitment, is not directly proportional to intellectual ability. The young and the uneducated often display greater religious devotion than the intellectually sophisticated. Extensive education is no guarantee that a person will make a strong religious commitment. In fact, the opposite seems to be the tendency. People often become less interested in religious matters as they become more educated. We often refer to the "simple faith" of children as an outstanding example of religious devotion, and their trust is characteristically untroubled by the complexities which occupy their elders.

Besides the facts of experience just mentioned, the nature of faith itself limits the extent to which reason can contribute to it. In Chapter 1 we described faith as having receptive, cognitive and volitional dimensions. It involves responding to God's gracious initiative, affirming the truth of certain propositions, and making a personal decision. The view that faith is the product of rational investigation conflicts with each of these essential dimensions.

The most obvious conflict involves the volitional character of faith. Faith presupposes freedom, and freedom requires the existence of genuine alternatives. If faith, or trust in God, were the only available position, if reason permitted no other choice, then faith would not be a free response to God's saving love. It would be nothing more than an admission of the obvious.

The view that reason can produce faith also conflicts with its receptive character. If faith could be attained solely by the operation of human reason, then it would represent a human achievement, a type of intellectual works righteousness, rather than an acceptance of divine grace. Moreover, if faith were simply the product of rational activity, we would expect the quality of one's faith to be directly proportional to one's intellectual abilities, or one's capacity for rational investigation. And if faith depended solely on our abilities to reach certain conclusions through rational inquiry, we would have to place a relatively low estimate on the quality of faith in the uneducated and the young, the very ones Jesus singled out as examples of trust in God.[26] Furthermore, the view that faith is the product of reason reduces the trust of such individuals as Job and Abraham to the level of stupidity, for they continued to rely on God when to all appearances it was the "unreasonable" thing to do.

The notion that reason can produce religious commitment also conflicts with the degree of confidence characteristic of genuine faith. We observed in Chapter 1 that faith involves absolute or unconditional confidence. It is the trusting certainty that its object is completely reliable. As John Henry Newman reminds us, however, rational investigation never achieves more than a high degree of probability, at least in matters of personal significance. We reach certainty only by going beyond inference alone. So, rational inference cannot produce the trusting certainty of faith. This is why we think of faith as going beyond the available evidence. It affirms and trusts in more than reason by itself could ever demonstrate. The discrepancy between what reason can achieve and what faith must affirm therefore contradicts the idea that reason could ever produce genuine religious commitment.

Another consideration which prevents us from regarding faith as a product of rational investigation is the type of evidence which provides faith with its strongest support. In Chapter 5 we examined the publicly accessible evidence which corroborates the contents of faith. We discovered, among other things, that the conclusions established by such evidence are extremely small in scope, when compared to the contents of special revelation. All that the evidence of our common human experience can establish is the minimal conclusion that it is reasonable to affirm the existence of a supreme personal being. Although it is not logically impossible that a person might respond to this evidence by exercising personal faith in God, it is highly unlikely. The factors that lead people to the point of commitment are typically private rather than public. They include such things as very personal experiences, the testimony of believers and the contents of particular religious traditions. As Stephen Davis remarks, "the evidence a person holds as grounds for his faith-propositions is typically private rather than public. That is, what convinces him that a faith-proposition is true would not necessarily convince anyone else."[27]

The romantic analogy may be applicable here. Ordinarily the specific factors which lead people to make a lifelong commitment to each other are highly personal in nature. There may be public evidence which makes such a decision understandable to other people, such as physical attractiveness, economic potential, and similar interests, but these reasons do not adequately explain why two particular people feel the way they do about each other. Only evidence of a private nature could do that. Lovers see things in each other that are imperceptible to anyone else.

Not only is the evidence which provides the strongest support for faith typically private, but it also presupposes the existence of faith to some degree. So, its role is less to generate faith than to enhance religious experience once faith is already present. To quote Ellen G. White once again, "the highest evidence of the divine authorship of the Bible" is the effect of its "vivifying power" on one's own mind and heart.[28] Similarly, she says that "the real evidence of a living God" lies in "the conviction that God has written on our hearts, illuminated and explained by His word. It is the living power in His created works, seen by the eye which the Holy Spirit has enlightened."[29] What Ellen White identifies here and elsewhere as the "highest evidence," the "real evidence," the most convincing evidence, for the claims of faith exhibits an intensely personal character. It is not perceptible from some neutral standpoint; it is not publicly accessible.

But if public evidence alone cannot produce faith, is it possible that *all* the evidence available to a person—private as well as public—could make faith logically necessary? Could a rational examination of everything that conduces to belief fully establish a person's trust in God? Bringing private as well as public evidence within the purview of rational inquiry would certainly expand the scope of available conclusions. And the rational examination of private evidence would no doubt contribute a good deal more to the establishment of faith than public evidence alone could do. Nevertheless, we would still have to conclude that faith could never be the product of rational investigation. If faith is really a free decision, there will always be a distance between the affirmations of faith and the deliverances of reason.

The fact that faith is not the product of rational inquiry has important consequences on the level of personal religious experience. Since the results of such investigation are not completely conclusive, there is always room for doubt. We can never reach the point where we are so secure in our convictions that we are beyond the possibility of losing them, or so close to God that we could never drift away. Just as each development of our experience can bring new evidence to support our trust in God, each phase of life can present us with new challenges to our confidence in him.

It may be significant that two of the most outstanding examples of faith in biblical literature faced their greatest test as mature believers. Job and Abraham each had their faith severely tried after they had been close to God for many years. This supports a point that existentialist Christian theologians have often made. Faith is never a permanent achievement. It is not something we acquire once and for all. Instead, it is something we must exercise again and again in the concrete experiences of life. As Rudolf Bultmann puts it, "Faith in the Creator can never be possessed once for all as a reassuring insight, but must constantly be won and realized anew."[30]

Another factor which restricts the contribution of reason to faith and prevents us from regarding faith as a product of reason is the limited results of rational inquiry into religion. In Chapter 5 we noticed the striking contrast between the God of religion and the God of philosophy. The God of religion is the concrete object of personal religious devotion. The God of philosophy is the object of philosophical reflection—the concept of God involved in the various theistic proofs, for example. It is the sort of idea of God that Thomas Aquinas has in mind in when he concludes each of the famous five ways by stating, "And all men call this God."[31] The religious notion of God is rich in detail, filled with the associations of specific religious traditions and personal religious experiences. The philosophical concept of God is comparatively abstract. It contains the minimal defining characteristics of the divine reality. The God of religion is my God here and now—the object of my personal religious devotion. The God of philosophy is anyone's God—God as he figures in the experience of every human being by virtue of his metaphysical status. The concept of God achieved by philosophical reflection will always fall short of the religious idea of God in its capacity to awaken devotion and serve as an object of worship.

The minimal results of philosophical inquiry into religion are rather typical of philosophical reflection generally. The stronger an argument is on logical grounds, the greater the theoretical confidence it generates, but the more abstract its conclusion will be. For example, nothing could be clearer than the assertion that two plus two is four, but its clarity is due to its abstractness. The relevance of this mathematical proposition to the issues which concern us most deeply is minimal. As we move toward the central concerns of life the logical clarity of the issues decreases, along with the possibility of attaining the theoretical certainty produced by rational argument. At the same time, however, the personal importance of the issues increases. On a purely logical or theoretical level, then, we can be most confident of things that matter least and least confident of the things in life that matter most. The more specific and concrete our religious beliefs, it seems, the less public evidence there is to support them and the weaker strictly rational arguments for them become. This does not necessarily mean that our personal confidence in such beliefs will be weaker, however. For, as we have seen, the evidence which provides the strongest support for personal convictions is typically private rather than public in nature.

It may be helpful to compare our views on this point with the position Gary Gutting takes in his interesting discussion, *Religious Belief and Religious Skepticism*. Gutting qualifies the contribution which rational justification can make to religious belief with two interesting distinctions. One involves different degrees of intellectual assent. As he describes them, "decisive assent" denies a need for further consideration of the claim assented to, while "interim assent" acknowledges such a need.[32] Gutting also differentiates between the "core" and the "outer belt" of religious belief. The inner core of religious belief has minimal propositional content. It consists of virtually nothing more than belief in the presence of a superhuman power and love in our lives, "an awareness of and an openness to the power and goodness of a divinity that remains essentially mysterious to us." All the more specific beliefs characteristic of particular religious creeds and traditions belong to the outer belt.[33]

Gutting argues that only the essential core of religious belief deserves decisive assent. In his words, "the assertion that there is a good and powerful being concerned about us is the *only* religious claim ... worthy of the decisive assent that is essential to religious belief as traditionally construed."[34] Accordingly, religious beliefs which form the outer belt appropriately receive only interim assent. This does not mean that such beliefs are unimportant or dispensable. To the contrary, they play an important role in religious experience. They enable us to participate in the life of religious communities, and they make religious belief a live option in the cultural context in which we live. But we should not give them the unqualified commitment we give to beliefs which comprise the inner core.[35] According to Gutting, this distinction between the core and the outer belt of religious belief is the key to rehabilitating the cognitive claims of religion. "The greatest cognitive failure of religions throughout history," he states, "has been their confusion ... of the core and the outer belt of their commitment," which results in "demands for decisive assent to claims that at best deserve interim assent."[36]

It is helpful to distinguish as Gutting does between central and peripheral aspects of our religious beliefs and between different levels of assent to what we believe. It is also helpful to correlate these distinctions. Ideally our confidence should be strongest about those aspects of belief which are truly most important, and we should be less insistent with respect to our claims about the rest. This position allows our faith to be strong even if we have doubts about matters of secondary importance, so long as the center of our beliefs is secure.

However, the way Gutting correlates these distinctions does not fit concrete religious experience precisely. The logical center of religious belief as he identifies it does not necessarily coincide with the actual center of personal religious faith. There is impressive public evidence for the reality of a supreme personal being, as we saw in Chapter 5, and private evidence supports it, too, as Gutting notes. But people also find compelling private evidence for a number of beliefs besides this one. And since believers are often just as confident in other things as they are in the reality of God, it is unrealistic to maintain that people should give decisive assent only to this one belief. To be faithful to actual religious experience, it seems we must either extend decisive assent to beliefs other than the logical core that Gutting identifies, or else expand the core of religion to include other beliefs. Either move would obscure Gutting's distinction.

I would like to preserve the distinction Gutting makes between the core and outer belt of religious belief without restricting the content of the core as he does, because this slights the influence of private evidence in personal religious experience. To do this we need to differentiate, as our discussion has done, among several configurations of belief. In Part 2 we carefully distinguished between philosophical and theological approaches to the contents of faith. Our examination of the experience of faith in Part 3 requires us to introduce another. For philosophical purposes, only evidence of a strictly public nature is appropriate—evidence accessible to any thinking person. For theological purposes, moderately private evidence comes into play. Expressions of the community's faith will draw from authorities accepted by the community and from common elements within its members' experiences. In the area of personal religion, evidence of a highly private nature plays a prominent role, and its influence is typically decisive.

Now, we will find a supreme reality of power and love at the core of all three configurations—philosophical, theological and personal. But this core will become progressively larger as we move from the philosophical to the personal sphere. Private evidence enters the picture, and it extends our confidence to other beliefs as well. In addition, the level of personal confidence in our core beliefs will rise in proportion to the amount of the total evidence that supports them and particularly in proportion to the strength of the private evidence. Even so, no matter how much evidence accumulates to support our beliefs, personal faith is always more than cognitive assent. There will always be a distance between the conclusions of reason and the commitment of faith.

Concept and Metaphor: Reason and The Language of Faith

The natural language of religion is one of the most important factors which limits the contribution of reason to faith. There is a stark contrast between the fundamental symbols and metaphors through which faith comes to expression and the conceptual language characteristic of rational inquiry. We will bring our discussion of faith and reason to a close by considering the relation between concepts and metaphors.

We just referred to two of the most familiar formal applications of reason to faith. Both theology and philosophy of religion involve the conceptual analysis of religion. Systematic or constructive theology examines the intellectual contents of a specific religious tradition. Christian theology attempts to identify and organize the essential beliefs expressed in the Bible, church doctrine and Christian experience. Philosophy of religion examines the most fundamental religious ideas from the perspective of human experience in general. We could also describe the two disciplines as exercises in conceptual translation. Christian theology seeks modern ways to express a message which was originally formulated within a completely different social and historical context. Its purpose is to express in terms and concepts that are meaningful today the message that the biblical writers originally expressed in the terms and concepts prevalent in their culture. Theology thus plays a mediating role. It moves between the thought-world of the Bible and that of modern times. The task of philosophy of religion is similar. It examines the manifold forms of religious expression, identifies the central ideas, and analyzes them in light of contemporary criteria of meaning and truth.

It is apparent that theology and philosophy of religion move between two contrasting realms of discourse—the realms of concept and metaphor. The two disciplines seek to express in straightforward, conceptual language meanings embodied in figurative speech—in symbols, metaphors, myths and parables. Both strive to develop a system of thought whose component ideas will be clear; coherent, or consistent with one another; adequate to the phenomenon under investigation; and convincing to the thoughtful observer. The two disciplines proceed by formulating questions, developing answers, constructing arguments and defending positions against objections and criticisms. Conceptual language therefore provides the natural means of theological and philosophical expression.

Conceptual language is not, however, the primary means of religious expression.[37] As the complex variety of material in the Bible reveals, the fundamental language, or languages, of religion are those of symbolic speech—parable, narrative, myth, and metaphor, to mention some of the more prominent categories. Occasionally, straightforward conceptual language may appear, but this is the exception. Theology and philosophy of religion thus apply reason to a dimension of life whose primary expressions are different from concepts.

Consider, for example, the biblical descriptions of God and the parables of Jesus. Some of the most familiar terms theology and philosophy apply to God, "omnipotent," "omnipresent" and "omniscient," do not appear in the Bible at all. We may see the idea of omnipotence in the words, "with God all things are possible,"[38] and find the notion of omniscience in the affirmation, "God is greater than our hearts, and he knows everything."[39] But these are hardly definitions of the concepts. Instead, we find God described as a father, a king, a shepherd, even a rock—expressions drawn from physical objects and familiar social relationships. To explain the meaning of the commandment, "Love thy neighbor," Jesus did not formulate theses on universal altruism, he told the story of the good Samaritan. To describe the eventual triumph of the kingdom of God—itself a figure of speech, by the way—he did not lecture on demographic growth or political transformation, he related the parable of the mustard seed. We could multiply examples, but it is clear that the characteristic languages of religious expression, as illustrated in biblical literature, are imaginative and suggestive rather than literal and conceptual.

Scholars today apply many different categories to the language, or "linguistic manifestations," of religion, but the one which is most inclusive, and which serves our purposes best, is "metaphor." One reason metaphors are important to religious experience is the fact that they are basic to all our experience. In order to determine the relation between reason and religious metaphor, therefore, it will be helpful to look at the influential role that metaphors in general play in our lives.

Most of us first heard of metaphors in introductory literature courses, since the use of metaphors is a familiar and widespread poetic device. A simile, our teachers told us, employs the words "like" and "as" in making a comparison, as in the line from Robert Burns, "My love is like a red, red rose."[40] In contrast, a metaphor dispenses with "like" and "as" and simply describes one thing as if it were something else. Literary metaphors may be relatively simple and straightforward. According to Samuel Daniel, for example, "love is a sickness full of woes, all remedies refusing."[41] Or they may be subtle and extended. In his poem "The Tiger," William Blake likens evil to that frightful beast of the jungle without ever actually saying so.[42] And in his complex poem "The Windhover" Gerard Manley Hopkins compares Jesus Christ to a falcon soaring on the morning breeze.[43] In general terms, then, a metaphor brings different things together and attributes to one the qualities and characteristics of the other.

The subject of metaphors has attracted a great deal of attention in recent years, and the evidence indicates that the use of metaphors in human thought extends far beyond their role in imaginative literature. Scholars have discovered that metaphors contribute to our thinking in many complex and multifaceted ways. And some believe that the formation of metaphors is one of the most important operations of our minds.

According to Mary Gerhart and Allan Russell, whom we mentioned in Chapter 2, the essential function of metaphor is not merely to illustrate but to generate meaning. In fact, they believe that we can best explain the way in which knowledge develops in science and religion as the result of forming new metaphors in these areas. An analogy is the discovery of similarities that already exist between different fields of meaning, but a metaphor is the forced conjunction of two fields of meaning, the imposition of one upon the other. When metaphors are deliberately created, they produce a willful distortion that requires us to look at things in new and potentially fruitful ways. A metaphor, then, is "inventive and constructive," rather than "expressive and descriptive."[44] It is much more than "a linguistic artifact," a clever way to illustrate something we already understand. A metaphor is nothing less than "a structural change in a field of meaning."[45]

While some metaphors are deliberate inventions, others seem to rise spontaneously from fundamental levels of our experience. In two books on the subject, Mark Johnson argues that we instinctively express ourselves in metaphorical terms.[46] Like Gerhart and Russell, he insists that a metaphor is not just a linguistic expression "used for artistic or rhetorical purposes," but "a process of human understanding by which we achieve meaningful experience that we can make sense of."[47] However, it is not the deliberate use of metaphors to generate meaning that interests him, but the natural way we rely on metaphors to interpret the world and express ourselves.

In *Metaphors We Live By*, Johnson and his coauthor George Lakoff explore the pervasiveness of metaphors in our experience. They discover that we think and speak in metaphors naturally and unself-consciously—attributing to one thing the qualities and characteristics of something else. Many metaphors are so familiar to us that we never recognize them as such until someone points it out. The familiar metaphor *time is money*, for example, lies behind such familiar expressions as "you're wasting my time"; "you need to budget your time"; and "thank you for your time."[48] Similarly, we rely on the metaphor *argument is war* when we make statements like these: "your claims are indefensible"; "his criticisms were right on target"; and "I've never won an argument with him."[49]

We use metaphors in great numbers, and we apply different metaphors to the same experience. Besides comparing argument to war, for example, we also describe it as a journey. We speak of an argument as "going somewhere," or "covering a distance," or "following a path," as these expressions show: "do you follow my argument?" "we've gone off in the wrong direction again"; "You're going around in circles."[50] No area of life inspires a greater variety of metaphors than the experience of love. We speak of love as a physical force ("they gravitated to each other immediately"), as a patient ("they have a strong, healthy relationship"), as a form of madness ("I'm crazy about her"), as magic ("she is bewitching"), and even as war ("she is beseiged by suitors").[51]

Although metaphors pervade our experience in great number, certain metaphors are so influential that they arise over and over in different areas of life. Consider the many ways we draw on the spatial orientation "up" versus "down." The metaphor *good is up*, along with its negative counterpart *bad is down*, lies behind many familiar expressions, such as "Things are looking up," and "He does high-quality work." We also see it in statements like these: "My income rose last year"; "The number of errors he made is incredibly low" (more is up; less is down); "He's at the height of his power"; "He is low man on the totem pole" (having control is up; being subject to control is down); "She has high standards"; "That was a low-down thing to do" (virtue is up; depravity is down).[52]

As these examples indicate, our use of metaphors is not artificial or contrived, and the basic metaphors we employ, such as *good is up*, are not arbitrarily invented. To the contrary, metaphors are the most spontaneous means we have of expressing ourselves. We grow up with them, and they are so natural to us that we never think of them as such. This means that metaphors do more than embellish our understanding, they constitute our understanding. In other words, human thought is intrinsically metaphorical; the way we understand things is to juxtapose them and attribute to one the qualities of another. The metaphorical nature of human thinking becomes clear when we perceive the intimate bond that exists between our bodily experience and the basic elements of our understanding.

As its subtitle suggests, "The Bodily Basis of Meaning, Imagination, and Reason," the thesis of Johnson's book *The Body in the Mind* is that the basic notions we use to interpret our world arise from the essential features of corporeal experience within the world. Elementary physical experiences such as a sense of bodily containment and a sense of force provide the material from which our concepts and ideas are constructed. The "simple" notion of containment, he argues, forms a basis for the fundamental operations of logic.[53]

In summary, metaphors not only express our experience, they shape and structure it. "Our ordinary conceptual system, in terms of which we both think and act, is fundamentally metaphorical in nature."[54] And our most basic attitudes and convictions arise from the metaphors with which we think. Consequently, it is not the case that we *have* experiences and *then* develop metaphors to describe them. Instead, our experience itself is intrinsically and incorrigibly metaphorical.

In religion, as in human experience generally, metaphors exhibit enormous variety, pervasiveness and influence. We can see the importance of metaphors in religious experience by comparing their influence to that of concepts. We do not acquire our basic religious metaphors through a process of self-conscious reflection. Instead, they typically emerge imperceptibly over a long period of time. People with a religious upbringing acquire their most influential religious metaphors within the first few years of life, and these metaphors determine the shape of their subsequent experience. So, our basic religious metaphors are pre-rational, and they speak to us on a deeper psychological and emotional level than concepts alone could ever do. Consequently, when metaphors and concepts come into conflict, metaphors almost always prevail.

Religious concepts and metaphors often clash within an individual's experience. Not infrequently people come to understand a doctrine intellectually yet fail to appropriate its truth personally. Consider, for example, Paul's famous doctrine of righteousness by faith, the belief that God saves sinful human beings solely on the basis of divine grace, independent of their success in keeping the law. The natural effect of this doctrine would be a sense of confidence and security, profound joy and relief at being accepted by God in spite of one's inherent sinfulness. But this is not the experience of a good many people who understand the Christian doctrine of salvation perfectly well.

The reason is that their basic religious metaphor is legalistic, even though their doctrinal conviction is evangelical. On an intellectual level they affirm that works contribute nothing to salvation. But on the deeper level of fundamental self-perception, they feel that God cannot accept them until they are worthy. So, when doctrinal concepts conflict with our basic religious metaphors, we may find them intellectually attractive, but we will not enjoy their experiential ramifications.

Because metaphors are so important in religion, significant religious change always involves a change of metaphors, not merely an adjustment of concepts or doctrines. A good deal of Jesus' teaching consisted of various attempts to alter people's religious metaphors. This was clearly his intention in telling the famous parables of Luke 15. Jesus' critics objected to his associating with sinners and tax collectors. They viewed such persons as sources of ritual defilement and therefore as objects to be avoided. In these parables Jesus attempted to change their perspective by applying a powerful new metaphor to these unfortunate people. He described them, not as threats to ritual cleanliness, but as objects of immense value, whose recovery brings joy to the heart of God. They were not merely "sinners," forever beyond the pale of divine favor, but lost sons and daughters of their heavenly Father, who longed for their return. By using dramatic metaphors to speak directly to the imaginations and emotions of his listeners, Jesus sought to transform their religious perspective.

An appreciation for the fundamental and formative role of religious metaphors has led many thinkers to reconsider the task of Christian theology. A while ago it was not unusual for theologians to regard their work as one of distilling the essence of religion from the raw material which primitive forms of religious expression provided. They seemed to assume that the essential aspect of religion was what could be stated with logical precision, and that theology performs the noble service of elevating religious matters from the rudimentary level of mythical and symbolic expression to the superior level of rational discourse, where questions concerning their truth could be effectively arbitrated.

The prevailing attitude toward religious symbols, myths, metaphors, and narratives has changed significantly within the past few years. Not only do theologians generally respect the unique religious significance of metaphor and narrative, but new types of theology—some would say new schools of theology—have developed in response to it. The list of articles, dissertations and books with words like "metaphorical theology" and "narrative theology" in their titles grows longer every year, not to mention those devoted to the exploration of specific religious metaphors, such as "liberation."

Indeed, in certain circles, the prevailing sentiment has not only turned away from the conceptually defined task of theology we outlined in Chapter 3, it has turned against it. A "postmodern" mentality regards attempts to achieve truth discursively with suspicion and emphatically rejects the view that concepts are superior to metaphors.[55] In the current climate the quest for cognitive precision and conceptual clarity is problematic, while the value of non-discursive means of expression like metaphors and symbols is taken for granted.

There have been impressive attempts in recent years to fashion a method for Christian theology in response to these developments,[56] but all we can do here is offer some general comments on the relation between concept and metaphor. We acknowledge the importance and the priority of metaphor in religious experience. But we also affirm the value of the rational inquiry into faith which theology and philosophy of religion involve.

Let us locate the possible extremes in relating metaphor and concept, then look for a place for ourselves between them. One extreme is to regard the two as merely different ways of saying the same thing. On this view, concepts and metaphors both serve to communicate information, but they transport their cognitive cargo differently. Concepts are practical, economic forms of expression. Their purpose is to convey meaning as efficiently as possible. Metaphors by comparison are elaborate. They follow a more circuitous route, but the trip is more interesting. A metaphor is thus a clever way to express something that could be more simply and clearly expressed with straightforward conceptual terms.

If one extreme construes metaphors and concepts as merely different ways of saying the same thing, the other regards the two as entirely diverse. According to this view, it is impossible to express something both metaphorically and conceptually, because two such expressions could never represent the same thing.

Metaphors and concepts belong to utterly different worlds of discourse, and there is no way to derive conceptual content from metaphors. The realm of metaphorical meaning is impervious to conceptual intrusion.

An acceptable position lies somewhere between these conflicting views of metaphor and concept. It neither collapses the two, giving metaphor the status of a fancy concept, nor does it isolate them from each other. Instead, it allows for some degree of overlap or coincidence between metaphorical and conceptual meaning. As we have seen, this is precisely the thrust of some recent studies of metaphor: metaphors serve a conceptual purpose. Indeed, they give our cognitive experience its basic structure and pattern. Consequently, while we can never reduce metaphors to concepts, metaphors have implicit conceptual content and we can identify and express this content without doing violence to them.

On the level of concrete religious experience, metaphors are indispensable. In fact, they take priority over concepts for a number of reasons. For one thing, metaphors surpass concepts in evocative power. They stimulate imagination and emotion. They awaken feelings and inspire actions. Concepts serve a different purpose. Their basic function is to promote intellectual comprehension, rather than arouse feeling or motivate to action. If the marks of a good metaphor are richness and evocative power, the marks of good concepts are clarity and precision. Metaphors sacrifice precision for emotional depth and evocative power, while concepts sacrifice emotional texture for accuracy and clarity. So, metaphors address a larger range of human experience than concepts do. They speak to the whole person as a feeling, acting being, not merely as an intellect.

Metaphors are also more inclusive and enduring than concepts. Just as they engage a broad range of human experience, metaphors also speak to a broad spectrum of human beings. Religious communities are more strongly united by the fundamental metaphors from which their members live than by the doctrinal formulas they develop. Symbols and metaphors form the original and originating expressions of Christianity, and they are its most enduring elements. Doctrinal formulas and theological systems change from generation to generation—some might say from year to year—but the central symbols of Christian faith abide. And one important reason for their endurance is the fact that they cannot be reduced to any given conceptual scheme. They constantly stimulate new intepretations.

Metaphors and symbols are essential to religion, then, because the experience of faith is too rich and complex to find adequate expression in the language of concepts alone. But this does not mean that conceptual language is unimportant to faith. Members of the Christian community have always expressed their faith conceptually as well as metaphorically, as we have often mentioned. And if we need religious metaphors because the whole person is involved in the experience of faith, we need concepts for the same reason. We are thinking beings, even though our experience always includes a great deal more than reflective thought. Margaret Miles is correct in maintaining that religion involves both a complex of concepts about the self, the world, and God and a different way of seeing, an altered perception of the meaning and value of the sensible world.[57] So, just as we cannot eliminate metaphors from religion in a quest for conceptual clarity, neither can we dispense with concepts in the quest for experiential depth or emotional intensity. Concepts, too, have a role to play in religious experience.

We need to apply concepts to religious metaphors to do three things—to clarify, organize and evaluate them. Whether or not it is their most important aspect, metaphors contain a cognitive element, and at times it becomes necessary to express this element as clearly as possible. For example, in the face of heretical views which could distort Christian faith, the cognitive element in its central religious symbols must be clarified in order to safeguard the experience. Even though a particular metaphor may generate a variety of interpretations, the possibilities are not endless. Conceptual analysis limits the number of meanings that can be appropriately derived from a symbol or metaphor. It defines the range of options which are compatible with the basic religious intuition which the symbol expresses.

In the New Testament, for example, the relation of father and son is arguably the most important metaphor for the relation between God and Jesus. In fact, this metaphor is basic to the Christian perspective on both God and Jesus. It is also vivid and suggestive. It awakens a number of personal responses, and it is open to a variety of interpretations. But certain interpretations of the father-son metaphor are inadmissable. One that Christians have never embraced is that of sexual generation. Another, which was rejected as heretical in the fourth century, is the notion that the Son of God began to exist at some point in time. Concepts are useful for identifying interpretations of Christian symbols which would distort the faith.

Concepts are also helpful in distinguishing between more and less important metaphors. As we mentioned, the biblical writings variously describe God as a rock, a shepherd and a father, to mention but a few examples. Most Christians believe that God is more like a shepherd than a rock, and more like a father than a shepherd. One purpose of theological analysis is to show why this is the case. What is there about God that makes father a better representation of divinity than either shepherd or rock? Concepts are helpful in answering this question. They help us to determine which of the various metaphors for God should have greater influence on the ways we think and feel about him. They can also help us to determine which among traditional Christian metaphors will be most effective in awakening and promoting faith.

Occasionally, concepts have an evaluative role to play in relation to religious metaphors. They provide the means for assessing the nature and consequences of individual metaphors. This is important, because without some such evaluation, we can be vulnerable to manipulation. The sheer evocative power of metaphors, their capacity to generate emotional intensity, can be a force for ill as well as for good. As an extreme example, think of the symbols which racist groups employ in order to win sympathy for their causes. A blazing cross on a dark night can have a powerful impact on people, even if the feelings it awakens are despicable. To protect our religious experience from exploitation, distortion and corruption, therefore, we need conceptual clarity as well as emotional intensity. We must subject our religious metaphors to conceptual analysis, not in an effort to eliminate them, but in order to safeguard their important role within the experience of faith.

An analogy of our own may help to clarify the point. If we compare the experience of faith to a ship, then religious metaphors are analogous to its engine and religious concepts have their counterpart in its rudder. Without an engine, of course, the ship cannot sail, no matter how well its steering mechanism functions. It lies dead in the water. On the other hand, without a rudder a ship under power is heading for disaster, even—in fact, especially—if it is operating with a full head of steam. A successful voyage requires both adequate drive and proper direction. Similarly, people with well-developed theological concepts may be spiritually dead if religious metaphors have no impact on their experience. And people who are wide open to the influence of various metaphors but have no concepts to guide their response may be headed for spiritual disaster. To paraphrase Kant's famous dictum, in the experience of faith concepts without metaphors are empty, but metaphors without concepts are blind. An ideal religious experience will give both metaphors and concepts a role to play.

Conclusion

In many ways the relation between religious metaphors and rational concepts we have just examined parallels the general relation between faith and reason. Just as concepts and metaphors are not incompatible even though they are different, rational inquiry is not inherently detrimental to faith, in spite of what certain thinkers have said. On the other hand, like the central metaphors through which it comes to expression, the experience of faith is too rich and complex to wrap in a neat conceptual package. There is a dimension of mystery in faith that resists conceptual analysis. Its depths are not transparent to rational investigation. Let us review both aspects of this relation.

We have seen that faith both allows and invites rational investigation, and we have found several ways in which reason can contribute to it. Once faith is present in someone's life, careful thinking can increase that person's comprehension and confidence. It can answer questions and meet objections to faith, marshall evidence to support its claims, and rearrange its contents for greater clarity and faithfulness to experience. In a similar way, rational inquiry can help prepare someone for religious commitment by removing obstacles to faith. Finding evidence for the claims of faith shows that the experience is intellectually responsible. People do not have to stop thinking in order to believe. Since it contributes to both the origin and development of faith, reason has a central role to play in religious experience. It is a serious mistake to discount its significance.

It is also a mistake to exaggerate what reason can do for religion, for in spite of its contributions to faith, rational investigation can only do so much. One thing that limits its role is the enormous variability of personal experience. Because faith is highly personal, it touches all aspects of human life—intellectual, emotional, social, and so on. Because faith affects everything about a person, and everything about a person affects his or her faith, the course of religious experience is typically just as circuitous as that of life itself. So, it is no surprise that people do not come to religious commitment through a process of deliberate investigation. In the actual course of life, faith never conforms to a clear, logical pattern.

In addition to the complexities of personal experience, the very nature of faith also limits the contributions reason can make. As we saw in our first chapter, the confidence characteristic of faith goes way beyond the supporting evidence, and the freedom essential to faith is incompatible with rational coercion. Consequently, faith never exists without some disproportion between the level of confidence a person has in what he or she affirms and the level of confidence which is fully justified by a critical review of the public evidence. Unless trust goes beyond the evidence, it is not faith.

A careful consideration of the nature of faith thus reveals that reason can contribute to the experience in several important ways, but the essential core of religious commitment, what Christians often call "saving faith," can never be the product of rational investigation, whether of public or private evidence. It makes sense to believe—that's what reason can show. But people never come to have faith just by exercising their powers of rational thought. To put it simply, faith is a *reasonable*, but not a *reasoned*, decision.

---

[1] Reinhold Niebuhr, *Leaves From the Notebook of a Tamed Cynic* (Cleveland and New York: Meridian Books, 1957), p. 188.
[2] V. Bailey Gillespie, *The Experience of Faith* (Birmingham, Alabama: Religious Education Press, 1988), p. 79.
[3] Ibid., p. 74.
[4] Ibid., p. 153.
[5] Karl Rahner, *Do You Believe in God?* (New York: Paulist Press, 1969), pp. 3-4.
[6] Lewis presents an account of his spiritual journey in *Surprised by Joy: The Shape of My Early Life* (New York: Harcourt, Brace & World, Inc., 1955).
[7] 2 Peter 1:5-7.
[8] Acts 17:11.
[9] Philippians 1:9.
[10] Colossians 1:9-10.
[11] See the articles on *ginosko* and *suniemi* in *Theological Dictionary of the New Testament*, ed. Gerhard Kittel and Gerhard Friedrich, trans. Geoffrey W. Bromiley (10 vols.; Grand Rapids, MI: Wm. B. Eerdmans Publishing Company, 1964-1976).
[12] Hebrews 5:11-13; 6:1.
[13] 1 Corinthians 3:2.
[14] See Kittel, 1:708.
[15] *Counsels to Writers and Editors* (Nashville, TN: Southern Publishing Association, 1946), p. 33.
[16] *Education* (Mountain View, CA: Pacific Press Publishing Association, 1903), pp. 107, 111.
[17] Ibid., p. 40; cf. Ellen G. White, *Testimonies For the Church*, (9 vols.; Mountain View, CA: Pacific Press Publishing Association, 1948), 5:581.
[18] Ellen G. White, *Steps to Christ* (Mountain View, CA: Pacific Press Publishing Association, 1956), p. 105.
[19] Ibid., pp. 107, 111.
[20] Bernard Lonergan, *Method in Theology* (New York: Herder and Herder, 1972), p. 339.
[21] *Proslogium*, Chapter 1; in *Saint Anselm: Basic Writings*, trans. S. N. Deane, with an introduction by Charles Hartshorne (2d ed.; LaSalle, IL: Open Court Publishing Company, 1966), p. 7.
[22] Ibid.
[23] *Concluding Unscientific Postscript to the Philosophical Fragments*, trans. David F. Swenson and Walter Lowrie (Princeton, NJ: Princeton University Press, 1941), p. 327.
[24] This does not invalidate the enterprise of formulating such proofs, in spite of what some people think (See, for example, John Hick, Introduction to *The Existence of God*, ed. John Hick [New York: Macmillan Publishing Company, 1964], p. 5). But it does show that the contribution of reason to the establishment of faith is limited.
[25] John 3:8.
[26] Jesus commended the Canaanite woman for her great faith (Matthew 15:28) and told his disciples they would never enter the kingdom of heaven unless they became like little children (Matthew 18:3).
[27] Stephen T. Davis, *Faith, Skepticism, and Evidence: An Essay in Religious Epistemology*

(Lewisburg: Bucknell University Press, 1978), p. 214.

[28] Ellen G. White, *Education* (Mountain View, CA: Pacific Press Publishing Company, 1903), p. 171.

[29] *Testimonies for the Church*, 8:325.

[30] Rudolf Bultmann, *Existence and Faith: Shorter Writings of Rudolf Bultmann*, selected, translated, and introduced by Schubert M. Ogden (Cleveland and New York: Meridian Books, 1960), p. 221.

[31] Thomas Aquinas, *Summa Theologiae*, I, Q. 2, Art. 3; in *Nature and Grace: Selections from the Summa Theologica of Thomas Aquinas*, trans. and ed. A. M. Faithweather, Volume XI in The Library of Christian Classics (Philadelphia: The Westminster Press, 1954), pp. 54-55.

[32] Gary Gutting, *Religious Belief and Religious Skepticism* (Notre Dame: University of Notre Dame Press, 1982), p. 4.

[33] Ibid., p. 175.

[34] Ibid., p. 178, italics original.

[35] Ibid., p. 175-176.

[36] Ibid., p. 175.

[37] Indeed, language in general may not be the most fundamental form of religious expression. Some would argue that ritual and ceremony are more basic. Margaret R. Miles presents a fascinating study of the role of art in religious experience in *Image as Insight: Visual Understanding in Western Christianity and Secular Culture* (Boston: Beacon Press, 1985).

[38] Matthew 19:26.

[39] 1 John 3:20.

[40] In *The New Oxford Book of English Verse: 1250-1950*, ed. Helen Gardner (Oxford University Press, 1972), p. 491.

[41] Ibid., p. 126.

[42] Ibid., p. 483.

[43] Ibid., p. 787.

[44] Mary Gerhart and Allan Melvin Russell, *Metaphoric Process: The Creation of Scientific and Religious Understanding* (Fort Worth: Texas Christian University Press, 1984), p. 108.

[45] Ibid., p. 95.

[46] *The Mind in the Body: The Bodily Basis of Meaning, Imagination, and Reason* (Chicago: University of Chicago Press, 1987).

[47] Ibid., p. 15.

[48] George Lakoff and Mark Johnson, *Metaphors We Live By* (Chicago and London: The University of Chicago Press, 1980), pp. 7-8.

[49] Ibid., p. 77.

[50] Ibid., pp. 89-91.

[51] Ibid., p. 49.

[52] Ibid., pp. 14-17.

[53] Compare the following sentences: if A implies B, and B implies C, then A implies C, as well; the book is in the briefcase and the briefcase is in the office, so the book is in the office, too.

[54] Lakoff and Johnson, *Metaphors We Live By*, p. 1.

[55] William Placher provides a helpful discussion of postmodernism and various theological responses to it in *Unapologetic Theology: A Christian Voice in a Pluralistic Conversation* (Louisville: Westminster/John Knox Press, 1989).

[56] The work of David Tracy is noteworthy in this connection. See especially his influential book, *The Analogical Imagination* (New York: The Crossroad Publishing Company, 1981).

[57] Margaret Miles, *Image as Insight*, p. 4.

CONCLUSION

The purpose of this project was to explore the complex relationships between faith and reason. Let us briefly retrace our steps and see where our efforts have brought us. We began, in Part 1, by examining the central terms in our discussion, and we found that each expression covers a broad range of meaning. "Faith" refers both to religious beliefs and religious experience, and "reason" can refer either to mental activity generally or to deliberate rational inquiry. The latter meaning of reason and the two meanings of faith provided the major themes of our study. We devoted Part 2 to reason and the contents of faith, and Part 3 to reason and the experience of faith. On the thesis that faith should neither be isolated from reason nor subordinated to it, our overall objective was an interpretation that would do justice to the importance and complexity of both faith and reason, so we tried to develop positions that would avoid rationalism and fideism at the same time.

In Part 1 we examined the various meanings of the central concepts in our discussion. In Chapter 1 we found that faith has cognitive and volitional dimensions. It involves both knowledge and commitment. We also found that faith manifests a confidence that goes beyond the evidence—something we called its "concessive" quality. In Chapter 2 we affirmed and qualified the role that reason plays in knowledge. We concluded that knowledge always includes a rational element, but it does not always satisfy "the rational ideal." Much that we can rightly claim to know does not sit squarely on a basis of clear rational justification. Given the concessive quality of faith, this is very important. Otherwise, religious believers could not be rationally responsible.

In Part 2 we found, *contra* fideism, that the contents of faith are accessible to reason, and that rational inquiry into faith yields results that are both positive and significant. We also found, *contra* rationalism, that these results are very limited in scope. Our discussion focused on two applications of reason to faith and the relation between them. In Chapter 3, we examined the task of Christian theology—the application of reason to Christian beliefs from a perspective which assumes their truth. Although the Bible is the principal source and criterion of Christian beliefs, we discovered that theology involves more than biblical exegesis. It always reflects the dynamic experience of the Christian community as well.

We also wanted to examine the contents of faith from a perspective which does not presuppose their truth, but first we asked if they would permit such an inquiry. Chapter 4 dealt with this question. Are the contents of faith open to rational investigation? Does the evidence of reason have any relation to religious beliefs? Our answer was affirmative. We found biblical support for general revelation and natural theology. Accordingly, in Chapter 5, we assessed the rational evidence for the contents of faith, centering on belief in God. Considered in its entirety, we concluded, the evidence for God is impressive, but falls short of logical demonstration. Moreover, the concept of God it points to is highly abstract, compared to the object of religious devotion. In Chapter 6, we turned to the relation between philosophy and theology. We asked if a rational examination of faith has a role to play in Christian theology, and we concluded that it does. The quest for public evidence can help us to understand and interpret the contents of faith. So, even though reason says less about God than religion does, what it has to say is important. It shows that faith and reason are not incompatible, in spite of their contrasts. The contents of faith meet the standard of responsible belief. In summary, our efforts in Part 2 showed that the application of reason to the contents of faith yields important, if minimal, results.

In Part 3, we turned our attention to the relation between reason and the experience of faith, and once again we found our way between fideism and rationalism. In Chapters 7 and 8, respectively, we asked if rational inquiry has any relevance to the experience of faith, and if so, what its role might be. We concluded that reason is indeed relevant to faith, but its contribution is limited. The indications that reason has a role to play in faith include the biblical emphasis on hearing and responding to the word of God, the prominent place that reflection occupies in the development of Christianity, and the fact that many people today find that intellectual challenges pose a formidable obstacle to religious commitment. The strongest objections to rational reflection on religion express a desire to preserve the uniqueness of the experience, but it is not necessary to reject reason in order to safeguard faith.

In Chapter 8 we saw that rational investigation can prepare the way for personal religious commitment, and once faith is present, it can help it to grow in a number of ways. On the negative side, reason can answer questions, remove obstacles, settle doubts. On the postive side, it can deepen understanding, increase confidence and assist faith in finding appropriate expression. But no matter what its accomplishments, there are limits to what reason can do. The plain facts of personal religious experience, the inherent qualities of faith, in particular its volitional character, the centrality of symbols and metaphors in its basic affirmation—all these factors demonstrate that people never make their way from unbelief to faith on the path of rational inquiry alone. They come to faith by a process that is much more subtle and complex. Faith is never the product of rational investigation.

We seem, then, to have reached our objective. We have considered a wide range of issues relating to faith and reason, and our conclusions have consistently avoided both rationalism and fideism. We have seen that it is a mistake to expect either too much or too little of reason in relation to faith, or to regard faith as either wholly continuous or wholly discontinuous with human experience generally. There is rational evidence which corroborates the contents of faith, but the conclusions it supports are minimal. As for the experience of faith, reason can help clear the way for personal trust in God, and once trust is present it can help a person's religious experience to develop. But it cannot produce this commitment in someone's life. Reason does not provide us with a non-stop flight from unbelief to faith. When all is said and done, faith remains a mystery and a gift. It is less a problem to be solved than a cause for wonder, and for thanks.

AFTERWORD

I began this investigation on a personal note, and it seems appropriate to bring it to a close in the same way. More than half my life has passed since I began to wonder about faith and reason, and I expect to be thinking about them still when it comes to an end. Like many writers on such topics, I suspect, the conclusion of this project leaves me feeling less impressed than ever with what I know. In fact, the more I think about faith and reason, it seems, the issues steadily grow more numerous and complicated, and the unexplored landscape now seems more vast than ever.

Consequently, this book is not definitive in any sense. In fact, it barely nicks the surface of any of the topics we have discussed. This project is best described as an inventory, a stock-taking, or to change the metaphor, a pause in the journey. It represents one person's attempt to sort through the various questions the subject raises, note some important contributions to their discussion, and identify the major pitfalls that need to be avoided in thinking about them. If it helps people to get a fix on their present position and plot a course for continuing reflection, it has fulfilled its purpose.

From our present vantage point, I see at least four areas we have touched on that call for further exploration, and I am sure there are others as well. One of these additional contours of faith is its developmental character. As we noticed, religious development and nurture is now a major field of study, with its own research centers, academic experts, scholarly societies and professional meetings. The well-established fact that people move through different stages in the course of their religious lives indicates that the relation between faith and reason is constantly changing. In fact, it would probably be more accurate to speak of a sequence of relations between the two. The dynamic nature of their interaction deserves much more attention.

The same is true of the social contour of faith. Actually, both faith and reason have a social side. One's religious experience inevitably reflects the expectations and aspirations of one's religious community, and this applies to one's intellectual experience, too. The concepts with which we think, the issues that concern us, the criteria we use to evaluate our thinking, the relative importance we attach to rational inquiry—all depend in some degree on our social environment. In this discussion we typically referred to faith as an individual experience. In fact, we often spoke of personal religious commitment as synonymous with faith. But this is not necessarily the case. Perhaps the fundamental religious reality is the believing community, rather than the individual believer, and instead of "I believe," the primary expression of faith is "We believe." If so, the impact on our understanding of faith and reason would be profound. So, we need to hear what the sociology of religion has to say about the interactions between faith and reason. It would no doubt require us to look at specific religious communities, and this leads us to yet another contour of faith.

Our discussion not only approached faith from a Christian perspective, it generally treated faith as a Christian phenomenon. But faith needs to be examined within the context of other religions as well. Each religion has a distinctive understanding of faith. From our perspective an intellectual element is central to faith, as the titles of this book and its chapters indicate. But in other religions, the intellectual element plays quite different roles, and these deserve attention, too.

Finally, in spite of all the attention it has received, the cognitive aspect of faith still calls for examination. For the most part, we approached the question of faith and reason along the traditional lines of theology and philosophy, with a fairly standard view of reason and its operations. During the past two decades, however, a new discipline has developed under the name of "cognitive science" which has important implications for all human knowledge, religious knowledge included. According to one account, this new endeavor represents "a contemporary, empirically-based effort to answer long-standing epistemological questions," and it draws from a wide range of disciplines, including philosophy, psychology, artificial intelligence, linguistics, anthropology and neuroscience.[1] A revisionary model of the mind and its operations cannot fail to affect our understanding of faith. So, here lies another important field for exploration.

All this sets an itinerary for future exploration. Let us close the log on this journey by reiterating two of our most important observations. First, we must appreciate the religious importance of reason. The claims of faith will never get a hearing in the modern world if there is nothing that recommends them to the inquiring mind. Indeed, given the challenges it currently faces, faith needs all the rational defense it can find. People need to realize that believers can think, and thinkers can believe.

At the same time, we must never exaggerate the religious importance of reason. It does violence to faith to expect too much of reason. In certain circles, people talk as if we could produce religious commitment through proper evangelistic or pedagogical techniques. They evaluate someone's ministry by the number of conversions it leads to, and they regard Christian education as a way to guarantee the spiritual destiny of the church's young people. What we have seen about faith, however, prevents us from sharing these views. Faith is not an intellectual accomplishment. In fact, it is not an accomplishment at all. We may encourage its development and nurture its growth, but we can never produce it. Faith is always a miracle, and a gift.

---

[1] Howard Gardner, *The Mind's New Science: A History of the Cognitive Revolution* (New York: Basic Books, Inc., Publishers, 1987), p. 6.

BIBLIOGRAPHY

Adler, Mortimer. *How to Think About God: A Guide for the 20th-Century Pagan.* New York: Macmillan Publishing Company, Inc., 1980.
Ayer, A.J. *Language, Truth and Logic.* 2d ed. New York: Dover Publications, Inc., 1952.
Baillie, John. *Our Knowledge of God.* New York: Charles Scribner's Sons, 1939.
Barth, Karl. *Church Dogmatics.* Translated by Geoffrey W. Bromiley et al. 4 vols. Edinburgh: T. & T. Clark, 1956-69.
_____. *The Knowledge of God and the Service of God According to the Teaching of the Reformation: Recalling the Scottish Confession of 1560.* Translated by J. L. M. Haire and Ian Henderson. London: Hodder and Stoughton Publishers, 1938.
Brown, Stuart C. Ed. *Reason and Religion.* Ithaca and London: Cornell University Press, 1977.
Brummer, Vincent. *Theology and Philosophical Inquiry: An Introduction.* Philadelphia: Westminster Press, 1982.
Brunner, Emil. *Revelation and Reason: The Christian Doctrine of Faith and Knowlege.* Translated by Olive Wyon. Philadelphia: Westminster Press, 1946.
_____. *The Christian Doctrine of God.* "Dogmatics," Volume 1. Translated by Olive Wyon. Philadelphia: Westminster Press, 1949.
Buckley, Michael. *At the Origins of Modern Atheism.* New Haven: Yale University Press, 1987.
Bultmann, Rudolf. *Existence and Faith: Shorter Writings of Rudolf Bultmann.* Selected, translated, and introduced by Schubert M. Odgen. Cleveland and New York: Meridian Books, 1960.

_____. "New Testament and Mythology." In *Kerygma and Myth: A Theological Debate*. Edited by Hans Werner Bartsch. New York: Harper & Row, Publishers, 1961.

Cahn, Steven M. and David Shatz. Eds. *Contemporary Philosophy of Religion*. New York: Oxford University Press, 1982.

Calvin, John. *Institutes of the Christian Religion*. Translated by Ford Lewis Battles. 2 vols. Philadelphia: Westminster Press, 1970.

Camus, Albert. *The Stranger*. Translated by Stuart Gilbert. New York: Vintage Books, 1946.

Chisholm, Roderick. *Theory of Knowledge*. 2d ed. Englewood Cliffs, NJ: Prentice-Hall, Inc., 1977.

Clifford, William Kingdon. "The Ethics of Belief." In *Lectures and Essays*. Edited by Leslie Stephen and Frederick Pollock. With an introduction by F. Pollock. 2 vols. London: Macmillan and Co., 1879. 2:177-211.

Cobb, John B., Jr. *A Christian Natural Theology Based on the Thought of Alfred North Whitehead*. Philadelphia: Westminster Press, 1965.

Collingwood, R. G. *Faith and Reason: Essays in the Philosophy of Religion*. Edited with an introduction by Lionel Rubinoff. Chicago: Quadrangle Books, 1968.

Collins, James. *The Mind of Kierkegaard*. Princeton, NJ: Princeton University Press, 1983.

Copi, Irving M. *Introduction to Logic*. 4th ed. New York: Macmillan Publishing Co., Inc., 1972.

Davis, Stephen T. *Faith, Skepticism and Evidence: An Essay in Religious Epistemology*. London: Associated University Presses, Inc., 1978.

Delaney, C. F. Ed. *Rationality and Religious Belief*. Notre Dame: University of Notre Dame Press, 1979.

Diamond, Malcolm and Thomas Litzenburg, Jr. Eds. *Logic and God: Theology and Verification*. Indianapolis: Bobbs-Merrill Company, Inc., 1975.

Edwards, Paul. Ed. *The Encyclopedia of Philosophy*. 8 vols. New York: Macmillan Publishing Co., Inc. & The Free Press, 1967.

Ely, Stephen. *The Religious Availability of Whitehead's God*. Madison: University of Wisconsin Press, 1942.

Erickson, Millard J. *Christian Theology*. 3 vols. Grand Rapids, MI: Baker Book House, 1983-85.
Evans, C. Stephen. *Subjectivity and Religious Belief: An Historical, Critical Study*. Washington, D.C.: University Press of America, Inc., 1982.
Farrer, Austin. *Faith and Speculation: An Essay in Philosophical Theology*. Edinburgh: T. & T. Clark, 1967.
Ferre, Frederick. *Basic Modern Philosophy of Religion*. New York: St. Martin's Press, 1965.
Ferreira, M. Jamie. *Doubt and Religious Commitment: The Role of the Will in Newman's Thought*. Oxford: Clarendon Press, 1980.
Flew, Antony and Alasdair MacIntyre. Eds. *New Essays in Philosophical Theology*. New York: The Macmillan Company, 1955.
Flew, Antony. *God and Philosophy*. New York: Delta, 1966.
Geach, P. T. *Reason and Argument*. Berkeley and Los Angeles: University of California Press, 1976.
Gerhart, Mary and Allan Russell. *Metaphoric Process: The Creation of Scientific and Religious Understanding*. Fort Worth, TX: Texas Christian University Press, 1984.
Gilkey, Langdon. *Naming the Whirlwind: The Renewal of God-Language*. Indianapolis and New York: Bobbs-Merrill Company, 1969.
Gill, Jerry H. *On Knowing God*. Philadelphia: Westminster Press, 1981.
Gillespie, V. Bailey. *Religious Conversion and Personal Identity*. Birmingham, Alabama: Religious Education Press, 1979.
_____. *The Experience of Faith*. Birmingham, Alabama: Religious Education Press, 1988.
Goodwin, George L. *The Ontological Argument of Charles Hartshorne*. Missoula, Montana: Scholars Press, 1978.
Gutting, Gary. *Religious Belief and Religious Skepticism*. Notre Dame: University of Notre Dame Press, 1982.
Hartshorne, Charles. *A Natural Theology For Our Time*. LaSalle, IL: Open Court Publishing Co., 1967.
_____. *Creative Synthesis and Philosophic Method*. LaSalle, IL: Open Court Publishing Co., 1970.

———. *Man's Vision of God and the Logic of Theism*. Chicago: Willett, Clark and Co., 1941.

———. *The Logic of Perfection and Other Essays in Neoclassical Metaphysics*. LaSalle, IL: Open Court Publishing Co., 1962.

Harvey, Van A. "The Ethics of Belief Reconsidered." *The Journal of Religion*, 59(1979): 406-420.

Hick, John H. and Arthur C. McGill. Eds. *The Many-faced Argument: Recent Studies on the Ontological Argument for the Existence of God*. New York: The Macmillan Company, 1967.

Hick, John. *Arguments for the Existence of God*. Volume 1 in "Philosophy of Religion Series." New York: The Seabury Press, 1971.

———. *Evil and the God of Love*. Rev. ed. New York and San Francisco: Harper & Row, Publishers, 1978.

———. *Faith and Knowledge*. Cleveland: Fontana Books, 1974.

Hick, John. Ed. *The Existence of God*. New York: Macmillan Publishing Co., Inc., 1964.

James, William. *The Will to Believe and Other Essays in Popular Philosophy*. New York: Dover Publications, Inc., 1956.

Johnson, Mark. *The Mind in the Body: The Bodily Basis of Meaning, Imagination, and Reason*. Chicago: University of Chicago Press, 1987.

Jones, W. T. *Kant and the Nineteenth Century*. 2d ed. rev. Volume 4 in "A History of Western Philosophy." New York: Harcourt Brace Jovanovich, Inc., 1975.

Kellenberger, J. *The Cognitivity of Religion*. Berkley and Los Angeles: University of California Press, 1985.

Kenny, Antony. *Faith and Reason*. New York: Columbia University Press, 1983.

Kierkegaard, Søren. *Concluding Unscientific Postscript to the Philosophical Fragments*. Translated by David F. Swenson and Walter Lowrie. Princeton, NJ: Princeton University Press, 1941.

———. *Philosophical Fragments or a Fragment of Philosophy*. Translated by David F. Swenson. 2d ed. Princeton, NJ: Princeton University Press, 1962.

Kuhn, Thomas S. *The Structure of Scientific Revolutions*. 2d ed. Chicago: University of Chicago Press, 1970.

Küng, Hans. *Does God Exist? An Answer for Today.* Translated by Edward Quinn. New York: Vintage Books, 1981.
Lakoff, George and Mark Johnson. *Metaphors We Live By.* Chicago and London: University of Chicago Press, 1980.
Leith, John. "Creeds and Their Role in the Church." *Creeds of the Churches: A Reader in Christian Doctrine From the Bible to the Present.* Garden City, NY: Anchor Books, 1963.
Lewis, C. S. *Mere Christianity.* New York: The Macmillan Company, 1960.
_____. *Miracles: A Preliminary Study.* New York: The Macmillan Company, 1947.
_____. *Surprised by Joy: The Shape of My Early Life.* New York: Harcourt, Brace & World, Inc., 1955.
Lonergan, Bernard. *Method in Theology.* New York: Herder and Herder, 1972.
Mackie, J. L. *The Miracle of Theism: Arguments For and Against the Existence of God.* Oxford: Clarendon Press, 1982.
Macquarrie, John. *Principles of Christian Theology.* 2d ed. New York: Charles Scribner's Sons, 1977.
Malcolm, Norman. *Thought and Knowledge: Essays by Norman Malcolm.* Ithaca and London: Cornell University Press, 1977.
Matson, Wallace. *The Existence of God.* Ithaca, NY: Cornell University Press, 1965.
Mavrodes, George I. *Belief in God: A Study in the Epistemology of Religion.* Washington, D.C.: University Press of America, 1970.
Maxwell, Graham. *Can God Be Trusted?* Nashville, TN: Southern Publishing Association, 1977.
Miles, Margaret R. *Image as Insight: Visual Understanding in Western Christianity and Secular Culture.* Boston: Beacon Press, 1985.
Mitchell, Basil. *The Justification of Belief.* New York: Oxford University Press, 1981.
Newman, John Henry. *An Essay in Aid of a Grammar of Assent.* Introduction by Nicholas Lash. Notre Dame: University of Notre Dame Press, 1979.
Niebuhr, Reinhold. *Leaves From the Notebook of a Tamed Cynic.* Cleveland and New York: Meridian Books, 1957.

Ogden, Schubert M. "Bultmann's Demythologizing and Hartshorne's Dipolar Theism." In *Process and Divinity: The Hartshorne Festschrift.* Edited by William L. Reese and Eugene Freeman. LaSalle, IL: Open Court Publishing Co., 1964.

_____. *The Reality of God and Other Essays.* New York: Harper & Row, Publishers, 1966.

_____. "What Is Theology?" *The Journal of Religion.* 44(1964): 1-16.

Pannenberg, Wolfhart. *Anthropology in Theological Perspective.* Translated by Matthew J. O'Connell. Philadelphia: Westminster Press, 1985.

Pelikan, Jaroslav. *The Emergence of the Catholic Tradition (100-600).* Volume 1 in "The Christian Tradition: A History of the Development of Doctrine." Chicago: University of Chicago Press, 1971.

Pinnock, Carles H. *The Scripture Principle.* San Francisco: Harper and Row, Publishers, 1984.

Plantinga, Alvin and Nicholas Wolterstorff. Eds. *Faith and Rationality: Reason and Belief in God.* Notre Dame: University of Notre Dame Press, 1983.

Polanyi, Michael. *Personal Knowledge: Towards a Post-Critical Philosophy.* Chicago: University of Chicago Press, 1962.

Price, H. H. "Belief 'In' and Belief 'That.'" *Religious Studies,* 1(1965): 1-27. Also in *The Philosophy of Religion.* Edited by Basil Mitchell. Oxford: Oxford University Press, 1971.

Proudfoot, Wayne. *Religious Experience.* Berkeley, Los Angeles, London: University of California Press, 1985.

Purtill, Richard L. *Reason to Believe.* Grand Rapids, MI: William B. Eerdmans Publishing Co., 1974.

Rahner, Karl. *Do You Believe in God?* Translated by Richard Strachan. New York: Paulist Press, 1969.

Ramm, Bernard. *After Fundamentalism: The Future of Evangelical Theology.* San Francisco: Harper & Row Publishers, 1983.

Reid, J. K. S. *Christian Apologetics.* Grand Rapids, MI: William B. Eerdmans Publishing Co., 1969.

Rorty, Richard. *Philosophy and the Mirror of Nature.* Princeton, NJ: Princeton University Press, 1979.

Ross, James F. *Introduction to the Philosophy of Religion.* New York: The Macmillan Company, 1969.
———. *Philosophical Theology.* Indianapolis and New York: The Bobbs-Merrill Company, Inc., 1969.
Rowe, William L. *Philosophy of Religion: An Introduction.* Belmont, CA: Wadsworth Publishing Company, Inc., 1978.
———. *The Cosmological Argument.* Princeton, NJ: Princeton University Press, 1975.
Runzo, Joseph. *Reason, Relativism and God.* New York: St. Martin's Press, 1986.
Schaeffer, Francis A. *Escape From Reason.* Downers Grove, IL: Inter-Varsity Press, 1968.
———. *He Is There and He Is Not Silent.* Wheaton, IL: Tyndale House Publishers, 1972.
Schleiermacher, Friedrich. *The Christian Faith.* Edited by H. R. Mackintoch and J. S. Stewart. 2d ed. Edinburgh: T. & T. Clark, 1928.
Smith, Wilfred Cantwell. *Faith and Belief.* Princeton, NJ: Princeton University Press, 1979.
Stoppard, Tom. *Jumpers.* New York: Grove Press, 1972.
Stout, Jeffrey. *The Flight From Authority: Religion, Morality, and the Quest for Autonomy.* Notre Dame: University of Notre Dame Press, 1981.
Swinburne, R.G. *Faith and Reason.* New York: Oxford University Press, 1981.
———. *The Coherence of Theism.* Oxford: Clarendon Press, 1977.
———. *The Existence of God.* Oxford: Clarendon Press, 1979.
Thulstrup, Niels. *Commentary on Kierkegaard's Concluding Unscientific Postscript With a New Introduction.* Translated by Robert J. Widenmann. Princeton, NJ: Princeton University Press, 1984.
Tillich, Paul. *Systematic Theology.* 3 vols. Chicago: University of Chicago Press, 1951-63.
Torrance, T. F. *Theology in Reconstruction.* Grand Rapids, MI: William B. Eerdmans Publishing Company, 1965.
Toulmin, Stephen Edelston. *An Examination of the Place of Reason in Ethics.* Cambridge: Cambridge University Press, 1968.

Tracy, David. *Blessed Rage For Order: The New Pluralism in Theology.* New York: The Seabury Press, 1975.

―――――. *The Analogical Imagination: Christian Theology and the Culture of Pluralism.* New York: The Crossroad Publishing Company, 1981.

Wood, Charles M. *The Formation of Christian Understanding: An Essay in Theological Hermeneutics.* Philadelphia: Westminster Press, 1981.

INDEX OF PERSONS

Adler, Mortimer, 136
Anderson, J. N. D., 206n.2
Anselm: faith and philosophy in, 185, 218, 254, 258; ontological argument of, 124, 149-51, 152
Aristotle, 185
Augustine, 75, 218, 254
Ayer, A. J., 20
Baillie, John, 165n.67
Barth, Karl, 111-13, 114, 118, 179-80, 208n.43
Blake, William, 271
Braithwaite, Richard B., 222
Brunner, Emil, 179-81, 208n.37, 208n.42, 208n.43
Buckley, Michael J., 104, 202-203
Bultmann, Rudolf, 185, 190, 265
Calvin, John: on relation between Bible and theology, 92-93; theology of, 75; on knowledge of God, 115; on revelation in nature, 109-11, 112-13, 115; on revelation in Scripture, 120
Camara, Helder, 209n.59
Camus, Albert, 146
Charnock, Stephen, 209n.62
Chesterton, G. K., 206n.2
Chisholm, Roderick M., 58
Clifford, W. K., 36, 37, 57, 58
Cobb, John B. Jr., 196, 210n.90
Collins, James, 240
Congar, Yves M.-J., 76
Copleston, F. C., 135
Davis, Stephen T., 50, 67n.26, 263

Descartes, René, 40
Erickson, Millard J., 79, 80
Flew, Antony, 21
Gerhart, Mary, 61, 271
Gilkey, Langdon, 177-178, 183, 192
Gillespie, V. Bailey, 250
Goodwin, George L., 210n.92
Gutierrez, Gustavo, 209n.59
Gutting, Gary, 155, 158, 266-68
Guy, Fritz, 163n.15
Hare, R. M., 29n.22, 222
Hartshorne, Charles, iii, 165n.56; on attributes of God, 100n.36; dipolar theism of, 191; on function of proof, 67n.22; global theistic argument of, 125, 155; on theistic proofs, *a priori* nature of, 163n.10; on theistic proofs, effect of, 159
Harvey, Van A., 48, 63
Hasel, Gerhard F., 83, 99n.19
Henry, Carl F. H., 83, 217
Hick, John, 27, 127, 137, 163n.7
Hopkins, Gerard Manley, 271
Hume, David, 34, 36, 124, 143
James, William, 29n.19, 40, 57-59, 68n.43
Johnson, Mark, 272, 273
Johnston, Robert K., 91
Justin, 170
Kant, Immanuel: on cosmological argument, 153-54; on theistic arguments, interdependence of, 153-54; moral argument of,

164n.50; on ontological argument, 150; on teleological argument, 125, 142, 163n.14; theistic argument of, 203
Kelsey, David H., 87
Kenny, Antony, 131, 132, 194
Kierkegaard, Søren, 223, 225-29, 243; on absurdity of faith, 244 n.29, 244n.31; on contradictions in Christianity, 244n.29, 244n.30, 244n.33; objections to, 238-40; on reason, critique of, 238; on faith, difficulty of, 244n.27, 260; on faith, uniqueness of 225-26, 228, 232, 239; on human existence, 244n.38; on paradox in religion, 245n.41; replies to, 239-40; on subjectivity, 226-27, 244n.40; on theistic arguments, 227
Kuhn, Thomas S., 60, 68n.47
Küng, Hans, 66, 224
Lakoff, George, 272
Leith, John, 99n.26
Lewis, C.S., 54, 252; as apologist, 170-71, 207n.3; conversion of, to Christianity, 252; on moral sensitivity, 145
Lindbeck, George A., 93, 94, 100n.27
Locke, John, 36
Lonergan, Bernard, 68n.46; on theistic proofs and religious experience, 258, 259; on theology, concept of, 74-76, 100n.37; on theology, functional specialities of, 98n.3
Luther, Martin, 86, 93
MacIntyre, Alisdair, 202
Mackie, J. L., 219, 236, 237
Macquarrie, John, 76, 77, 92, 205
Malcolm, Norman, 55, 56, 151, 152
Marcel, Gabriel, 6, 7n.5

Marx, Karl, 209n.59
Matson, Wallace I., 7n.4, 219, 236, 237
Maxwell, A. Graham, 7n.2
Miles, Margaret R., 278, 283n.37
Newman, John Henry: on assent and inference, 233-35, 263; on certainty (or "certitude"), 234, 235, 242; on valid reasoning, criterion of, 236; on reasonableness of faith, 233, 236, 242; on similarity of faith to reason, 242
Niebuhr, Reinhold, 249
Ogden, Schubert M.: on atheism, extent of, 193; on concept of theology, 76, 83, 189-90, 205; on idea of God, 104, 191; on knowledge of God, 198; natural theology of, 198; theistic argument of, 191; use of philosophy by, 186, 192
Paley, William, 125, 139, 140, 164n.35, 164n.38, 259
Pannenberg, Wolfhart, 30n.29, 193
Pascal, Blaise: on faith and reason, 237-38; on God of religion and God of philosophy, 161, 224; on reasons of the heart, 67n.27, 223; on the uniqueness of faith, 237-38, 243; wager of, 224-25
Pelikan, Jaroslav, 89
Placher, William, 283n.55
Plantinga, Alvin, 56, 68n.38, 210n.88
Polanyi, Michael, 61
Price, H. H., 66n.3
Proudfoot, Wayne, 232, 242
Purtill, Richard L., 157
Rahner, Karl, 107, 252
Ramm, Bernard, 179, 196
Randall, John Herman, Jr., 68n.45
Ritschl, Dietrich, 92

Ross, James F., 53-54, 127-128, 130
Rowe, William L., 124, 158
Runzo, Joseph, 218, 231, 241
Russell, Allan Melvin, 61, 271, 272
Russell, Bertrand, 7n.3, 36, 136, 137
Schaeffer, Francis A., 173, 193, 207n.10
Schleiermacher, Friedrich, 75, 203; on basis of Christian doctrines, 207n.13; on theology, concept of, 174-75; on feeling of absolute dependence, 175-76; Tillich's objection to, 187
Segundo, Juan Louis, 209n.59
Smith, Wilfred Cantwell, 229-31, 240-241
Socrates, 42, 228
Stoppard, Tom, 220
Stout, Jeffrey, 202, 204
Swinburne, Richard, 34, 47, 66n.4, 158, 159
Tennant, F. R., 142
Tertullian, 25, 170
Thomas Aquinas: on God, concept of, 265; on knowledge of God, 198; as philosopher, 185; philosophical theology of, 123, 172-74, 195; on use of reason in theology, 220; on natural theology, scope of 198; theistic arguments of, 195, 258, 207n.11; theological achievement of, 75
Tillich, Paul: on theology, concept of 76, 78, 92; on constructive theology, importance of, 193; method of correlation in, 187-88; on method of correlation, dangers of, 201, 210n.94; use of philosophy by, 187-89, 192; on philosophy of religion, types of, 160; on theistic arguments, 188-89

Torrance, Thomas F., 76, 80
Tracy, David, 186, 283n.56
White, Ellen G.: on Christ, universal influence of, 120n.9; on doubt, 29n.27, 256; on faith, evidence for, 29n.27, 256, 264; on God, creative power of, 120n.13; on Holy Spirit, influence of, 30n.31; on intellectual responsibility of Christians, 243n.1; on role of reason in religion, 254-55, 256
Whitehead, Alfred North, 186, 191
Wood, Charles M., 81

Index of Persons 303

INDEX OF SUBJECTS

A priori statements, 39
Abraham, 24, 25
Analytic philosophy, 20
Analytic statements, 39
Anti-foundationalism, 131, 194, 223
Apologetics, 169-171, 218, 207n.2
Argument, 42; *a priori* versus *a posteriori*, 124, 163n.7; limits of, 53-54, 266; purpose of, 53, 67n.22, 127-128, 129; qualities of, 130-131, 132; soundness versus persuasiveness in, 128; standards of, 128; versus proof, 129
Arguments for the existence of God. *See* Theistic arguments
Atheism, 219; contribution of natural theology to, 203; modern pervasiveness of, 104-105, 193
Basic beliefs, 40, 49, 56, 132; and belief in God, 153; belief in God as one of, 131-133; and foundationalism, 56; elusiveness of, 133; justification of, 64; and theistic proofs, 134
Belief in and *belief that*, 13, 27, 33
Belief, 23, 34, 66n.4
Belief, responsible: criterion of, 65; acquisition of, 53, 62; criterion of rationality of, 157; development of meaning of, 230; distinct from faith, 229, 230; groundlessness of, 55-57; importance in Christianity, 251; justification of, 63; mediated and immediate, 56; non-rational factors in, 57-59; not produced by argument(s), 53; rational, categories of, 46-47; relation to evidence, 55; relation to investigation, 55-57; responsible belief, 61-65
Bible: as Word of God, 85; authority, 81, 93; basis of theology, 79; cognitive content of, 83; doctrinal authority of, 97; historical nature of, 83; human character of, 85; in theology, 73; importance of *Word* in, 217; interpretation of, influenced by doctrine, 92; Reformation view of, 93; theological authority of, 99n.26; theological center of, 85-86; theological function of, 87-88; worldview of, 219
Cause: types of, 134
Certainty: absolute, 46; and faith, 215, 231, 258; as intellectually responsible, 242; in Newman, 233, 234; objective versus trusting, 30n.29; as product of informal reasoning, 235
Christian faith: cumulative case for, 210n.93
Cognitive structure, 132
Cognitivism, and non-cognitivism, 221
Common human experience:

continuity of, with faith, 183; and knowledge of God, 119; and religious language, 178; importance of, to faith, 184; supports existence of God, 173; theological role of, 184-85. *See also* Public evidence
Community, religious: relation to theology, 78
Concepts: application to religious metaphors, 278; importance to Christianity, 278; role in theology and philosophy, 269
Configuration of belief, 256, 266
Continuities between faith and reason, 3, 102, 162, 182, 206; scope of, 263
Conversion: imperceptible nature of, 261
Cosmological argument, 156; basic structure, 136; objections to, 136-137; sense of wonder, 139; strength and weakness, 154; theological function in Aquinas, 172; Tillich's assessment, 189
Creed, 23. *See also* Doctrines
Death-of-God theology, 22, 201, 223
Deduction, 42, 44, 67n.21
Doctrines: change of, 96-97; influence on Biblical interpretation, 92; interconnections among, 198; interpretations of, 93-94; object of theological interpretation, 94; relation of, to beliefs, 95-96; relation of, to Bible and church, 89-90; relative importance of, 95
Doubt, 46, 256, 264
Education: effect of, on faith, 262
Epistemology, 33
Ethics of belief, 48, 62

Evidence: for God, religious versus philosophical, 203; for religious beliefs, different evaluations of, 2; for religious beliefs, scarcity of, 44; natural quest for, 234; needed by faith, 19; presupposed by faith, 24; surpassed by faith, 25; and the rational idea, 36-37; role of, in knowledge, 38-41; role of, in argument, 42-43; and rationality, 64-65; changing shape of, 54-55; scientific, 59. *See also* Private evidence, Public evidence, Public and private evidence
Evil, 141, 143-145, 219
Existence of God: as philosophical and theological concern, 186
Existentialism, 186, 226-27, 244n.31
Experience: common human, 74
Faith: as basic existential faith, in Schubert M. Ogden, 191; cognitive dimension of, 18-23, 240-241; concessive quality of, 23-27, 45, 281, 285; concessive quality of, in Kierkegaard, 228; concessive quality of, incompatible with rationalism, 263; development of, 249; developmental character of, 289; dimensions of, 215, 262, 285; dynamic nature of, 265; elusive character of, 261, 281; in children, 249; includes intellectual assent, 217; not an intellectual achievement, 217; as mystery, 288; obstacles to, 218-219; problematic status of, in modern world, 220; not the product of reason, 253, 260, 287, 291; propositional view of, 240; receptive character of, incompatible with rationalism, 262;

receptive dimension of, 16-18; relation of, to reason, 285; as rationally responsible, 221, 286; religious faith, meanings of, 71; and revelation, in neo-orthodoxy, 180; similarity of, to reason, 233, 242; social aspect of, 290; as trust, 71, 215; volitional dimension of, 26-29, 240, 262
Falsification, 222
Feeling: of absolute dependence, place in theology, 175-176
Fideism, 2, 3, 216
Foundationalism, 55-56, 67n.20, 131
Free will: relation to evil, 144
General revelation, 167, 286; Biblical support for, 106-109; human response, 115-116; and natural theology, 117; original purpose, 117; possibility of, 102; purpose of, 113-114; question of, 105; relation to Bible (Calvin), 110; relation to natural theology, 106, 109; relation to special revelation, 120; sin and human perception of, 113
God: as basic belief, 133, 194; as being itself (in Tillich's thought), 188; as creator, 107; dipolar concept of, 191; evidence for, religious versus philosophical, 203; existence of, as philosophical and theological concern, 186; idea of, 103; importance to Christian faith, 103-104, 190, 199; knowledge of, subjective condition for, 106; natural knowledge of, 161, 173, 198; of philosophy, 181, 224; of religion and God of philosophy, 265; proofs for, *See* Theistic arguments; reality of, 3; revealed knowledge of, 161-162; as supreme reality, source of life, 108; universal experience of, 107, 108; universal salvific will of, 117
Heart, 223-24
Heresy, 90, 100n.27
Historical-critical method, 84-85
Holy Spirit, 28, 115-116
Induction, 42-44
Intellectual responsibility, 62, 220, 242
Intelligence: relation to religious experience, 250
Intuition, 41, 51, 224
Job, 24, 25
Justification, 35-36; of basic beliefs, 64; needed for contents of faith, 241; when required, 63-65
Kerygma, 22-23
Knowledge, 16, 35, 38-41, 44, 55-56
Language analysis: as theological resource, 178
Leap of faith, 226, 228
Marxism, 186, 209n,59
Memory, 39
Metaphors: basic function of, 271; and concepts, religious importance of, 280; and creation of meaning, 271; difference of, from concepts, 277; different views of, 276-77; importance of, 273; importance of, to religion, 270; pervasiveness of, 272; power of, 279; relation of, to concept, 276; relation of, to theology, 275; religious, conflict with concepts, 274 religious, power of, 274; role in religious community, 277-78; in science, 61; spontaneity of, 273

Metaphysics, 138
Method of correlation, 187-88, 201, 210n.94
Modernity, 220-221, 241, 243, 252
Moral argument, 145, 149, 154, 156, 164n.50
Morality, moral obligation, 22; and consequences, 148; objective validity, 147; objective validity, objections to, 147; universality, 145
Mystery, 6, 261, 280
Natural knowledge of God, 161; biblical support for, 116; essential idea of, 119; evidence for, 116, 119; in Paul, 117; relation of, to Christian mission, 114, 118; relation of, to human salvation, 118
Natural theology, iii, 4, 286; Barth's rejection of, 180; basic question of, 123; Catholic position on, 171; central question of, 103; definition of, 197; difference of, from revealed theology, 201; objections to, 112-113; philosophical versus theological question of, 168; possibility of, 123; rejected by Barth, 112; role of, in systematic theology, 197-98; strategy of, 123; task of, 102; theological question of, 102-103; view of God in, 161; views of, summarized, 192
Necessary existence, 151
Neo-orthodoxy: concept of faith in, 180; concept of revelation in, 179; concept of theology in, 205; contributions of, 182; critique of reason in, 181; problems of, 183-84
Nihilism, 145

Non-cognitivism, 19, 223, 236-37
Ockham's razor, 156, 165n.60
Ontological argument, 125, 150, 154, 189
Paradigm, 60, 68n.47
Passion, passional nature, 68n.43, 227
Philosophical theology, *See* Natural theology
Philosophy of religion, 4-5, 73, 74, 167; basic task, 269-70; dependence on public evidence, 268; task of, 102. *See also* Natural theology
Philosophy: role in Christian theology, 204; role in theology, 168-169, 175, 286; role in theology, according to Tillich, 187-188; theological need for, 196; theological role, limitations of, 201; traditional concept of, 167
Piety, 110, 176
Post-modernism, 276
Private evidence, 50-51, 65; importance of, to faith, 263; importance, 51-52; influence of, 266; influence on faith, 268; often presupposes faith, 264; role in theology, 206, 268; theological significance of, 73, 78
Probability: role in reasoning, 235
Process philosophy, 186
Proof. *See* Argument
Psycho-sociological objections to religion, 260
Public and private evidence, 50-53; contrast between, in scope and kind, 72, 248; contributions of, to religious experience, 255; respective contents of, 247; respective relations of, to theology and philosophy of religion, 216.

Index of Subjects 309

See also Private evidence, Public evidence

Public evidence: and arguments, 128; for Christian faith, 108; for religion, 102; for theism, 160; importance to Christian theology, 78, 194, 197, 204; importance to faith, 184; importance to faith, 240; importance within church, 195; limited support for faith, 259; relation of, to theology, 168; relevance to faith, 242; role in apologetics, 170; role in philosophy of religion, 268; role in theology, 171, 174, 205, 206; role in theology, rejected by neo-orthodoxy, 179; supports idea of God, 200; theological contribution of, 184, 192, 194, 199, 200; theological role, for Paul Tillich, 189

Rational ideal: description of, 36-37, 42, 63; relation of, to reason, 44; reliance of, on argument, 53; problems with, 47-50, 53, 57, 61

Rational responsibility, 48, 285. *See also* Ethics of belief

Rationalism, 2, 3, 216, 285; incompatible with faith, 262; Kierkegaard's rejection of, 228

Rationality: levels of, 46-48, 64-65; and religious maturity, 258

Reason: as "clearing-house for faith", 259-60; contribution of, to faith, 250-52, 254-55, 280-81, 287; critique of, in neo-orthodoxy, 180; effect of, on configuration of belief, 256; effect of, on religious doubts, 256; effect of, on theism, 225; importance of, to faith, 231-32, 237, 291; importance of, to theology, 197; inability of, to produce faith, 253, 260, 287, 291; informal operation of, 235; limitations of, in relation to faith, 281-82, 287; meaning of, 72, 216, 247; relevance of, to faith, 247, 287; risk of, when applied to faith, 257; role of, in theology, 174, 176; similarity of, to religion, 233; social aspect of, 290; as source of truth, 171, 172; and stages of life, 249; suppression of, danger in, 257; validity of, criterion of, 236

Religion and philosophy, 160-61

Religious experience, 74; as evidence, 52-53; place of, in theology, 176; variations in, 255; variety within, 248

Religious language, 177-78, 232, 270, 283n.37

Religious metaphors: and religious change, 275

Responsible belief, 42, 44, 53; and theism, 127, 133

Revelation: general revelation, concept of, 4; general revelation, basis for natural theology in, 105-109; general revelation, Barth's critique of, 111-12; special revelation, 108; revelation in nature, 109-111; Christian concept of, 105; concept of, in neo-orthodox theology, 179, 184; as source of truth, 171; as universal, for Schubert M. Ogden, 190; role of, in Tillich's theology, 187

Salvation, 1, 15, 16, 18

Science: discoveries of, 60; use of induction by, 43; influence of, 59, 68n.45; and rational ideal, 59; role of imagination in, 61; shortcomings of, 59; scientific evi-

comings of, 59; scientific evidence, 50; scientific revolutions, 60

Scripture. *See* Bible

Secularism: as challenge to Christian faith, 177

Sin: in neo-orthodox theology, 182

Skepticism, 62

sola scriptura, 93

Subjectivity, 239

System (of beliefs), 55-56

Teleological argument, 139, 140, 142, 154, 156

Theism: comparative value of, 156; evidence for, effect of, 168; explanatory power of, 156; as responsible belief, 127, 133; universal implications of, 159

Theistic arguments: circularity of, 138; complexity of, 124; controversiality of, 124, 126; as counterproductive, 202; cumulative effect of, 155, 158, 160, 259; origin of, within faith, 258; importance of, 237; ineffectiveness of, 261; interrelation of, 153-155; concept of God in, 160; popularity of, 125; problems with, 177; purpose of, 129, 130, 132, 157, 159; rejection of, by Kierkegaard, 227; rejection of, by Pascal, 224; rejection of, by neo-orthodoxy, 181; relative success of, 157; resiliency of, 126; formulation of, by Schubert M. Ogden, 191; strategy of, 153, 156, 159, 177; Tillich's assessment of, 188; types of, 124. *See also* Cosmological argument; Moral argument; Ontological argument; Teleological argument

Theistic proofs. *See* Theistic arguments

Theodicy, 164n.47

Theology (systematic theology): approaches to, 78, 80, 205; as arrangement of Christian doctrines and beliefs, 95, 167, 169, 269-70; assumptions of, 98; basic task of, 4, 73, 168; as biblical interpretation, 80, 98; characteristics of, 77; concept of, in neo-orthodoxy 179; concept of, in Schleiermacher, 174; concept of, in Schubert M. Ogden, 189; concepts of, liberal and conservative, 82-83; definitions of, 74-75, 76; constructive task of, 96, 100n.37; dependence of, on private evidence, 268; historicity of, 193; in current intellectual climate, 193, 195; independence of, from philosophy, 201; meanings of, 94; object of, 79; perspective of, "from inside" faith, 206, 286; relation of, to Bible and church, 90-91; relation of, to doctrines, 94; relation of, to metaphors, 275; relation of, to religious commitment, 77-78, 79; as exercise of reason, 101; role of Bible in, 82, 83, 85; role of tradition in, 91-92; two-story concept of, 173, 175; use of evidence in, 216; use of philosophy in, dangers of, 201-202. *See also* Natural theology

Trust, 11, 16, 45

Understanding, 33

Universe. *See* World

Validity, formal, 42

Verification, 20

Will to believe, 29n.19, 57-59, 68n.43

World, 135, 142

www.ingramcontent.com/pod-product-compliance
Lightning Source LLC
Chambersburg PA
CBHW061428300426
44114CB00014B/1586